Media Bias in Reporting Social Research?

In recent years, the importance of disseminating the findings of social research has been given increased emphasis. The most effective way in which research findings can be disseminated to a wide audience is via the mass media.

However, there are frequent complaints that media coverage of social and educational research is very limited and often distorted. Through a detailed analysis of a particular case, about ethnic inequalities in educational achievement, this book examines some of the processes involved in the reporting of research findings, and their implications for judgements about media distortion and bias.

Martyn Hammersley, a well known and respected scholar, unravels some of the complexities which are frequently ignored in claims about media bias. Relevant to many fields – including education, media studies, cultural studies, sociology and social policy – this book will generate wide interest.

Martyn Hammersley is Professor of Educational and Social Research at the Open University, UK. His most recent books are: *Taking Sides in Social Research* (also published by Routledge), and *Educational Research, Policy Making and Practice*.

Routledge Advances in Sociology

This series aims to present cutting-edge developments and debates within the field of sociology. It will provide a broad range of case studies and the latest theoretical perspectives, while covering a variety of topics, theories and issues from around the world. It is not confined to any particular school of thought.

Media Bias in Reporting Social Research?

The case of reviewing ethnic inequalities in education

Martyn Hammersley

Routledge
Taylor & Francis Group

LONDON AND NEW YORK

First published 2006
by Routledge
2 Park Square, Milton Park,
Abingdon, Oxon OX14 4RN

Simultaneously published in the USA and Canada
by Routledge
270 Madison Avenue, New York, NY 10016

Routledge is an imprint of the Taylor & Francis Group, an informa business

© 2006 Martyn Hammersley

Typeset in Times by Keyword Group Ltd
Printed and bound in Great Britain by Biddles Ltd, King's Lynn

British Library Cataloguing in Publication Data
A catalogue record for this book is available from the British Library

Library of Congress Cataloging in Publication Data
A catalog record for this book has been requested

ISBN10: 0-415-37274-7 (hbk)
ISBN10: 0-203-96659-7 (ebk)

ISBN13: 978-0-415-37274-9 (hbk)
ISBN13: 978-0-203-96659-4 (ebk)

Contents

List of tables

Acknowledgements

I am indebted to David Gillborn, Caroline Gipps and some of the journalists involved in reporting the Review for their willingness to be interviewed about it and for the information they provided. I would also like to thank Roger Gomm for his interest and support over many years in this and other projects. The spirit of our late colleague and friend, Peter Foster, also inhabits these pages. Finally, thanks go to participants at a session of the British Educational Research Association conference, Cardiff University, September 2000 and at a weekend conference of the Open University EdD Programme, where earlier versions of some of the analysis were presented.

The authors and publishers would like to thank the following for granting permission to reproduce material in this work:

HMSO/Office of Public Sector Information for permission to reprint material from one of their publications:
Gillborn, D. and Gipps, C. (1996) *Recent Research on the Achievements of Ethnic Minority Pupils*, London: Office for Standards in Education/Her Majesty's Stationery Office.
This is covered by Core Licence number C02W0008216.
www.opsi.gov.uk

Introduction

The central concern of this book is with how the results of social research are represented in the media. This is explored through a detailed case study of the ways in which the mass media reported a review of research dealing with the educational achievement of ethnic groups in Britain (Gillborn and Gipps 1996, henceforth referred to as 'the Review'). I compare this review, and the press release that announced its publication, as a source, with the various reports that appeared on the radio, on television, and in a wide range of newspapers. I try to use this case as a kind of tracer to highlight some of the processes of selection and formulation involved in news media reporting, and the factors that could shape these. Above all, the analysis offers a basis for examining what is involved in researchers' complaints about media distortion and bias – against the background of a particular model of how the media ought to operate.

The issue of how research findings are represented in the media is important because social research is widely seen, by social scientists themselves and by others, as properly playing a key role in shaping policymaking and various forms of occupational practice, and/or as informing public discussion of political issues. Being reported in the mass media is the most direct means by which the findings of social and educational research can reach a wide audience. In their study of media reporting of research findings in the United States, Weiss and Singer (1988: 1) note that media reports are a crucial way in which even politicians and policymakers hear about such findings:

> Although they may have their own research and analysis staffs, and sit at the nodes of specialised communication networks, often it is not until the media carry a story about social science that [politicians] become aware of it. A report from their own aides may lie unnoticed on their desk, but a story in the *Washington Post* or on CBS television news demands – and receives – immediate attention.

If this is true of policymakers, and there seems little reason to doubt it even in the British context, then it is also likely to be true of occupational practitioners of various kinds to whom the research concerned may be relevant, and even more so of the general public, who have fewer resources available to help keep themselves informed.[1] Weiss and Singer conclude: 'if the social sciences want to get their messages to a mass audience, then the mass media are pretty much the only wheel in town' (Weiss and Singer 1988: 155).

Moreover, this mode of disseminating the findings of research is an especially important one from the perspective of those who see the key role of research as informing public debate about social, economic, or political issues – rather than as simply providing information for direct use by policymakers or occupational practitioners. In this democratic model of the role of research, rational discussion or deliberation among the public about key issues is believed to be the proper basis for policymaking; and the function of research is to provide the main, or at least some highly significant, informational resources for that discussion. From this point of view, the role of both research and the media is to build 'an informed, responsible and active public opinion', which is central 'to the establishment of viable democracy and the good society' (Lacey and Longman 1997: 2). Or, put another way, the social science disciplines are 'a potentially important source of society's understanding of itself', and how their findings are represented in the media is part of 'the wider issue of how citizenship can be promoted and enhanced' (Fenton *et al.* 1998: ix).[2]

At least two requirements must be met if social science is to play this key role in discursive democracy.[3] An obvious first one is that social science findings actually get reported by the mass media. The second is that they are presented accurately. However, social scientists frequently complain that the media fail in one or both of these respects. It has been noted that only a small proportion of social science studies get coverage, even though there is much research relevant to many of the issues dealt with each day by the media. Even more commonly, social scientists argue that when research findings *are* actually reported they are distorted.

Such complaints have been made over many years. Here for example are Cohen and Young, writing bitterly about their experiences with journalists over

---

1 Weiss and Singer also note: 'The media are a potent channel for conveying social science not only because they carry information but also because they create incentives for attending to the information' (Weiss and Singer 1988: 1). Professional practitioners and citizens are, perhaps, less likely to feel compelled to attend to what is reported in the media; though sometimes they will do so.

2 Probably the most developed version of this democratic model of the role of the media in relation to social science research findings was presented by John Dewey in the 1930s, in his debate with Walter Lippman: see Westbrook 1991. Of course, the idea that the media themselves play a central role in democracy is widely accepted; see for example Curran 1991: 2.

3 I am using the term 'discursive democracy' in a very broad way here to refer to policymaking that involves public discussion of the issues concerned. Many advocates would define the term more narrowly, by stipulating conditions as to the extent of public participation, in terms of both numbers or representation and power. An alternative term sometimes used is 'deliberative democracy'. See Dryzek 1990; Thompson 1995; Bohman 1996; Guttman and Thompson 1996; Nino 1996; and Elster 1998. On the role of the media in relation to democracy generally, see Keane 1991.

a quarter of a century ago:

> It is important to understand ... the institutionalized bad faith which journalism perhaps more than any other occupation is prone to. Over the years, we have been interviewed on numerous occasions by reporters on such matters as the 'drug problem' and the 'violence problem'; each time we have been earnestly assured that the reporter privately absolutely agrees with our views, is determined to write up a fair and balanced story, is only taking an aggressive and philistine line of questioning to put himself in the hypothetical position of his readers and viewers, and that any distortion or unfair selection which appears is the fault of the sub-editors, producers and other such nasties. And when the highly selective story does appear or the taped interview judiciously edited, we know that it is too simple to dismiss all reporters as either fools or knaves ... but where does the responsibility lie?

> (Cohen and Young 1973: 20)

Rather more recently, Dunning has also complained about the difficulties that social scientists face in 'getting their message across', this stemming from the reliance of many parts of the media on 'sensation and sentiment as news values' (Dunning 1994: 59). And other sociologists have made similar points (Walum 1975; Haslam and Bryman 1994a). Nor is this kind of criticism restricted to sociologists; it is to be found in other academic disciplines and across theoretical and political divides. Thus, Ussher comments that the media's role as gatekeepers 'acts to ensure that only particular forms of psychological research come to the public attention, distorting the very perception [among the public] of what psychologists do ...' (Ussher 1994: 128; see also Rubin 1980); while Eysenck has complained of 'misrepresentations, inaccuracies, irrelevancies and downright lies' in the media's treatment of his own work (Eysenck 1994: 71–2).[4]

There is an interesting question, though, about how we are to approach these views on the part of social scientists. Do they constitute social scientific analyses of the media's operation, or are they complaints by one occupational group about the behaviour of another group on whom they depend? In practice, the criticisms are generally based on personal experience rather than on systematic research, though they are in line with some more general sociological analyses of the operation of the media. In fact, while there has been considerable investigation of the media's treatment of natural science findings, there has been very little empirical work on the reporting of social scientific research in the media. There have been just two main studies, one in the United States and the other in Britain.

---

4 As in most situations where complaints are made, they are not limited to one side. Journalists are often critical of social research, and especially of the way that research reports are written. See, for example, Toynbee 1999.

THE LITERATURE ON MEDIA TREATMENT OF
SOCIAL RESEARCH

Investigating the representation of social science in the US media, Weiss and Singer commented on how research findings are processed as they move from the academy into the world of news reports (Weiss and Singer 1988). Here, as elsewhere, the media operate as a filter, selecting and reformulating what is to be reported. Anything judged likely to be unintelligible to the audience is stripped out, and the story will be written in a way that is designed to be not only accessible but also interesting to that audience. In particular, it will be structured in terms of a news 'angle'. Weiss and Singer report that newspapers tend to carry more social-science-based stories than do news magazines, and that television carries still fewer. The reports are usually produced by general reporters or those who specialize in economic affairs, political news, or social issues. Thus the research is not normally the main focus of the stories, but rather is called in to illuminate some issue that is currently newsworthy. These authors argue that social science is not a category that is salient in itself for journalists. There is a contrast here with the reporting of natural science findings, since these tend to be the main stimulus for and focus of the stories drawing on them, and to be covered by specialist science reporters, even though reports may sometimes relate the findings to practical or political issues of wider interest.[5]

Weiss and Singer document a high level of general criticism of media reports of social science research among social scientists, the criticisms being very similar to those made by natural scientists: that there is extreme selectivity in what is reported, that reports are oversimplified, that the validity of the findings is exaggerated (presenting an inaccurate image of certainty and universal application), and that there is inadequate scrutiny of the evidence involved (indeed, a tendency to rely simply on the press release). At the same time, perhaps surprisingly, researchers were found to be less critical of media reports dealing with their own work than of coverage of social science generally. Weiss and Singer, writing in the 1980s, argue that media reports display a bias towards quantitative rather than qualitative studies, towards findings which favour the status quo, and towards those which support a 'liberal' (by which they mean a Centre or Centre–Left) political perspective. Moreover, they see this as in line with the findings of sociological research on the media generally, which they summarize as documenting how the media focus on individuals rather than on larger economic and social forces, and how they are preoccupied with drama and conflict rather than with long-term processes, the result of these characteristics being that what is supplied is a 'superficial and fragmented picture of reality' (p. 13).

---

5 An important feature of the relationship between social scientists and journalists is that their areas of claimed expertise overlap considerably, much more so than those of journalists and natural scientists. However, there are also complaints by natural scientists about the inadequate amount and character of the coverage their work is given.

Subsequent to the work of Weiss and Singer, Fenton *et al.* (1998) carried out a major study of the treatment of social research in the British media. Using work on the sociology of the media as a framework, they set out to cover the whole process of media representation of research: from the role of social scientists, research units, and funding bodies as news sources, through the work of journalists in producing their reports, to the responses of audiences. They provide a content analysis of the British media over a defined period, looking at the extent to which – and ways in which – social science research has been reported, as compared both with the coverage of natural science and with the treatment of social science in the United States. And they also carried out qualitative analysis of a sample of media items, showing how these tend to open social science up to commonsense criticism for either 'discovering the obvious' or reaching conclusions that are 'ridiculous'. In order to understand how social science gets represented in the media the authors look at the roles of social scientists and journalists, and of the various agencies and institutions associated with each, against the background of changes over time in the UK's economic and political climate. They document variations in the representation of social science findings in the media, and in researchers' perceptions of how the media report their work, along with journalists' attitudes towards such work and its newsworthiness. Like Weiss and Singer, these authors note that, by contrast with natural science, most reporting of social science research is usually subordinated to journalistic agendas, though they emphasize that the relationship is a contingent one. In other words, where most natural science items focus on the results of the research, much reporting of social science operates in the context of general journalistic concern with issues. One might say that, whereas natural scientific research findings are usually treated as the topic, social science research findings tend to be used by journalists as a resource in discussing some currently topical social problem.

ETHNIC MINORITIES IN THE MEDIA

While my general focus in this book is on the representation of social science research in the media, the specific case I am investigating concerns research on the educational achievements of ethnic minority pupils. Given this, the study can also be located within the body of work concerned with how ethnic minorities are portrayed in the British media.[6] In effect, this has usually taken the form of evaluations, concerned with the extent to which media reports provide accurate coverage of ethnic minority groups, their circumstances and activities, with whether they offer fair or just accounts of them compared with other groups, and/or with the likely implications and effects of the coverage. With few exceptions, the conclusions reached have been negative ones, pointing to distortion

6 For reviews, see Allan 1999:ch. 7 and Cottle 2000: Introduction.

and bias in the representation of many ethnic minorities, this being characterized or explained in terms of the operation of white racism.[7]

All the studies in this field claim that ethnic minorities tend to be referred to in ways that carry negative implications, and reinforce popular stereotypes about these groups. For instance, reportage about them is typically included in stories about immigration, social problems, violence and crime. Cottle comments that 'the collective findings of this research effort generally make for depressing reading. Under-representation and stereotypical characterization within entertainment genres and negative problem-oriented portrayal within factuality and news forms, and a tendency to ignore structural inequalities and lived racism experienced by ethnic minorities in both, are recurring research findings' (Cottle 2000: 7–8). Similarly, Allan (1991) reports: 'News media representations of race in "western" societies, one study after the next suggests, are recurrently framed within the boundaries of dominant white cultural attitudes' (p. 157). Moreover, in line with many of these studies, Allan claims that this ideological framing of news reports serves to reinforce commonsensical racism on the part of white audiences, and thereby to reproduce the fundamental structures of a racist society.

In one of the studies, van Dijk (1991) is concerned with the way in which British newspaper reports are constructed in a manner that reflects the racist attitudes of political elites, and thereby serve to mobilize public support for racist policies. His data consisted of newspaper reports about issues involving ethnic minorities. He looks in quantitative terms at the coverage of topics, but also provides detailed analysis of the discursive strategies that are employed, and what he takes to be their sources and political implications or consequences. In a similar way, but this time relating to local news sources in the United States, Campbell (1995) focuses on the 'myths' that are purveyed by the media, arguing that these both reflect and reproduce racism in US society.

While studies in this field document change over time in the mode of reporting, they usually characterize this as a shift from blatant racism to a new form of racism that is more subtle. For example, following Stuart Hall, Allan argues that the ideological framing of news reports is not evident simply in overtly racist formulations but also takes the form of 'inferential racism', where representations rely on implicit racist assumptions that enable audiences to draw racist conclusions *for themselves* (pp. 159–60; see Hall 1990: 13). Whereas, in earlier reporting, terms were used and attitudes expressed of a directly racist kind, for example referring to skin colour and attributing negative characteristics to minority groups, today it is more common for the focus to be on cultural differences, with these serving as proxy for racial differentiation. Accounts may also involve disclaimers and other devices that seek to protect the reports from accusations of racism (van Dijk 1998: 41).

---

7 For a now rather old, but more sophisticated, assessment, see Braham 1982.

So, much of the literature argues that while there might seem to have been progress, this is not actually the case. Racism has become more subtle and disguised, and perhaps thereby works its effects even more powerfully than before. In fact, there are some commentators who argue that even the immediate consequences of this new racism are at least as damaging, and perhaps even more damaging, than more overt versions. Van Dijk writes that many forms of the new racism are discursive, being 'enacted and confirmed by text and talk', and that while 'they appear "mere" talk, and far removed from the open violence and forceful segregation of the "old" racism ... they may be just as effective to marginalize and exclude minorities'. Indeed, he suggests that 'they may hurt even more, especially when they seem to be so "normal", so "natural", and so "commonsensical" to those who engage in such discourse and interaction' (van Dijk 1998: 34).

Much of the research in this field operates within a social reproduction model. For example, in his studies of the representation of ethnic minorities in British national newspapers, van Dijk is primarily concerned with how 'discourse [is] involved in the reproduction of (or resistance against) racism'. He recognizes that, in order to determine whether the news media reproduce or resist racism, 'we must know what racism is'. In defining it, he writes: 'Summarizing a complex theory, we shall simply assume here that racism is a social system of "ethnic" or "racial" inequality, just like sexism, or inequality based on class' (van Dijk 1998: 35). In this literature, then, media coverage of ethnic minorities is treated as governed by racist ideology, this being viewed as part of a broader socio-cultural process whereby the political status quo, characterized by ethnic and other kinds of social inequality, is preserved.[8]

So, what is involved in this work is a portrayal of the mass media as purveying ideological messages that reproduce existing inequalities, and thereby serve powerful groups within the society. In factual terms, the concept of ideology employed here involves several claims: about how media reports are shaped to serve this reproductive function, about the misrepresentation of ethnic minorities in those reports, and about the actual effects of the reports on audiences. Generally speaking, the evidence provided in these studies relates to the middle claim: it is argued that the reports are factually incorrect, involve unequal treatment of different ethnic groups, and/or imply attitudes or policies that are discriminatory. From this it is inferred that media reports are generated and function so as to reproduce the marginalized or oppressed position of certain ethnic minorities within the wider society.

Analysis of its ideological role has been an important part of research on other aspects of the news media in the past, and to some extent such work continues today. However, there have been important developments that raise questions

---

8 For an account of the sort of reproduction theory that underpins this approach, see Bennett 1982: 51–3.

about, and create problems for, this kind of analysis. I will examine these briefly in the next section.

RECENT DEVELOPMENTS IN RESEARCH ON MEDIA NEWS

As noted earlier, social scientists' complaints about the distortion of research findings by journalists link to a broader tradition of sociological research on media news reports, much of which has been concerned with the issue of bias.[9] Where journalists have often sought to justify their work in terms of serving the public's right to know about what is happening in the world, claiming that it enhances democracy, many sociologists have argued that media news reporting performs latent functions that are at odds with these journalistic self-perceptions, the latter being part of an occupational ideology. Work in this tradition has claimed that what is reported, and how it is reported, serves the interests of dominant groups and/or the needs of the capitalist or neo-imperialist system. Key mechanisms here are the routinized practices by which journalists identify sources, and the 'news values' by which they select from the material provided by these sources and formulate stories. These practices and values, it is suggested, are designed consciously, unconsciously, or through institutional mechanisms to avoid what will offend powerful agents (the news sources on which journalists rely as well as media organization proprietors), and to boost newspaper sales. Thus, news values effectively screen out stories that might, from other perspectives, be judged of great significance. Similarly, *how* events are reported reflects the same concerns and priorities, despite expressed commitments to objectivity. This occurs not necessarily because of the personal views of journalists, but because of biases built into the organizational structures within which they operate, and the functional location of media organizations in Western societies.[10] Much of the research in Britain along these lines has purported to show how the media operate within a framework that presents a picture of the world constrained within conventional political boundaries, ruling out information and images that would constitute any fundamental political challenge to the status quo.

However, in more recent research on media news there has been a move away from a focus on bias or distortion, since this concept assumes both the desirability and possibility of objectivity. There are various grounds for challenging the ideal of objectivity. One is the argument, characteristic of Frankfurt School

9 The best known early examples in Britain are probably the work of the Glasgow University Media Group: see Glasgow University Media Group 1976, 1980, 1982 and 1985. For a critical assessment of this research, see Harrison 1985, and see the response from Philo 1987. A different tradition, but one that shares this concern with bias, or 'systematically distorted communication', is that developed by the Centre for Contemporary Cultural Studies, see, for example, Hall *et al.* 1978.
10 For studies focusing on the contexts and practices of news journalism, see Epstein 1973; Altheide 1974; Tuchman 1978; Gans 1979; Golding and Elliott 1979; Schlesinger 1987.

Critical Theory, that even portraying the world as it actually is effectively supports the status quo, because it gives no hint that alternative social arrangements are possible. In terms of this argument, even if the media were to present events accurately, they would nevertheless operate in such a way as to have a conservative effect by portraying it as natural. Here the possibility of objectivity is accepted, but its desirability – or at least its priority – is denied.

Another argument dismisses the idea of an objective, unbiased picture of society as spurious, as part of the occupational ideology of journalists. From this point of view, it is emphasized that any news report is a construction: it cannot simply reproduce what it purports to represent. Different accounts are always possible, and there is no definitive way of identifying one as true and all the rest as false.[11] Where, previously, analytic efforts had sometimes been made to show the mismatch between 'what actually happened' and what was reported in the media, and the bias involved in this, it came to be argued by some media researchers that any report of particular events is necessarily an arbitrary construction in representational terms. As a result, analysis has focused on the processes through which journalistic reports are produced and the forms they take, and perhaps also on why one particular account is generated rather than another, and the effects of this. Here, much of the ideology model is retained, but what is abandoned is the claim that it is through misrepresenting the world that media reports aid social reproduction.

While much social constructionist work has been concerned with the content of news reports themselves, analysing these as semiotic or discursive products, another important line of research has focused on the *reception* of media reports by audiences. In some ways, this offers a more fundamental challenge to older views about the ideological function of media news. The latter assumed a relatively passive response on the part of audiences, imbibing the messages transmitted; though the possibility of resistance was usually recognized, at least in principle. By contrast, subsequent work emphasized the 'active' role of audiences, and their differential responses to 'the same' message. In fact, it is often suggested that, in many ways, audiences construct the messages that are 'received'.[12]

In part this emphasis on the active audience arises from empirical research, but it also stems from a shift in theoretical assumptions.[13] It draws on work in literary theory which has emphasized the role of 'reader reception' and in particular the sense in which readers 'write' the books they read (see Tompkins 1980 and

11 The sources of this relativism are to be found not just in various kinds of constructionism, such as that arising within symbolic interactionism (Hammersley 1992: ch. 3), but also from structuralism, with its emphasis on the arbitrariness of signs (see, for example, Hartley 1982).
12 See Morley 1986; Moores 1993; Abercrombie and Longhurst 1998; and Brooker and Jermyn 2003.
13 As Curran 1997: 264–7 points out, many accounts of the rise of audience research caricature earlier work on the effects of the mass media, which also emphasized the active, and socially located, role of audiences.

Bennett 1995). Subjected to fundamental challenge here is the idea that writers produce texts that carry a fixed, intended message which is decodable by readers – if the latter have the necessary resources and the right attitude to 'receive' it. There is a long tradition of work which has focused on the complexities of identifying messages in texts, especially literary texts, and of the constitutive role of reading (see Holub 1984).

In more recent times there has been a reaction against the notion of the active audience, reverting to the idea that media products tend to impose a preferred reading. Fenton *et al.* outline how the idea that media messages are polysemic, being open to free construction by audiences, came to be criticized as implying that texts have no force at all. They comment that, 'as a result of a growing awareness of the framing power of texts and an understanding that the text must be viewed in relation to hegemonic culture, more circumscribed accounts of audience activity have emerged'. Thus, accounts have been produced that

> recognise that differently located audiences may derive particular interpre-
> tations of texts but that the text itself is rarely subverted. In other words,
> the essential power of authors to frame audience reception is accepted; audi-
> ences do engage in interpretation but that interpretation is marginal to the
> denotative structuring of the text. In this manner ideology remains a crucial
> reference point but not in the form favoured in purely structuralist analyses.

> (Fenton *et al.* 1998: 119–20)

These developments in research on media news are an important backdrop to my analysis of the portrayal of research findings in the media. However, the particular sociological orientation I have adopted here differs in some important respects from that represented by much of this literature. My focus is a limited one, concerned with the extent to which media reports differ from source material in ways that are open to evaluation as inaccuracy, distortion or bias. I am not offering a practical evaluation of media coverage of the Review as good or bad. Nor will I make any claims about the role of media reporting in ideological processes of social reproduction.[14]

This limited focus reflects a Weberian perspective that treats social research as properly guided by the principle of value neutrality, though also as necessar-ily framed by value relevancies (see Hammersley 1995 and 2000). In my case, this means that I am concerned with documenting how social research is rep-resented in the media, in ways relevant to any claim that the media distort its message, as well as with why media reports take the forms they do. Only in the Epilogue, once the analysis is complete, will I look at the issue from a normative

---

14 This is partly because I share many of the concerns that Anderson and Sharrock (1979) expressed many years ago in their critique of critical media studies. I discuss some of the issues in the Epilogue.

perspective, concerned with the proper public role of the media and of social research. And, even here, my primary aim will not be to put forward a particular evaluation but rather to explore some of the complexities involved in making judgements about these issues.

So, my approach differs sharply from that adopted by many authors in this field.[15] It contrasts very sharply, for example, with the work of van Dijk, whose book *Racism and the Press* is described on its back cover as 'scholarly, partisan and topical'. It is clear that neither the author of this description, Charles Husband, nor van Dijk himself, sees any contradiction between scholarship and partisanship. Van Dijk describes his work as 'research against racism' (p. xi), and comments in the Preface to his book: 'I hardly need ... to justify my criticism of the Press, and especially of the sometimes appalling practices of right-wing journalists in Britain, who may be second to none in the world in propagating racial hatred' (pp. xi–xii). Moreover, much of van Dijk's analysis amounts to evaluative judgements about how stories were formulated by contrast with how they *ought to have been* formulated if racism was to be avoided and anti-racism supported. By contrast with this, my aim in this book is neither to counter racism nor even to persuade journalists to treat social science research more favourably. Rather, I simply want to understand how the particular research findings I am concerned with were reported, to consider why they were reported in the ways that they were, and to explore what more general conclusions might be drawn from this.

THE CASE INVESTIGATED HERE AND THE APPROACH ADOPTED

My focus in this book is quite limited in another sense, in that I deal almost entirely with the relationship between one research publication, as a news source, and how the media represented the information it provided in their reports. As indicated earlier, this source is *Recent Research on the Achievements of Ethnic Minority Pupils*, authored by David Gillborn and Caroline Gipps, and sponsored by the Office for Standards in Education (OFSTED) (Gillborn and Gipps 1996). This case is worth detailed examination for at least three reasons.

First, it involves a *review* of research studies in a particular field, rather than a report of findings from a single study. Some commentators have argued that reviews are the most appropriate way for research findings to be communicated to lay audiences (Weigel and Pappas 1981; McIntyre 1998; see also Foster and

---

15 It does not conform to the 'pluralist', 'radical', or to either of the two forms of 'revisionism' identified by Curran (1997) since all of these rely on acceptance or rejection of some conception of how the media *ought* to operate. My aim here is to suspend any such commitment, and also any assumption that the larger society is strongly integrated such that the media function consistently in some predetermined way.

Hammersley 1998). This is because they draw on a range of studies and on collective assessment of these studies by the research community.

A second reason for focusing on the Review is that it attracted far more attention than most reports of social science research do (and, indeed, most reviews of such research).[16] The day after it was published it was one of the top stories in the early morning *Today* programme on BBC Radio 4. In addition, items dealing with it appeared on all the BBC television news programmes, and it was also included in ITV and Channel 4 news programmes that day. Furthermore, it was covered in all of the main national daily newspapers, in two national Sunday newspapers, in many ethnic minority newspapers, and in the regional press as well. Thus a considerable number of media reports are available for analysis, representing quite a wide range of outlets, varying in both medium and intended audience.

Finally, unlike most research publications that are given attention by the news media, the Review was itself the focus of many of the reports, rather than being used as a resource in reporting some newsworthy issue. In other words, its publication *made* the news, rather than being drawn on by journalists to report other events. As noted earlier, this is relatively unusual for social science research.

Of course, I am not suggesting that analysis of this single case can, on its own, provide us with a secure basis for drawing general conclusions about how the media treat social and educational research, even specifically in relation to late twentieth century Britain. Nevertheless, it will allow us to derive some tentative conclusions, against the background of other work in the field. In this respect, the case study presented here will provide important material that can be used for exploring social scientists' arguments about media bias in general, as well as their more specific complaints about the media's treatment of social research findings.

The main task of the analysis will be to compare media reports with the source material on which they were based: the Review, and the press release issued at the time of its publication.[17] My aim will be to look at the processes of selection and reformulation involved in the production of these media reports. I will approach this task via a form of discourse analysis. Such analysis can, of course, take a variety of forms.[18] My approach here is an eclectic one: I have drawn on whatever resources in the literature seemed useful for my task, and ignored what

16 It is worth noting that most of the research findings reported in the Review had been available for some time, and had been given little or no attention by the media.
17 There are some gaps in the data that were available to me, largely resulting from the fact that this was an opportunistic, rather than a pre-planned, piece of research. I did not have direct access to what was said at the press conference and in interviews with the press by the lead researcher and OFSTED officials; though I have managed to gather some indirect information about this. Also, it is unlikely that I managed to record all of the news and current affairs coverage of the Review on radio and television, but the most prominent and detailed reports were probably recorded. Coverage of newspapers has been as close to exhaustive as I could make it.
18 For an outline and bibliography, see Hammersley 2003a.

was not. Furthermore, my approach departs, in at least one important respect, from what is common among discourse analysts in that I do not treat this form of analysis as self-sufficient.[19] Thus I draw on some other sources of information, notably interviews with the authors of the Review, with some of those involved in producing the news reports, as well as with informants who were able to provide me with background information about the operation of various segments of the media. I have also drawn heavily on previous research about media organizations, and about the work of journalists, in order to understand what seems likely to have been involved in the production of the news reports I analyse.

Nevertheless, my main source of information about the processes by which journalists selected and formulated material from the Review has been the reports they produced. In analysing these I have had to rely on my own readings in trying to understand the intended messages as well as what conclusions readers might draw from them. This was unavoidable. Of course, my conclusions would have been strengthened if I had been able to study journalists while they were producing news reports about the Review. Unfortunately, this was not possible in practical terms, since the research only began after the news reports had been published. But, in any case, it would have been very difficult to have observed the production of reports across a wide range of news media. There are similar limitations in relation to how the reports were 'read' by a variety of audiences. Fenton *et al.* (1998) investigated audience response by setting up focus groups and documenting their responses to particular news items. Unfortunately, I did not have the resources available to do this. It would have been of considerable value, even though there are clearly problems with using such data as a basis for drawing inferences about how people normally respond to news reports in everyday life.

In analysing both the Review and media reports as texts, I have assumed that they carry messages, though not that these are always clear and unambiguous or invariant across audiences. Furthermore, by contrast with structuralist approaches that treat meaning as coded into texts, I have assumed instead that making sense of messages is always an active process on the part of audiences, just as much as conveying a message is an active process on the part of an author. Indeed, it seems to me that design features built into a text are a crucial source of evidence for audiences in coming to conclusions about what the intended message was. In other words, audiences usually assume a rational communicative orientation on the part of authors, albeit one operating within certain conventions. Grice has indicated the importance of these conventions, some of which can be summarized as: do not say less, but equally important say no more, than is necessary to communicate the message; do not communicate as true what you know to be false or even what you do not have good evidence for; and so on (see Grice 1978; see also Sperber and Wilson 1986: 33–4 and *passim*). Habermas has suggested that conventions like these inform all communication, and in a sense this is true (see Finlayson 2005: ch. 3). However, Grice points out that much talk and writing

19 I have explained elsewhere why I regard this as counterproductive: Hammersley 2003b.

actually breaches these conventions, its meaning relying precisely on the fact that it can be seen by audiences to involve such a breach. One can, for example, snub, insult, or amuse someone by breaching expectations. For the most part, such strategies are not involved in news media reporting, but they do arise in some contexts.

What this model of communication means for the 'mediation' of the Review by news reports is that both the Review and the reports themselves are discursive sites in which at least a two-way process occurs. The authors of the Review wrote in anticipation of how various audiences might interpret what they were writing, the media interpreted the source material they used in terms of what its intended message seemed to be but also according to how they could produce a report about the Review that would be 'news' to their audiences; and, presumably, media audiences interpreted the reports in terms of what seemed to be the intended message of these reports, and of the Review, and how this related to their own attitudes and interests. Moreover, in all three phases, the interpretations may well have been produced through interaction with other people; and, in making and sharing their interpretations, all parties will have drawn on a variety of cultural resources relevant to the topic of the Review.

THE STRUCTURE OF THE BOOK

In Chapter 1 I look at the Review itself, how it is organized textually, and what seems to be its central message. In particular, I focus on the summaries that it contains, and also the summary presented in the press release. The next two chapters examine reports of the Review on radio and television news programmes, analysing what is included in headlines and how these are formulated, as well as how information about the Review is structured in the body of the reports. Chapter 4 is concerned with newspaper coverage. There was much greater range here, and I analyse the reports in mass circulation Sunday and daily newspapers, in publications directed specifically at education professionals, in ethnic minority newspapers, and in the local press. A variety of interpretations of the Review's message can be found in these publications, much more diverse than in the other media. In the Conclusion I bring the evidence together to consider in what ways, and to what degree, the message of the Review might be judged to have been distorted by media coverage, and explore the issues involved in coming to a conclusion about this. There is also an Epilogue, where I interrogate some of the assumptions about the role of the mass media, and indeed about that of social research, which lie behind my focus on the media's accuracy in reporting social research findings.

1 From Review to press release

In studying the media, there has been increasing recognition of the role that sources play. Where before these tended to be treated as passive, with journalists selecting from what they offered, the relationship has come to be seen as rather more dynamic, and indeed as sometimes conflictual.[1] Some agencies that provide source material play an active role in seeking to manage the news so as to serve their own goals. This forms part of the burgeoning 'public relations' industry and the rise of 'political spin'. Of course, on the other side, journalists do still pursue and select from sources in order to get access to, and to extract, what they need for their stories. And each side is aware that the other may be engaged in strategic action that could amount to manipulation. Sometimes the goals of the two sides will be in close alignment, so that collusion is facilitated. At other times, there will be direct confrontation. Usually, though, the situation is somewhere between these two extremes, and each side may seek to work on the other to further its own goals.

Generally speaking, academics are not very active in their role as sources of news material (see Fenton *et al.* 1998: 91–2). However, there are increasing pressures on them to become so, as part of demonstrating the value of their work. Moreover, some of the organizations with which they are involved – universities, funding bodies, professional associations, etc. – now play a more pro-active role than in the past, at least in seeking to attract the attention of the media to newly emerging research material.

The case of *Recent Research on the Achievements of Ethnic Minority Pupils* is significant in this respect. Its lead author made considerable effort to get the Review reported, and in ways that represented its message accurately; and both authors worked in a university institution whose Press Office is widely regarded as highly effective. Much more importantly, though, the Review was commissioned

---

1 The Hutton Inquiry (2003) into the events surrounding the death of the government scientist David Kelly, which reported while I was completing this chapter, could be characterized as concerned with the highly conflictual relationship between a media organization, the BBC, and one of its key sources, the British government. On the whole issue of the relationship between journalists and their sources, see Sigal 1986 and Manning 2001.

by the Office for Standards in Education (OFSTED), a non-departmental government agency that is responsible for school inspection in England and Wales. And OFSTED has a strong track record in publicizing its reports. As we shall see, the link with OFSTED, and thereby with the UK Government, seems to have played a key role in the level of coverage given to the Review by the media.

In this chapter I want to look at the Review itself, in terms of how it was structured for its projected audience, and also at its presentation to the media via a press release and press conference.

THE REVIEW: FORM AND CONTENT

Reviews of research literature can vary considerably in form. This will reflect the purposes that motivated them and the audience(s) they were directed towards (Foster and Hammersley 1998; Bassey 2000). They necessarily involve selection from a body of work in a field, in terms of what will be included, and usually also the assignment of differential importance to particular studies. In addition, the reviewer must summarize the findings of these research studies, either individually or by integrating them in some way. Reviews may be designed to reflect a consensus among researchers in the field; though, of course, consensus is almost always partial and sometimes there is little agreement on key issues. On other occasions, reviewers may take a more independent line as regards what parts of the field are most important, as well as in judging the validity of particular findings. Reviews also vary in the extent to which they limit themselves to stating the factual conclusions of research, or go on to draw policy recommendations. Reviews that are directed at a lay audience are especially likely to extend discussion to policy implications – on the grounds that this audience may be primarily interested in these.[2]

Up to now my discussion has ignored the fact that reviewers may act under various constraints, that they do not simply make these decisions on their own account. And the authors of the Review did work under some significant constraints. It was produced on the basis of a commissioning brief prepared by OFSTED, and after it had been written there were extended negotiations before it was finally published. Indeed, according to one of the authors (David Gillborn, personal communication), publication was only forced by a public statement from the then head of the Commission for Racial Equality, who criticized the delay in publishing it (*Times Educational Supplement*, 3 May 1996, p. 1).[3]

---

2 There is considerable dispute currently among social scientists about the proper nature of reviews of the research literature: see Hammersley 2004a.

3 See also Smith 2000: 343. A first draft had been completed more than a year prior to publication, and had been sent to the CRE for comment. Among the issues involved in the delay, though perhaps not the only one, was the fact that the draft was much longer than specified in the original tender, and the belief on the part of OFSTED that this would reduce the likelihood of the Review being read by schoolteachers.

As already noted, one of the most important dimensions along which reviews of research vary is in terms of their target audience. Some are aimed mainly at fellow researchers and at students doing research projects in the field. Others are explicitly directed towards audiences beyond the research community. The nature of the sponsoring organization would suggest that the review I am concerned with here falls into the latter category. And, indeed, on the Review's back cover we find the following statement:

> Recent Research in the Achievement of Ethnic Minority Pupils *is another in the series of OFSTED Reviews of Research. OFSTED has commissioned these reviews in order to make published research findings more accessible to teachers and trainee teachers.*

Furthermore, within the body of the Review, it is stated by the authors that the focus is on 'issues that directly influence pupils' achievements which relate to education or school policy or matters that teachers might want to address as part of their work (Gillborn and Gipps 1996: 7). However, from interviews with the authors it is clear that they expected the readership to include fellow academics, perhaps even more than teachers. This illustrates a general point: even when there is a specific target audience, it is unlikely that this will be the only one taken into account in producing a review. And sometimes the officially stated audience is not the expected one. Writers are often addressing multiple audiences, simultaneously or in different parts of the documents they produce. Nevertheless, who are the intended or expected audiences will shape the character, and also to some extent the content, of reviews.

In large part, then, my aim in this chapter is to identify the intended message of the Review and how it has been shaped for audience reception. At the same time, I am also concerned with how readers might approach and interpret the Review, especially – but not exclusively – media journalists: in other words, with what messages they might reasonably draw from it. So there is an important sense in which my analysis seeks to operate in two directions at once, in order to grasp the role of the Review in mediating the findings of research to the news media, and in turn to their audiences.

Let me begin by outlining the Review's structure and content, beginning with what Genette refers to as the paratext – in particular, the cover and initial pages (Genette 1997).[4]

The cover and the initial pages

The cover of the Review is what any reader will first come into contact with. The format here is A4 portrait, as against the smaller format that is more common

---

4 Genette describes the paratext as 'those liminal devices and conventions ... that mediate the book to the reader' (Macksey 1997: xviii).

for books and pamphlets. This seems calculated to attract attention, and much the same function probably lies behind the design of the cover – in particular the use of multi-colour printing (six colours, plus black and white).

Of course, readers will not necessarily take much notice of the cover, and we cannot know what parts of it they will read, or how. Still, it seems reasonable to assume that they might start with the front, and would read from left to right and from top to bottom, as readers of English do in approaching other texts.[5] Following this path, the first item on the cover of the Review is the OFSTED icon, and the full name of this organization; these are placed in the top right hand corner. Next comes the title of the review – *Recent Research on the Achievements of Ethnic Minority Pupils* – which occupies the second third of the cover down from the top. This is printed in much larger type than everything else, white on a dark blue background. In the bottom left hand corner are the names of the authors and their institutional affiliation. Finally, running vertically down the left hand side of the front cover there is a purple strip on which is printed in capitals, in landscape orientation, 'OFSTED REVIEWS OF RESEARCH'. The background of the front cover is a red diamond-shaped pattern of abstract design, with small light blue square and oblong markings (some joined together) within each diamond.

The back cover of the Review might be the next port of call for some readers. Here, following the same reading procedure, first of all there is a summary of the Review's findings, printed in the top left third of the cover, in purple print on a light blue background. We will examine the content of this summary later. Below there is a further specification of the series from which the Review comes (this was quoted earlier) which indicates that the target audience is teachers and trainee teachers. This is in white print on a dark blue background. In the bottom half of the back cover, on the left, are details, including addresses of bookshops, of the publisher: HMSO. The background pattern is the same as on the front. Finally, on the spine, is the title of the Review and the publisher's name.

Looking at the front and back covers together, we can try to make an assessment of the salience to readers of their different components. Most prominent of all is likely to be the title, as a result of the size of the print and the use of white letters on a dark background. After this, the name 'OFSTED' seems most striking, given that it is mentioned in two places on the front, once quite prominently in spatial location and the other in the largest print used (though in landscape orientation). Furthermore, OFSTED is already a widely known name, and is therefore more likely to be registered by readers than some other elements. For these reasons, OFSTED would probably be more salient to most readers than the names of the authors; and this is perhaps reinforced by the fact that those names do not appear on the back cover, whereas the name of OFSTED does. HMSO as publisher probably comes below the authors in terms of prominence, since it does not appear on the front cover, though it is included on the spine as well as on the back cover.

---

5 This is what Kress and van Leeuwen 1998: 189, 205–9 refer to as the 'reading path'.

On opening the Review, readers are likely to go to the title page first. This is a black, grey (five shades), and white replica of the front cover. There are two typographical changes, however. One is that the names and affiliations of the authors are now in black print, with the names themselves in bold. As a result, these stand out more sharply than on the cover, though they are still in the bottom left corner. The other change is that 'LONDON: HMSO' now appears at the bottom of the page to the right of the authors' names, in the same level of bold type as their affiliations, but in a slightly smaller typeface. The OFSTED logo and name are still in the top right position, and the vertical band referring to OFSTED reviews of research is also presented again. Given this, it seems likely that, here too, this will be the most prominent feature – after the title – for many readers.

The obverse of the title page assigns the copyright of the review to the Crown, carries the ISBN number, and has the name, address, telephone and fax numbers of OFSTED. The next of the preliminary pages is a dedication to Barry Troyna, an educational researcher whose work was concerned with ethnic inequalities, who died in 1996, the year in which the Review was published. The next preliminary page is blank apart from the page number. Following this, there is the list of contents, which takes up two pages. As is normal, this presents the chapter titles and within-chapter headings, along with page numbers.

As a whole, the Review is 91 pages long (including references), and is broken down into six sections. It begins with what is sometimes referred to as an 'executive summary' and ends with a section entitled 'Conclusions', whose sub-heading is 'ways forward: policy and practice'. Between the opening summary and the conclusion, there is an introduction followed by separate chapters on: the achievement levels of ethnic groups; research dealing with the relative educational progress of different groups and the significance of school effectiveness as a factor in this; the findings of qualitative research on multi-ethnic schools; and evidence about the situation in post-compulsory education. Each of these chapters begins with a title printed in white on a purple strip, and this is followed by a summary of the chapter's main points (which is close in content to the relevant section of the executive summary). These chapter summaries are printed in purple on a mauve background.

In the body of the chapters there are sub-headings, often printed in capitals, in white on a purple background. In addition, some sentences in the body of the text are picked out for emphasis. In some chapters this is done by printing them in italics in mauve on a white background. There is also considerable other use made of italicization of clauses and sentences, as well as bullet points printed in black on a mauve background, or simply on a white background.

What should emerge clearly from this description is that considerable effort went into making the Review attract and engage the attention of potential readers, far more so than is the case with most research reports, and even most literature reviews. Furthermore, within the Review, the use of multi-colour printing, italics, bold print and bullet points, plus the provision of summaries, seems designed to focus attention on what are intended to be its key points. While some of these devices are common in academic research reports, there is much greater use of them here.

The content of the Review

Writing a review for a lay audience involves the reviewer in working backwards and forwards between a body of research and an audience potentially interested in the issues to which it can be related. However, it is important not to think of either the research or the audience as fixed and completely defined from the beginning, though at the same time they are not simply inventions of the reviewer. He or she must delineate, and in a sense construct, both the research field to be reviewed and the desired and likely audiences. On this basis, the reviewer must select and summarize what seems likely to be relevant and of interest to target audiences, but the target audience will also be defined, and redefined, as those who will be or should be interested in this research. And these processes of construction and reconstruction will be carried out within parameters set by what the researcher takes to be fixed features of both research and audience, as well as any external constraints that must be taken into account.

One aspect of defining the research field is setting its temporal boundaries. *Recent Research on the Achievements of Ethnic Minority Pupils* does not state any time period explicitly, but it does refer to the fact that 'more than a decade has passed since the last major review of the educational experiences and achievements of ethnic minority pupils' (Gillborn and Gipps 1996: 1).[6] The reference is to the Swann Report (Swann 1985), which included a discussion of the research findings that were then available about the educational experience of ethnic minority children. In addition, it commissioned a series of reviews of research findings relating to the educational experience of different ethnic minorities and factors affecting this (Taylor 1981, Taylor with Hegarty 1985; Taylor 1987, 1986, 1988). So, the implication is that the new review is intended to cover research since the publication of the Swann Report, and the associated reviews (though, in fact, the latter are not mentioned in the Review). And this is confirmed by the fact that if we look at the references included in the Review, we find that over 90 per cent of them are to work published in the 1980s and 1990s.

It is worth noting that one of the effects of this temporal framing is that most of the research available for review focuses on processes within the education system, rather than on home and community background, which had been the main focus of previous research on the education of ethnic minority children. This reflects a fundamental change in the research field, and perhaps more widely. Earlier reviews had underlined the neglect of institutional processes and called for more research in that area. However, what followed was an almost complete switch in focus motivated by other factors as well as the desire to remedy a gap

---

6 In fact, this seems to have been the justification for commissioning the review given by OFSTED in inviting bids to carry out the task.

in the literature. It reflected a general change in the intellectual and political climate, away from explanations for differential educational achievement in terms of pupils' home or community backgrounds, and towards a focus on the operation of the education system as itself generating differences in educational outcome across social class and ethnic groups. This shift resulted partly from theoretical and methodological developments within educational research, but also from a change in wider political views about where the responsibility for educational failure lies. On the political Left this arose from rejection of any explanation for pupil failure which could be interpreted as 'blaming the victim'. On the Right, and increasingly too among those on the Centre Left, there was greater emphasis on the accountability of public institutions, and demands that they provide a better service for clients.

Another criterion, besides time period, that is often used in selecting studies for inclusion in reviews, or in deciding the extent to which they are discussed, is methodological. Studies whose findings are judged to be very questionable as a result of likely error or bias will be excluded or given no more than a mention. Gillborn and Gipps discuss methodological problems briefly in the 'Summary' that opens their review, though they do not indicate what methodological criteria they employed in selecting studies for inclusion. While they cover both quantitative and qualitative studies of school processes, there is a suggestion that they regard qualitative work as superior. At one point, having noted some of its disadvantages, they write: 'Despite these weaknesses, qualitative research frequently offers a more revealing perspective, highlighting patterns of experience and achievement that are not visible in quantitative studies' (Gillborn and Gipps 1996: 49). They also downplay the findings of one study which were at odds with those of many others in the field, and dismiss the author's criticism of these other studies on the grounds that he requires too demanding a level of evidential warrant, and misinterprets others' work as blaming teachers for educational inequalities (ibid.: 55–6).

In the main section of this chapter I will look at the content of the Review and how it is presented, particularly through examining the various summaries it contains.

Summaries in the Review

It is of significance for media reporting that this text is a relatively long one, in which a large number of points are made. This has at least two implications. One concerns its accessibility to lay audiences, even to journalists. Although it was publicly available for purchase, many people who have an interest in the issue will not have had the inclination to buy it or the time to read the whole of it. Furthermore, there is also likely to have been variation among journalists covering the story in how much, and how carefully, it was read, given its length. One likely axis of variation here is between those who are general reporters and those who are specialist education correspondents (see Fenton *et al.* 1998: 96–100). Given the time pressures under which journalists work, and in particular their need to be able to assess rapidly what news status any source has, the length of the Review could be an obstacle to its being reported, as well as shaping *how* it was reported.

The second implication of the length and complexity of the text is that the Review provides a great deal of scope for different selections and interpretations on the part of readers. And, as we shall see, there was some variation in what media reports focused on.

Against this background, a notable feature of the Review is its provision of several summaries. As already noted, there is a summary on the back cover, an executive summary at the start of the Review, and an opening summary at the start of each chapter. In addition, a further summary is provided at the start of the Conclusion.

Summaries are an example of what is sometimes referred to as 'meta-discourse': discourse which refers to the discourse in which it is itself embedded or to which it is attached, providing some sort of gloss on this. We can identify at least two functions of summaries. One is to substitute for the whole text – for those unable or unwilling to read it. Another is to guide the interpretations of those who do read the whole text or substantial parts of it, structuring their understanding of what are the key points and implications. Indeed, very often, meta-discourse is specifically concerned with clarification and/or with correcting possible misinterpretations. We can expect, then, that the various summaries provided were intended to play, and probably did play, a significant role in the 'reception' of the Review.

The summaries included in the Review differ from one another to varying degrees and in various respects. While those on the back cover and in the Conclusion are quite similar in content, they diverge considerably from the executive summary, not least in length. We can think of what is involved here as a process of filtering and reformulation. In these terms, the summaries can be organized in a sequence, in terms of increasing distance from the main text, as follows: the executive summary (which re-presents the chapter summaries); the summary contained in the Conclusion; and, finally, the summary on the back page of the Review. Looked at in this order, each of these texts is shorter than the previous one, and on that basis perhaps nearer to the world of the intended lay reader. I will look at each of these summaries in turn, starting with the fullest one: the executive summary.

The executive summary[7]

The executive summary is placed at the start of the Review, and takes the form of 68 bullet points, covering just over five pages. It is organized under a series of headings and sub-headings that broadly conform to those within the

---

7 Of course, here I am also myself providing a summary of the Review. My purpose is to provide readers with a sufficiently detailed knowledge of the content of the Review to understand the

main body of the Review's text. Thus, to begin with, there is a summary of the context of the Review, which corresponds to the Introduction, followed by points about differential achievement, educational progress and school effectiveness, the findings of qualitative research, and those relating to post-compulsory education. As a result, this summary provides very brief résumés of each chapter, in the order in which they occur. Of course, as with any précis, a great deal is left out, and in some places I will mention some points that only appear in the body of the text – especially where these were picked up by the media.

The message of the executive summary is, inevitably, a complex one. The many points are grouped under five main topic headings, with between two and four sub-headings in most of the sections. Furthermore, many of the bullet points themselves have more than one component, and sometimes these are balanced against one another.

The opening section of the executive summary outlines its context, and thereby seeks to justify its importance in the following terms:

- A decade has passed since the last review:

  – New findings and techniques have emerged
  – Massive reforms have taken place
  – Race and equal opportunity have slipped from policy agendas

The initial implication here is perhaps that reviews of research in this field are necessary at regular intervals, and that the information provided by the previous review has become out of date. The next two points support this interpretation, pointing to developments in the fields of both research and educational policy.

The third sub-argument is of a rather different kind. Here, it is implied that the purpose of reviews is not simply to provide up-to-date information but actually to shape the policy agenda. This is reinforced in the Review itself. The summary at the start of the Introduction reads:

> It is now more than ten years since the publication of the final report of the Committee of Inquiry into the Education of Children from Ethnic Minority Groups – widely known as the 'Swann Report'.

> In the intervening years, new research techniques have been devised and recent data have shed light on issues that were poorly understood a decade ago. However, the question of race and equality of opportunity has fallen from the prominent position it once held. This review, therefore, offers an

---

selections and reformulations made by media reports. In doing this I will relate what is in the executive summary to relevant parts of the body of the Review itself.

important chance to take stock of recent changes in the educational achievements of ethnic minority pupils.

Here the Review is presented as equivalent to the Swann Report, which was not simply a review of research literature but the product of a Committee of Inquiry set up by the government and charged with making policy recommendations. And in a few places in the body of the text, and especially in the final chapter, the authors move from reporting research findings to outlining what they take to be the policy implications. Thus, on the opening page of the Introduction, they present the following two sentences, the second highlighted by being printed in italics and mauve on white:

> Differences in the age structures of minority communities are such that the number and proportion of people from ethnic minority backgrounds will grow in the future: it is estimated that by the year 2020 the minority population will have doubled.

> *One of the clearest findings of this review is that if ethnic diversity is ignored, if differences in educational achievement and experience are not examined, then considerable injustices will be sanctioned and enormous potential wasted.*

The first paragraph is designed to indicate that the issue addressed by the Review is not simply of present significance, that its importance will grow in the future. The second paragraph is a statement of a 'headline' finding, which has the form of a policy conclusion. This is presumably one that the authors regard as of primary importance, even though it does not appear in any of the summaries. Moreover, it is an evaluative conclusion, indicating that the function of the Review is not seen as simply to report the factual conclusions that can be grounded in extant research but as interpreting those conclusions in order to reach policy recommendations.

The next section of the executive summary is concerned with achievement levels across ethnic groups, and corresponds to Chapter 2 of the Review. It opens with three general points, and is then broken up into two sub-sections, one quite short – two bullet points – on 'Achievement in the early key stages', and one much longer – eleven bullet points – on 'Achievement at the end of compulsory education'.

The opening three bullet points set out the orientation of the Review. The first indicates that its focus is on differences in levels of achievement among ethnic groups, plus the influence of social class and gender. The second and third points are more concerned with what might be referred to as the authors' policy in examining such differences. First, it is declared that 'underachievement' is 'a relatively crude term' and 'has long been misunderstood as implying that some groups are better or worse than others'; and, by implication, that it will therefore be avoided in the text. Second, it is stated that any 'significant differences in performance' will be interpreted as 'a cause for concern, highlighting areas where minority pupils might face additional unjustifiable barriers to success'. This tells us something about how the authors see the function of their work: very much in terms of providing information necessary for effective and socially just policy and practice in the field.

The authors' concern about the term 'underachievement' is spelled out in the body of the Review, and this too gives a sense of their guiding orientation.[8] In the opening section of Chapter 2 they point out that in its technical usage 'underachievement' 'says nothing about the specific potential or achievements of any individual pupil' but relates rather to relative outcomes achieved by different groups, and to inferences drawn from these about whether equality of opportunity has been achieved. They outline how the term came to be misunderstood as 'blaming the victim', and then state their policy in relation to usage of the term:

> Conscious of these problems, we do not generally refer to *'underachievement'* in this review. We prefer instead to focus on the relative achievements of pupils in different ethnic groups, conscious that total equality of outcome may be neither possible, nor just – for instance, if some ethnic groups have better attendance records, tend to spend longer on their homework and are more highly motivated (as some black and Asian groups appear when given questionnaire-based assessments), we might expect them to do better than less motivated groups. Reliable information on such differences is scarce. Our position is that, in practice, *significant differences in the relative achievements of different ethnic groups may reasonably be taken as a cause for concern.* In reviewing the available evidence, attention will be drawn to discrepancies between the relative performance of different ethnic groups. Where differences are significant it is likely that the lower achieving group does not enjoy equal educational opportunities; they may face additional barriers that prevent them fulfilling their potential.[9]

Turning back to the executive summary, the first two bullet points that deal specifically with findings about achievement levels are as follows:

- Research on the performance of infant and junior school pupils does not paint a clear picture: on average African Caribbean pupils appear to achieve less well than whites, although the situation is reversed in recent material from Birmingham.
- A more consistent pattern concerns the lower average attainment of Bangladeshi and Pakistani pupils in the early key stages: this may

---

8 Much material was cut from this section as a result of pressure from OFSTED to reduce the overall length of the Review (David Gillborn, personal communication).

9 'Significant' here presumably means 'sufficiently large to be noted', or it may refer to educational or political significance. Statistical significance is not intended.

reflect the significance of levels of fluency in English, which are strongly associated with performance at this stage.

Here, in reviewing the available research, as is common in other fields, the authors are forced to make judgements about where there is and is not a 'clear picture' or 'consistent pattern'.

In the body of the Review, at the end of this section, the authors provide the following:

> To summarise, the overall picture is complex and changing. There is evidence that at the primary phase, in London at least, the performance of African Caribbean and some Asian pupils gives considerable cause for concern. Interestingly, this is not replicated in Birmingham. The good performance of young African Caribbean pupils in Birmingham merits continuing attention.

The sub-section of the executive summary concerned with 'Achievement at the end of compulsory education' opens with a justification for the importance of this topic: 'Performance in GCSE examinations at 16 can be vital to young people's future educational and employment chances'. The remaining two sentences in the first point present general findings not specifically related to ethnic differences, though no doubt serving as important background:

> Results show that, regardless of ethnic origin, pupils from more economically advantaged backgrounds achieve the highest averages. Girls also tend to do rather better than boys from the same social class background.

The second and third points present what is perhaps the most general and abstract, and certainly the briefest, formulation of what were taken to be the main findings of the whole review:

> Recent years have seen widespread improvements in average GCSE performance. However, not all pupils have shared equally in this trend.

> In many LEAs the gap between the highest and lowest achieving groups has increased.

While there is no explicit mention of ethnicity here, it can be read as referring to differences among ethnic groups.

The fourth bullet point in this section is methodological. It concerns the absence of 'nationally representative figures on GCSE performance'. However, the authors state that 'our review of research and new LEA data has identified some common patterns'. Here, then, a problem with the knowledge base is acknowledged, but it is made clear that this weakness does not stand in the way of reaching conclusions. In the body of the Review, data are used which *are* from a national sample (the Youth Cohort study), though these refer to the mid-1980s. More recent evidence is then presented from data collected by the authors of the Review from local authorities.[10]

In the executive summary, a series of findings based on these data is presented:

> Indian pupils appear consistently to achieve more highly, on average, than pupils from other South Asian backgrounds.

> Indian pupils achieve higher average rates of success than their white counterparts in some (but not all) urban areas.

> Bangladeshi pupils are known on average to have less fluency in English, and to experience greater levels of poverty, than other South Asian groups. Their relative achievements are often less than those of other ethnic groups. In one London borough, however, dramatic improvements in performance have been made – here Bangladeshis are now the highest achieving of all major ethnic groups.[11]

> African Caribbean pupils have not shared equally in the increasing rates of educational achievement: in many LEAs their average achievements are significantly lower than other groups.

> The achievements of African Caribbean young men are a particular cause for concern.

> In some areas there is a growing gap between the achievements of African Caribbean pupils and their peers.

It is worth noting that many of the formulations here are very much in line with the policy adopted by the Review's authors, as signalled in their discussion of 'underachievement'. Phrases such as 'appear consistently to achieve more highly, on average ...', 'relative achievements', 'have not shared equally in the increasing rates of educational achievement', 'average achievements are significantly lower', and 'growing gap between the achievements of African Caribbean pupils and their peers' are clearly designed to avoid what the authors previously identified as the danger of 'blaming the victim'.

These formulations imply what I will refer to as the distribution model. This represents education as a social good that is in some sense distributed among groups or individuals. In these terms, any inequalities in educational achievement among ethnic groups are to be regarded as mal-distribution. The distribution

---

10 One of the authors went on to produce further evidence designed to provide a national picture, drawing on local authority figures: Gillborn and Mirza 2000.

11 The borough is Tower Hamlets.

model contrasts with accounts that explain differential educational achievement in terms of the characteristics (ability, effort, character) of pupils or features of their home and community backgrounds – in other words, the kind of account that the authors fear the term 'underachievement' will stimulate.

Even findings reporting a *higher* level of average achievement on the part of ethnic minority groups, or an improvement in performance, are presented in terms that are relatively neutral as regards explanations for this. However, some of the phrases used, for instance 'Indian pupils appear consistently to achieve more highly . . .', are open to interpretation in terms of what I will call the competition model, simply because (as used here) 'achieve' is an active verb. Even 'dramatic improvements in performance have been made', while passive in grammatical structure, probably implies an active role on the part of those whose performance has improved. The competition model portrays educational performance in terms of a team race, with ethnic groups competing, rather in the manner that children in a class might compete, to achieve the highest level of performance.[12] And, unless it is qualified, it can be taken to imply the allocation of praise or blame to ethnic groups (the pupils themselves or parent communities) according to their relative performance. As we shall see, these contrasting models were reflected in media coverage of the Review.

It is also worth noting here the section in the body of the Review dealing with Bangladeshi pupils, since it is picked up by some of the media. This includes a figure, for Tower Hamlets, showing the change in average exam scores for Bangladeshi, Caribbean and English/Scottish/Welsh pupils from 1990 to 1994. Bangladeshi pupils start off at the bottom of the rank order but are well ahead of the other groups by the end of this period. The following commentary is provided by the authors:

> The London Borough of Tower Hamlets houses almost a quarter of all Bangladeshi children aged 5–15 in England. The borough has made a priority of identifying and targeting the needs of Bangladeshi pupils, especially through the use of Section 11 funds. Recent years have seen improvements in the average exam scores of pupils in each of the borough's major ethnic groups, but the achievements of Bangladeshi pupils are especially dramatic: as a group, Bangladeshi pupils now achieve higher average exam scores than both white and 'Caribbean' pupils in the borough. This is despite experiencing greater levels of economic disadvantage. It would appear, therefore, that Bangladeshi pupils in Tower Hamlets are able to transcend social class relatively more than their white and Caribbean peers; nevertheless, social class continues to be strongly associated with achievement in as much as each group attains below the national average. . . .

---

12 There are, of course, some parallels between educational and sporting achievement, as well as significant differences: see Mackinnon 1986.

The results from Tower Hamlets are especially significant because they illustrate the complexity of achievement. Here Bangladeshi pupils, the group most usually associated with high levels of disadvantage and low average achievements, have become the most successful ethnic group in the LEA – despite continued economic disadvantages. The findings warn against over-simplifying the achievements of pupils in any ethnic group.

The performance of Bangladeshi children in Tower Hamlets is presented here as signalling that schools are able to make a difference and eradicate (in fact, reverse) local outcome inequalities. At the same time, a note of caution is added that underlines the continuing role of economic disadvantage.

The next sub-section in the body of the Review deals with African and African Caribbean pupils, and it is worth noting the points that are highlighted. An initial discussion of findings is summarized in two bullet points:

- The situation is too varied for simple talk of 'black underachievement'.
- Nevertheless, recent research tends to show African Caribbean pupils as relatively less successful than their 'Asian' and white peers.

Data from the London Borough of Lambeth are drawn on, leading to two further bullet points:

- *Pupils of 'Black African' background often achieve relatively higher results than their peers of 'Black Caribbean' origin – where statistics allow distinctions to be made.* It seems likely that both social class and gender play a part in this, but further research is required.
- *On average, Caribbean young men in particular appear to be achieving considerably below their potential.*

And later there are two further bullet points that summarize the general findings on African Caribbean pupils:

- On average, black pupils have not shared equally in the increasing rates of educational achievement: in many LEAs their average achievements are significantly lower than other groups.
- Black pupils generally may be falling further behind the average achievements of the majority of their peers.

The concluding paragraph in this sub-section begins as follows:

As with the Bangladeshi group, this pattern is not inevitable. One LEA, for example, provided details of a special project (funded using Section 11 resources) that uses a targeted programme of support and tuition: the project has produced real improvements in the average achievements of Caribbean pupils …. The project includes three secondary schools at present (so the numbers involved are small) and, of course, the improvements only refer to a single year. Nevertheless, the gains are significant and confirm that differences in rates of achievement are not in any way fixed.

The next section of the executive summary is on 'Educational progress and school effectiveness', and the chapter of the Review to which it corresponds draws on quantitative studies of school effectiveness, some of which have measured differential rates of progress through the educational system, in terms of test and examination scores, on the part of different ethnic groups. The findings listed on educational progress in the executive summary are worth noting:

Social class is strongly associated with differences in pupil progress.

The higher rates of unemployment among some ethnic minority groups may have important educational consequences.

In primary schools over time the gap widens between the performance of pupils from different social class backgrounds.

Whites tend to make greater progress than ethnic minority pupils in primary schools.

In secondary schools Asian pupils make rather better progress than whites of the same social class background. The performance of African Caribbean pupils is less consistent.

Despite the greater progress made by some ethnic minority groups, studies outside London tend to show white pupils leaving school with the highest average achievements.

The next section of the executive summary relates to Chapter 4 of the Review, which is concerned with the findings of qualitative research in multi-ethnic schools. The opening three points are about the nature of qualitative research. The rest of this section is broken down into four sub-sections. The first is concerned with racial violence and harassment. The three points listed here are as follows.

- Qualitative studies highlight the widespread incidence of racial harassment against some pupils.
- Racist harassment is not always recognised as such by teachers, who may mistakenly view it as simple boisterousness.
- Asian pupils seem especially likely to be victimized by their white peers. This echoes the pattern in society more generally and points to the urgent need for action against racial violence and harassment.

The first point does not indicate who the perpetrators of the harassment are, and these might even be interpreted as including teachers. However, this impression seems to be countered in the following two points. In the last point harassment of Asian pupils by white pupils is picked out and there is, once again, a shift from the reporting of factual findings into the drawing of policy conclusions.

The next section deals with exclusions from school:

- Statistics indicate that exclusion from school is being used with increasing frequency. Exclusion is the most serious punishment available to headteachers: two out of every three pupils who are permanently excluded never return to full-time mainstream education.
- African Caribbean pupils are between three and six times more likely to be excluded than whites of the same sex: a pattern that is true for boys and girls in both primary and secondary schools.
- Qualitative research documents individual cases where pupils and their families feel that racial discrimination has occurred. In the future, qualitative research could offer a way of exploring whether issues of ethnicity are involved (directly or indirectly) in the wider use of exclusions at the school level.

The first point here is concerned to underline the significance of exclusion as an issue. The second provides factual information about ethnic differences in exclusion rates which is picked up as a key finding in many media reports. The third point highlights the contribution that qualitative research can make to documenting the causes of ethnic differentials in exclusion rates.

The next sub-section of the summary is about ethnic variation in teacher/pupil interactions. The findings here are as follows:

- Research in infant, primary and secondary schools has recorded an unusually high degree of conflict between white teachers and African Caribbean pupils.
- School case studies describe processes where, despite their best intentions, teachers' actions can create and amplify conflict with African Caribbean pupils.
- In comparison with African Caribbeans, teachers often have more positive expectations of Asians – as relatively quiet, well behaved and highly motivated.
- South Asian pupils are sometimes subject to negative and patronising stereotypes – especially concerning language abilities and the nature of their home communities.
- These stereotypes can be especially damaging for Asian girls.

Here there are outlined several potential causes of outcome inequalities relating to the attitudes and expectations of teachers and their actions in relation to African Caribbean and South Asian pupils.

The final sub-section is entitled 'Understanding success: qualitative perspectives', and contains the following points:

- In relation to the high achievements of certain ethnic minority pupils, existing research suggests that social class, gender and ethnic origin may all play an important role; unfortunately, the relative significance of these factors is not always clear.
- Some ethnic minority pupils respond negatively to school; this is sometimes seen as a means of resisting perceived injustices. Others adapt differently, seeing achievement as a sign of their worth and independence.
- Research suggests that a combination of gender- and race-specific stereotypes might make success especially difficult for African Caribbean young men.
- Qualitative research documents the long, uncertain and sometimes painful processes of change in schools.
- Case studies of primary and secondary schools highlight the potential for school-based change that involves teachers, pupils and local communities in a positive re-evaluation of the role and work of schools in a multi-ethnic society.

Despite the heading of this sub-section, the main emphasis continues to be on the problems faced by ethnic minority pupils. The value of qualitative research is also underlined once again, and 'school-based change' is declared to be both possible and, by implication, desirable.

The final section of the executive summary deals with post-compulsory education. A range of findings is presented about differences between ethnic groups in the likelihood of their staying in the education system beyond 16. It is noted that participation rates generally have been increasing, but that these vary by ethnicity. The findings include the following:

- The participation of Asian young people is especially high; even three years after the end of compulsory schooling, a majority of Asians are still in full time education [. . . .]
- Asian young people tend to follow traditional 'academic' courses. Consequently, by age 18 Asians are the most highly qualified of all groups (including whites).
- African Caribbean young people are more likely to follow vocational courses.

Following this, there are some findings about access to higher education. These include:

- Relatively more people of ethnic minority origin apply to enter Higher Education.

- Whites are more likely than their ethnic minority peers to be accepted by the 'old' universities; Black Caribbean and African applicants are accepted least often.
- Even when previous achievement is taken into account, people do not share an equal chance of admission; being male, attending a selective school and having parents in professional/managerial occupations all increase the probability of success.
- Taking all these factors into account, it is still the case that certain ethnic minority groups experience significantly different rates of admission to university: Chinese young people are more likely to be admitted than other groups; Black Caribbeans and Pakistanis are less likely to gain a place at university.

Looking at the executive summary as a whole, there is no single, clear overall message. What is offered is a long list of points relating to various aspects of the field, summarizing achievement and progress, indicating where inequalities in outcome persist and possible causes for these. However, there are some potential overall messages embedded in this summary. One of these concerns the complexity of the patterns being reported, with progress having been made in some respects, but little or no progress in others, so that there is continuing 'cause for concern'. Another message is that inequalities in educational outcome should be seen as generated by the education system, and that change within that system can lead to significant improvements.

The summary in the conclusion

By comparison with the executive summary, the conclusion summary is much shorter. It also differs in its *structure*. The main part of it reads as follows:

Many things have changed in the decade since the Swann Committee reported: among the many encouraging developments that our review highlights are:

- Generally higher levels of achievement, increasing year on year;
- Improving levels of attainment among ethnic minority groups in many areas of the country;
- Dramatic increases in the examination performance of certain minority groups, even in LEAs where there is significant poverty;
- In higher education, people of ethnic minority background are generally well represented among those continuing their education to degree level.

However, the review also illustrates the need for critical consideration of changes, keeping sight of the continuing differences in educational experience and achievement between certain groups. We have noted, for example:

- The gap is growing between the highest and lowest achieving ethnic groups in many LEAs;
- African Caribbean young people, especially boys, have not shared fully in the increasing rates of achievement; in some areas their performance has actually worsened;
- The sharp rise in the number of exclusions from school affects a disproportionately large number of black pupils;
- Even when differences in qualifications, social class and gender are taken into account, ethnic groups do not enjoy equal chances of success in their applications to enter university.

Like the executive summary, this one starts with the temporal context of the Review, formulated in terms of the time that has passed since 'the last major review' in the area. However, the changes that are mentioned here relate to the performance of ethnic minority pupils.

The specific points that make up the body of this summary are very much descriptive factual information about ethnic variations in educational performance. Furthermore, the formulations tend to be in terms of what I referred to earlier as the distribution model: notably, 'have not shared fully', and 'do not enjoy equal chances of success', though here again reference to highest and lowest achieving groups may be open to interpretation in competition model terms.

The conclusions are grouped into two sections, one labelled as 'encouraging developments', and explicitly contrasted with the other, referred to as 'continuing differences in educational achievement and experience between certain groups'. What is presented here, then, is not just a summary of factual findings but also an evaluation, with a mixed overall message suggesting that there is both good and bad news.

A question that might arise in relation to the conclusion summary on the part of readers is: which half of the message is being given priority – the good news or the bad news? In the case of media presentations, it is generally assumed that what is presented first, notably headlines, is treated by readers as carrying the greatest weight. This would suggest that the good news is being prioritized in this summary. However, this interpretation has to be qualified, given widespread public awareness of the good news/bad news format. It seems likely that, in reading the first section, readers familiar with this format will have the expectation that bad news is to follow. And it is possible that, as a result, they will give greater weight to the latter. Where this occurs, the good news is turned into a preface to the bad news. Furthermore, it is worth noting – in thinking of journalists as readers – that, in the media, bad news is generally treated as more newsworthy than good news, no doubt because it may point to a need for action (see Braham 1982: 275) – and the need for the latter is made explicit in this summary.

The back cover summary

The summary on the back cover of the Review is similar in structure and formulation to that in the conclusion. It reads as follows:

> This is the first major review of research on the educational achievements of ethnic minority pupils for over ten years.
>
> It points to improving levels of attainment among ethnic minority groups in many areas of the country and dramatic increases in the examination performance of certain groups, even in LEAs where there are significant levels of disadvantage.
>
> It also suggests that people of ethnic minority background are generally well represented among those continuing their education to degree level.
>
> However, the review also highlights the growing gap between the highest and lowest achieving ethnic groups; African Caribbean young people, especially boys, have not shared equally in the increasing rates of achievement and in some areas their performance has actually worsened.
>
> The report also shows that the sharp rise in the number of exclusions from school affects a disproportionately large number of black pupils, and that ethnic groups do not enjoy equal chances of success in their applications to enter university.

While the good news/bad news structure is not as strongly signalled here, the ordering of the points is the same as in the conclusion summary: the first two paragraphs outline what are likely to be taken as positive changes, the second two paragraphs refer to negative features. And, as in the conclusion summary, the two 'halves' are separated by a 'However', indicating contrast. Moreover, the points included are the same, with only minor variations in phrasing.

All three summaries presumably draw out what the authors see as the main points of their Review. Moreover, they provide a much more limited array from which journalists might select items for inclusion in their reports than the Review as a whole. However, there is one further part of the Review that we need to give attention to: the section which follows the conclusion summary and takes up the final pages. This is entitled 'Ways forward: policy and practice'.

Ways forward: policy and practice

As the title implies, this section is largely concerned with what are taken to be the implications of the Review's findings for policy and practice, broadly interpreted.

It begins with a prefatory paragraph emphasizing that there are 'no simple answers to the range of educational issues raised by ethnic diversity'. It is also noted that there are gaps in the research evidence. The final two sentences read: 'This review charts the importance of ethnic origin as a factor in educational achievement from infant school to university. It is crucial that ethnicity is considered when new agendas are debated or targets set'. Here the authors are taking up a point made in the first section of the executive summary and in the Introduction, about the policy importance of ethnic differences in achievement. And, once again, they are moving from reporting factual findings to drawing policy conclusions, or at least offering policy advice.

What follows in this concluding section is a series of bullet point recommendations, each accompanied by a paragraph or so of explication. The bullet point headings are listed below (and I have also provided a summary of each of the explicatory paragraphs, with the exception of the final one where I have reproduced the original text, since this covers a point that was picked up by some of the media):

- Monitoring achievements and needs
  [Here the importance of monitoring is emphasized and also that the results must be used to good effect.]
- A focus on ethnicity
  [The fact that ethnicity is not a 'cities-only' issue is stressed, and recommendations made about how OFSTED could encourage this issue to be addressed.]
- Achievement for all
  [Here the unevenness in performance of different ethnic groups is emphasized and the need for this problem to be remedied is underlined.]
- Ethnicity and the whole school
  Failure to address ethnic diversity has proved counter-productive at the school level. Where schools have adopted 'colour-blind' policies, for example, inequalities of opportunity have been seen to continue. In contrast, research has begun to examine the benefits of addressing diversity as an important and changing part of school life. In this country 'multiculturalism' has received some support at a national level (though often marginal and focused mainly on the curriculum). The word 'anti-racism' has been applied rather loosely and, in many cases, its practical application at the school level is uncertain. Nevertheless, some local authorities and individual schools have worked seriously at developing practical and workable approaches to ethnic diversity. Research shows that the past has produced both failure and success and suggests that there are no easy formulae, but a wide ranging attempt to address ethnicity is long overdue in many schools. It also suggests that, sensitively and self-critically handled, schools' approaches to multiculturalism and anti-racism can

make a real impact; reducing racial harassment and involving pupils in genuine and supportive ways.[13]

The argument presented in this last point is a complex one that, I suspect, may not have been easy for many readers to fully grasp. First, a contrast is set up between 'colour-blind' policies and 'addressing ethnic diversity'. Then a second pair of terms is mentioned: 'multi-culturalism' and 'anti-racism', and some but perhaps not all readers will know that these too are often taken to form a contrast. However, the two sets of terms do not map on to one another in any obvious way, other than that multi-culturalism can be seen as 'addressing ethnic diversity' in at least some sense. There is also the problem for interpretation that racism too 'addresses ethnic diversity' in the sense that it is specifically not 'colour-blind'. And implicit here as well is the question of the relationship between ethnicity and 'colour'.

In the middle of the paragraph a further contrast is created, between the 'uncertain' practical application of anti-racism at school level and the way that 'some local authorities and individual schools have worked seriously at developing practical and workable approaches to ethnic diversity'. It is implied that this has not always produced success (presumably in terms of equalizing average achievement levels across ethnic groups), but that many schools have not even attempted to do this, and ought to. The last quarter of the paragraph makes claims about what research has 'shown', and that it suggests that multi-culturalist and anti-racist policies 'can make a real impact; reducing racial harassment and involving pupils in genuine and supportive ways'. However, it is not clear what research is being referred to here: it does not seem to have been highlighted in the body of the Review.

Clearly the summaries included in the Review are likely to have played an important role in shaping media reporting of it, and I have used this account of their content as a way of outlining what seem to be presented by the authors of the Review as their main findings. There were, however, two even more direct bridges between the Review and the media: the press release and the press conference.

PRESENTING THE REVIEW TO THE MEDIA: THE PRESS RELEASE AND PRESS CONFERENCE

Considerable effort went into publicizing the Review, much more than with most reports of primary research, and indeed most research reviews. OFSTED, the Review's sponsor, has well-established procedures for getting media coverage of its reports – through prior notification of journalists, production of press releases that are available on its website and distributed to media agencies, and through the calling of press conferences. Furthermore, because it and the then Chief Inspector

---

13 The remaining bullet points outline areas where there are gaps in research knowledge.

of Schools had a high media profile, it was usually successful in attracting media attention. At the point of publication a press release was prepared and a press conference arranged at the offices of OFSTED. Press releases and conferences can, of course, be very important in shaping media coverage.[14]

The Review was presented at the press conference by the Chief Inspector of Schools, Chris Woodhead, along with David Gillborn, its lead author.[15] An internal briefing document had been prepared for them, identifying possible questions and suggesting answers. There were around twenty journalists present, plus television cameras. The Chief Inspector made a brief presentation focusing on the implications for schools, and this was followed by questions, some of which were redirected by Woodhead to Gillborn, notably those that related to the specifics of the Review. The conference was followed by individual television interviews with both Woodhead and Gillborn, and then further radio interviews. The conference lasted around 30 minutes, though the interviews went on for some time after that.[16]

The press release was prepared by OFSTED, with no input from the authors, though they saw it beforehand. It was headed: ' "Colour blind" school policies do not help ethnic minority pupils says OFSTED report'. It is not unusual for titles of texts to play a key role in signalling key points, and shaping audience responses. The heading here focused on what is the main practical conclusion of the Review, though it is not included in any of the summaries, and is only presented explicitly in the 'Ways forward: policy and practice' section of the conclusion. What is highlighted in the title of the press release, then, is not a factual research finding but a policy conclusion that is presented as following from the results of the Review.

The body of the press release is in five parts, though these are not labelled. The first amounts to an introduction. There are two paragraphs here, with the opening one announcing that 'the achievement of ethnic minority pupils is the subject of a report, commissioned by the Office for Standards in Education, which is published today'. It is striking that at this point the Review is attributed to OFSTED, albeit as commissioner, rather than to the authors – mention of their names only comes much later.

The second paragraph of the press release reads as follows:

> Recent Research on the Achievements of Ethnic Minority Pupils looks at research published in the last ten years and finds that there have been many encouraging developments since the Swann Report of 1985. However, the

---

14 Alexander reports that at the press conference dealing with the publication of the report of the 'Three Wise Men' journalists were encouraged to rely on the press release: see Alexander 1997: 218–19.

15 Originally, the authors were not to have been involved in the press conference but they exerted pressure to be included in it (personal communication, David Gillborn).

16 My information about the press conference is second-hand, coming from some of those who attended.

review also illustrates the need to consider the reasons for the changes and the continuing differences in educational experience and achievement between certain groups. The review charts the importance of ethnic origin as a factor in educational achievement from infant school to university.

Here we have a summary of the findings of the Review that is even more condensed than that on its back cover, though it has the same 'good news'/'bad news' format. And the last sentence comes from the opening part of the 'Ways forward' section of the conclusion, indicating the comprehensiveness of the Review.

The next section of the press release is a more detailed presentation of the findings, and this follows closely the bullet points listed in the conclusion review:

The report found encouraging developments over the last ten years. These include:

- improving levels of attainment among ethnic minority groups in many areas of the country;
- dramatic increases in examination performance in certain minority groups experiencing economic disadvantage such as Bangladeshi pupils in the London Borough of Tower Hamlets;
- in higher education, people of ethnic minority background are generally well represented among those continuing education to degree level, although there are significantly different university admission rates between the ethnic groups.

However, over these same ten years the report also finds that:

- the gap is growing between the highest and lowest achieving ethnic groups in many LEAs, for example, in the London Borough of Brent between Asian and African Caribbean pupils respectively;
- African Caribbean young people, especially boys, have not shared equally in the increasing levels of achievement;
- a disproportionately high number of black pupils have been excluded from school.

Here, the four points of good and bad news from the conclusion summary have been reduced to three each, by elimination of a point from each section. However, the mode of formulation is very similar to the other short summaries.

Following this, there is a list of the policy implications, derived largely from the 'Ways forward' section of the conclusion. This reads as follows:

The report calls for:

- greater monitoring of educational achievements and experiences of ethnic minority pupils;

- schools to address ethnicity;
- a research agenda to address gaps in data;
- systematic studies of teaching and learning in multi-ethnic schools; and
- research into exclusions at school level.

The remainder of this section consists of two paragraphs providing slightly more information about the policy implications. These link back to the press release headline through a repeated reference to 'colour-blind policies':

> Schools must address ethnic diversity as failure to do so has proved to be counterproductive. Where schools have adopted colour-blind policies, inequalities of opportunity have continued. Sensitive and self-critical approaches by schools to multi-culturalism and anti-racism can make a real impact.

> The gathering of reliable information about the experiences, achievements and needs of ethnic minority groups is essential to improving standards for all. This requires the cooperation of pupils and parents. (OFSTED inspections reveal that ethnic monitoring is carried out in less than 0.5 per cent or one in 200 of schools inspected.)

These two paragraphs appear to relate to the first two bullet points listing recommendations (though research is perhaps also seen as playing a crucial role in ethnic monitoring). Thus, in the press release, by contrast with the Review itself and the summaries it contains, it is the policy implications of the Review that are foregrounded for the media and the audiences they serve.

The penultimate section of the press release is a reported statement from the head of OFSTED:

> Welcoming the report Chris Woodhead, HM Inspector of Schools in England, said:

> 'This review shows that ethnicity is an important factor to be considered when new agendas are debated or targets are being set. In a complex educational area such as this, however, where so many factors and influences come into play, there are no quick and easy answers as to what produces high and low achievement.'

> 'OFSTED inspections are aimed at improving education for all. The new Framework for Inspection takes a much tougher line on equal opportunity issues and requires inspectors to report any significant variations in attainment of pupils of different ethnic backgrounds. Schools are expected to have procedures in place to monitor achievement by different ethnic groups and failure to do this would be regarded as a significant weakness.'

'For its part, OFSTED is preparing a report on exclusions, conducting an assessment of bilingual pupils based on a study of nearly 20 local education authorities, and preparing a further report on achievement in urban schools of which at least half have significant minority ethnic populations. These reports will be published during 1997 and 1998.'

It is worth noting how the Chief Inspector, and thereby OFSTED, are positioned here as external commentators on the Review. Yet we have seen how strongly the Review was identified with OFSTED in other places, both on its cover and in the opening section of the press release. And not only did that organization commission the Review but its officers were involved in negotiating the character of the final draft. Moreover, while the opening sentence of the Chief Inspector's commentary simply summarizes what has been presented as one of the Review's key policy implications, the second sentence can be read as qualifying the message. Woodhead refers to a 'complex educational issue' to which there are 'no quick and easy answers'. This echoes what is written in the opening part of the 'ways forward' section of the Review, but does so in a way that suggests there are limits to what can reasonably be expected from public policy in this field – a message that is not that of the Review. We might perhaps read this as an attempt to downgrade expectations about, and therefore any negative evaluation of, OFSTED's work. The message seems to be that OFSTED is active in this field, though it should not be blamed for the fact that there is still a problem. And there is also an indication in what the Chief Inspector says that the main responsibility lies with schools, and that OFSTED will hold them to account.

The final section of the press release is entitled 'NOTES TO EDITORS'. It gives the publication details of the Review, the names of the authors and their institutional affiliation, details about the 'Swann Report' which is referred to in the Release, and a description of OFSTED.

As already noted, what is striking about the press release is how much emphasis is given to what are taken to be the practical implications of the research findings, by comparison with the Review itself. This may reflect a concern on the part of OFSTED to make clear the relevance of the Review to an audience, the mass media, whose interest is anticipated to be not so much the research findings themselves as their implications for government policy and the operation of its institutions, including OFSTED. But of course it also relates to the policy orientation of that organization itself as a government agency.

CONCLUSION

In this chapter I have looked at some of the ways in which the Review was designed and structured, and how it was presented to a media audience, along with the implications of this for how it might be read. The Review was clearly designed to attract public attention; and, while it is a long and complex text, it is broken up into chapters and sections, parts of it are highlighted in various ways, and multiple summaries are provided. All these features enable readers to get some sense of the salience of the various research findings presented. In these ways, a lengthy document is made more usable by non-academic audiences, including the media – whose own target audiences are very diverse. Of course, the other side of this recipient design was an effort to control the use that was made of the Review: not only to make clear what are – and perhaps even more importantly, *what are not* – the main points, but also to indicate what policy conclusions should be drawn. In other words, the Review is designed not just to put research evidence into the public domain in an attractive and accessible way, but also to shape the policy agenda. Despite this, the Review is still open to differing interpretations, and in subsequent chapters we shall see how this leeway was used by the media.

2 The Review on the radio: the *Today* programme and *The World at One*

In Britain, the media profile of education as a policy issue increased considerably in the last two decades of the twentieth century (Baker 1994). In large part, this resulted from its move up the political agenda to become one of the top priorities for government. But the causal relationship probably ran in both directions, with the media playing a key role in raising education's public profile by mounting various campaigns about failures in the state education system (see Alexander 1997: Part II). Of course, both government and the media usually claim to be speaking on behalf of 'ordinary people', but it also seems likely that many people's views – about the importance of education, about what is wrong with schools, about what should be done, etc. – have been shaped by the mass media's treatment of educational issues, including their reporting of government statements and policies.[1] A predominant theme in this period was an attack on 'progressivism' within the teaching profession, and on the 'educational establishment' more generally.

However, while the high public profile of education led to an increased number of news items and current affairs programmes dealing with education on radio and television, it did not lead to much coverage of the findings of educational research.[2] The substantial coverage received by the Review was very much the exception. The main radio coverage here was on the national BBC station Radio 4, in particular on the early morning *Today* programme, the day after the Review was published.[3]

---

1 Some recent research has suggested that the media can have a substantial impact on people's attitudes to key political issues: see Lacey and Longman 1997.
2 In an interview with Mike Baker, one of the BBC's education correspondents, he reported some research he had done on his use of different sources for stories, and he comments: 'what did surprise me was how *few* stories we do on the basis of educational research' (M. Baker, personal communication, August 1999).
3 I did not collect data on coverage by other BBC radio channels or on commercial stations. However, it seems likely that this would have been limited to brief headlines at most. For a discussion of the distinctive characteristics of radio news and current affairs programmes, see Crisell 1994: chs 1, 3 and 5. For a detailed account of the production processes behind BBC radio and television news, albeit from a slightly earlier period, see Schlesinger 1987; while there would have been some significant changes, notably in the number of education correspondents, much of his analysis probably still applies.

THE *TODAY* PROGRAMME

Today is a news programme which is broadcast live on weekdays from 6.30 a.m. to 8.40 a.m., and on Saturdays from 7.00 a.m. to 9.00 a.m.[4] It starts with news headlines and a news bulletin; and the programme is broken up into half-hour segments by the presentation of news summaries on the half-hour and full news presentations at 7.00 a.m. and 8.00 a.m. The headlines are also sometimes summarized between these times.

As Crisell (1986) points out, one of the distinctive characteristics of radio news, by comparison with newspapers, is that the audience has less capacity for selection among news items. One cannot go immediately to the items one is interested in, ignoring the rest. Most people will hear, though perhaps not listen very attentively to, many items in which they have little initial interest. Yet, of course, they may discover that they *do* have an interest in some of these items and begin to pay more attention. In this way, radio, and also television, news may have a wider impact than newspapers. Of course, particular radio channels and programmes have distinctive audiences, and this limits who is likely to be reached. The audience for the *Today* programme is, in crude terms, typically rather middle-aged and middle-class.

The main body of the *Today* programme consists of several types of item. First, there are those which follow up stories in the news bulletins, usually through correspondents' reports and/or interviews. On the day I am concerned with here, besides coverage of the Review, there were items of this kind dealing with cruise missiles over Iraq and the American Secretary of State seeking European support for action against that country, about Conservative and Labour Party electioneering over tax, about a call from the chief executives of some large companies in favour of European monetary union, as well as news stories about the Irish political situation, about Israel, and about South Africa. Some of the top news stories are covered on the *Today* programme by more than one item. Thus the Iraq story had a spot in every segment of it; and the Review itself was covered by two items.

There are also some stories on *Today* that are not related to public policy issues. For instance, on this day, there was an item dealing with a conference about the Big Bang theory of the origin of the universe, one about the discovery of a new prime number, and one about a study claiming that pets can anticipate their owners' return from work. Occasionally, too, there may be special features that are not directly news-led, dealing with an issue in depth through items that occur on consecutive days. Finally, there are some regular features: weather forecasts, the sports news, the business news, a report on the day's newspapers, and *Thought for the Day*.[5]

---

4 The timings have changed slightly since 1996.
5 In the past, *Today* was much more of a 'magazine' programme, and carried more items like this. From the 1970s onwards, however, it came to be more and more dominated by news-led items

I will begin by looking at the headlines, news summaries and bulletins dealing with the Review. Later, I will examine the two follow-up items within the *Today* programme.

The Review in the news

News of the publication of the Review was included in the headlines and the initial news bulletin on the *Today* programme at 6.30 a.m. It was the second item in both lists. Two items followed it in the headlines, and six followed it in the news bulletin. In a later summary of the headlines at 6.44 a.m. it was also in second place, one of three items. In the 7.00 a.m. news, it moved to third spot; but it was back in second slot at 7.30 a.m. It was missing from the opening headlines at 8.00 a.m., but was included in the bulletin, albeit down in fourth slot. However, it was back to third slot in the 8.30 a.m. summary.

What is selected for inclusion in news headlines and bulletins, and the order in which items are presented, probably gives a rough indication of journalistic judgements about its relative newsworthiness. On this basis, we can conclude that the story about the Review was initially given relatively high priority among the items chosen for inclusion that day, this declining slightly over the course of the programme.[6]

In order to analyse the relationship between the Review as source and news coverage of it, I will look first at the content of the relevant headline at 6.30 a.m., the 6.30 news bulletin item, and the 6.44 a.m. headline summary. These are transcribed in full below:

[6.30 a.m. headlines:]
Research on the educational achievements of ethnic minorities suggests Asian pupils are outshining their classmates. We talk to two headteachers.

[6.30 a.m. news bulletin:]
Research published by the Schools' Inspectorate says that pupils from some Asian groups are out-performing their classmates. The study, comparing the academic achievement of ethnic minority pupils, also suggests that Afro-Caribbean students are underachieving.

dealing with political issues. This is documented by a set of cassettes entitled *BBC Radio Collection: Today – Forty Years of the News Programme that set the Nation's Agenda*, BBC Worldwide Ltd, 1997.
6 The length of treatment of different items may also indicate news value. In terms of wordage across headlines, summaries and bulletins, the Review comes at fourth or fifth in position. The story on Iraq is a long way ahead (1425 words across all the headlines and news summaries). The story on political parties, their election campaigns and tax comes second. Following this, there are three stories, including that dealing with the Review, in the range 400–464 words.

[Headline summary at 6.44 a.m.:]
A new study from the Schools' Inspectorate concludes that boys of Afro-Caribbean origin are under-performing at school.

A number of points can be made about this coverage. First of all, while in the opening headlines the research is not specifically attributed to anyone, in the news bulletin and in later headlines it is attributed to 'the Schools' Inspectorate'. It is noticeable that no reference is made to the fact that the study was produced by independent, academic researchers. This attribution of the Review to OFSTED, or to School Inspectors, is a common feature of the media coverage, as we shall see. It probably reflects not just OFSTED's commissioning of the Review, the salience of its name on the cover, and the fact that the Review was launched at an OFSTED press conference, but also this organization's high media profile.[7] Either the journalists themselves, or some of them, assumed that OFSTED was the author of the Review, or (more probably) they decided that this was the best way to introduce it to an audience who were much more likely already to have heard of that organization than of the Institute of Education at the University of London, or of the actual authors of the Review.

It is a commonly noted feature of media coverage that a great deal of it concerns the sayings and doings of official agencies. So we might also suspect that the Review was attributed to OFSTED because this signifies its relation to government, and thereby its newsworthiness. This reflects the fact that, for the media especially, the significance of what is said often depends a good deal on who said it. Indeed, it seems very likely that the extent of media coverage of the Review arises from the link with OFSTED. This conclusion is supported by the fact that, for the most part, the Review deals with research which had been published over the previous ten years; and none of these individual studies had received much media coverage.[8]

A second point to be made about the content of the news reports is that they focus on the *findings* of the Review, rather than on its policy recommendations. There is no mention at all of the latter, though they *are* mentioned in the education correspondent's account later during the *Today* programme, discussed below. This is discrepant with what seemed to be the main emphasis of the press release.

A third point is that there are clear differences between how the findings are reported here, and how they were presented in the press release and in the two

---

7 However, it is striking that the OFSTED acronym is not used by the BBC; 'the Schools' Inspectorate' was presumably judged to be more informative to a wider audience.

8 There is further evidence for this conclusion, in that three years after publication of the Review, OFSTED produced another report on the education of ethnic minority pupils, this time based on the results of inspections rather than research; and this too received a great deal of coverage. For example, the front page headline of the *Daily Express* on Monday 8 March 1999 was 'Schools failing black pupils'. We should note, though, that this not only followed the change of government but also the Macpherson Inquiry into Stephen Lawrence's death (Macpherson 1999).

short summaries that can be found in the Review. Most obviously, first of all, the BBC's three initial accounts of the Review's findings are highly selective, even compared with the summary in the press release. This reflects the pressure on 'space' within headlines and bulletins, along with the relative priority given to this story. Equally important, the BBC reports involved some reformulation of the selected points.[9]

Given this process of selection and reformulation, I want to look fairly closely at the account of the Review provided by each of these initial BBC news reports/headlines.[10] The opening headline offers a comparison between the performance of Asian pupils and 'their classmates', summarized in the description that they are 'outshining' them. Even if we accept that the selection of just one item from the findings of the Review was technically unavoidable for a headline, we can still ask why this particular point was highlighted. After all, many other headlines were possible on the basis of the Review: for instance, that there were improving levels of attainment among ethnic minority groups in many areas of the country; that in higher education ethnic minorities are generally well represented; and/or that a disproportionately high number of black pupils continue to be excluded from school. Furthermore, the finding that was selected was not one that was highlighted in the press release summary or the summaries within the Review, or even in the body of the Review itself.

To some degree, the selection of headlines about the Review will reflect a concern on the part of journalists to represent its content accurately. Thus, one reason for the selection that was made may be that it was taken to capture the main focus of the Review, as implied by its title. In other words, the latter's emphasis on the *achievements* of ethnic minority pupils may have led to selection of the high achievement levels of some Asian pupils as the key finding, though we should note that what is presented is an unqualified formulation of a finding that is formulated in the Review as relating only to Indian pupils in *some* areas. Journalists are also likely to be concerned with the relative newsworthiness of what *could be* reported about the Review. And we must remember that they are competing with one another to get a slot for their stories, and a slot as high up the priority list of news items as possible. So this particular item was probably also selected because it was judged to have intrinsic news value: that some Asian groups are achieving at higher levels than ethnic majority pupils was perhaps judged to be not widely known. In these terms, the Review could be seen as

---

9 Pressure on 'space' operates across all mass media, though it is probably greater for broadcast news than for newspapers. See Bell 1991: 76–7 on how pressure on space leads to the editing down of newspaper reports. On how the problem is dealt with in the broadcast media, see Schlesinger 1987: chs 3 and 4.

10 It is important to remember that the production of broadcast news headlines and reports, even more than in the case of newspapers, is a collective process, by no means limited to those journalists who appear on air (see Schlesinger 1987).

newsworthy not just in being the pronouncement of an official agency but also because it offered some striking new information.

As already noted, this finding was not one that was highlighted in the summaries. The only place where it appears in these is in the first item of the 'bad news' component of the press release summary, where the example is given that in the London Borough of Brent the gap is growing between the highest-achieving ethnic group – Asian pupils – and the lowest-achieving ethnic group – African Caribbean pupils.

Possible sources for this headline can also be found within the Review itself, and it may have been drawn from there rather than from the press release. For example, in the executive summary there are the following statements: 'Indian pupils achieve higher average rates of success than their white counterparts in some (but not all) urban areas' and 'In secondary schools Asian pupils make rather better progress than whites of the same social class background'. It should be noted, though, that these are two among 68 bullet points; and the second of them is not only about progress rather than achievement but is also sandwiched between the findings that whites 'tend to make greater progress than ethnic minority pupils in primary schools' and that 'despite the greater progress made by some ethnic minority groups, studies outside London tend to show white pupils leaving school with the highest average achievements'.

Within the body of the Review, if we look at the opening summary to Chapter 2, which is concerned with achievement, there is no mention of the relatively high level achievement of some Asian groups. However, on the ninth page into that chapter, we find the following highlighted sentence (mauve print on a white background): 'Asian pupils ... achieved almost as well as, or better than, whites of the same class and gender' (p. 18). There then follows a discussion of the data from Brent, including a graph showing the relative performance of Asian, African Caribbean and white pupils (p. 20). The discussion here points to problems in generalizing about national levels of educational achievement for different ethnic groups. This is then followed by two bullet points, one of which matches that in the executive summary:

- Indian pupils are achieving levels of success consistently in excess of their white counterparts in some (but not all) urban areas.

In a later section of the Review, it is reported that '*By the age of 18 Asian young people are the most highly qualified group*, placing them in a relatively strong position for entry into higher education' (p. 70, italics in original).

What seems to have happened here, then, is that journalists have identified as the key finding one that was not prioritized by the authors of the Review, and one about which the latter make important qualifications; though it does fit with the emphasis of the title of the Review on the achievements of ethnic minority pupils. Indeed, it seems likely that the BBC have taken a subordinate part of one of the points made in the press release summary as the first part of their main news about the Review.

We might ask why the headline names the high-achieving group, rather than simply noting that one ethnic minority group seems to be achieving at a higher level than the majority population. One explanation for this may be the belief that headlines should be relatively specific and self-contained in the information they convey. To say that 'some ethnic minority groups are achieving at a high level' immediately raises the question of *which* groups these are. On some occasions, such lack of specificity might be used by radio and television journalists to draw their audience into listening to the full bulletin. But, even in doing this, sufficient information needs to be provided to attract interest. Furthermore, journalists working on the *Today* programme will be aware that people are doing other things while listening to the programme, such as preparing and eating breakfast.[11] This heightens what may be necessary to attract attention, but also indicates that many people will only hear the headlines, so that these need to contain the gist of the news if journalists are to fulfil their task of informing the public.

Rather more significant perhaps, is the fact that Asian pupils are described in the opening headline as 'outshining' others. This is not a term that is used in the Review, or in the press release. There, Asian pupils are generally described as 'achieving higher rates of success' or 'making rather better progress'. This journalistic reformulation probably stems from a desire to make the meaning more immediately accessible to a wide audience. Not only does it reduce several words to one, but the term 'outshining' is vivid and colloquial. Of course, as with all simplifications, the effect may be to change the message, subtly or dramatically. And there is an issue here to do with what I will call the explanatory implications of this term. The metaphor underlying 'outshining' is that of competition: it implies that the difference between Asian pupils and their classmates lies with *them*: they are 'brighter', they 'shine' more. Such explanatory implications are a key issue in considering whether media reports distorted the message of the Review.

In summary, in their initial headline, the BBC chose to focus on the findings rather than the recommendations of the Review, on just one of the findings out of six listed in the press release – and a subordinate one at that. Moreover, in naming the highest achieving group they adopted a more global term ('Asian' rather than 'Indian') and stripped out significant qualifications. Furthermore, the finding was reformulated in terms that may be more accessible to the public, but which could carry rather different explanatory implications from the formulations in the Review and press release.

In the news bulletin itself, which followed very soon after the initial headline, the same finding from the Review is repeated, but there are three changes. First,

---

11 This is the other side of what Crisell describes as one of the advantages of radio, as against other media: its flexibility, in the sense that, even more than with television, one can perform other activities while listening (Crisell 1994: 11). He points out that 'the freedom that radio affords us to pursue other activities while listening can, and frequently does, detract from our full understanding of what it purveys. Listening is a good deal easier than ever before but by the same token often a good deal less attentive – much of the message can be ignored' (p. 14).

it is *some* rather than all Asian pupils who are now presented as the highest achieving group. Second, the word 'outshining' is replaced by 'outperforming'. Third, this finding about Asian pupils is supplemented with another: that 'Afro-Caribbean students are underachieving'.

The first change adds a qualification that was to be found in the press release and *Review* summaries. We can perhaps explain this on the grounds that qualifications often get omitted from headlines because of the need for extreme brevity, and because they must dramatize their newsworthiness. The reason for the second change is less obvious, but it may stem from a concern with including some variety in headlines and news bulletins. Nevertheless, 'outperforming' can be read as a close synonym to 'outshining', and it seems to carry similar, though perhaps slightly weaker, explanatory implications. It may (though it need not) be taken to suggest that it is active effort, or intrinsic superiority, on the part of (some) Asian pupils which has led them to achieve at higher levels than other groups.

As regards the third change, it should be noted that the new element which is introduced is also to be found in the component of the press release summary that I suggested earlier might have been the source for the headline. There, not only were Asian pupils identified as the higher achieving group (in Brent), but African Caribbean pupils were also identified as the lower achieving group. However, the second point in the 'bad news' section of that summary also relates to the lower average level achievement of African Caribbean pupils: 'African Caribbean young people, especially boys, have not shared equally in the increasing rates of achievement'. Here, then, one of the main points listed in the summaries is being reported.

It is worth paying close attention to this new two-element message used in the news report, since it recurs in most of the remaining headline summaries and bulletins during the *Today* programme.[12] We should note that this message involves one comparison laid upon two others. As in the headline, the performance of Asian pupils is compared to that of all other pupils. And, by implication at least, the performance of African Caribbean pupils is also being compared to that of everyone else.[13] Over and above these two comparisons, the performance of Asian and African Caribbean pupils is also being contrasted, albeit implicitly. Their achievement levels are presented as mirror images of one another: one is 'outperforming', the other is 'underachieving'.

As already noted, different language is used by the BBC from that in the press release and the *Review*. And this is true of the clause about African Caribbean

---

12 The formulation varies somewhat, but Asians 'outperforming' and African Caribbeans 'underachieving' are the modal forms.

13 'Underachieving' could be interpreted in other ways, notably in relation to some pre-defined standard, but this does not seem to be the case here.

as well as of that about Asian pupils. They are described as 'underachiev-ing', whereas in the press release they were described as 'the lowest achieving group [in Brent]' and as 'not sharing equally in the increasing rates of achieve-ment'. This latter formulation is also found in both the conclusion and back cover summaries, with the addition that: 'in some areas [African Caribbean pupils'] performance has actually worsened'. Once again, the different formula-tions vary, potentially, in the explanatory implications they carry. As I indicated in Chapter 1, 'Having not shared equally' implies unequal distribution, whereas 'underachieving' can (though need not) be interpreted as implying failure on the part of African Caribbean pupils. In particular, to underachieve might be interpreted as failing to work hard enough, even though this is not automati-cally implied. Indeed, in the previous chapter, we saw that the authors of the Review specifically warn against use of the term 'underachievement' for these reasons.

Earlier, I suggested that the high level of achievement of some Asian groups may have been selected by the BBC as the main finding of the Review because of its intrinsic news value. It seems likely that the 'underachievement' of African Caribbean pupils was not seen to have as high a news value.[14] Indeed, later during the *Today* programme one of the presenters refers to it as indicating that 'not much has changed'. In any case, it is clear that the *combination* of the two items *is* regarded as having news value, over and above that of the first item on its own and the fact that what is being reported can be presented as an official pronouncement. The very contrast between *some* ethnic minority groups doing better than white pupils, while others continue to do worse, may be taken to have considerable interest. For one thing, it indicates diversity where the audience might perhaps be expected to assume similarity. More than this, the contrast *could* be taken to count against any suggestion that the lower level of performance of African Caribbean pupils is a product of 'racial' discrimination against them. If there is such discrimination, it could be asked, how is it that Asian pupils are doing so well?[15] No such message is presented by the BBC, but the contrast format used could raise this question for some listeners. And, to the extent that it does, it is at odds with the interpretative policy adopted by the Review's authors, which as we saw focused on the role of the education system in generating outcome inequalities.

Finally, it must be noted that in the 6.44 a.m. headline summary there is, once again, only one finding presented from the Review. But this time it relates to

---

14 At the same time, it perhaps constituted news as part of a continuing story, and probably also benefited from the media's preference for bad news.

15 This presupposes a spurious argument, since because other factors also shape educational achieve-ment, discrimination is compatible with relatively high achievement on the part of the group discriminated against. Furthermore, in some circumstances, discrimination may increase motiva-tion and thereby stimulate higher levels of achievement: see Fuller 1980 and 1982, though also Gomm 2001.

African Caribbean rather than to Asian pupils. Furthermore, here rather more specificity is introduced, the reference being to African Caribbean *boys*. In addition, 'underachieving' is replaced with 'underperforming'. These changes seem likely to be a matter of stylistic variation rather than reflecting any intended shift in meaning. Indeed, it may even be that the switch in headline stems from the same motive; though it should be noted that, throughout the rest of the programme, the two-part contrast between Asian and African Caribbean pupils is used. It may even be that the presentation of the second item alone on this occasion was intended to balance the initial presentation of the first part of the contrast on its own.

In the case of this headline, we might reasonably conclude that newsworthiness is enhanced by the specific reference to African Caribbean *boys*. This is because the underachievement of boys, generally, was an issue quite frequently addressed in the media, and indeed it was an issue whose profile was still on the rise (Smith 2003: 283).

In summary, then, it seems that the need for a headline, and for a very brief account of the Review in the news bulletin, has led to selection of just two items from among the findings listed in the press release summary and in the Review. Furthermore, some reformulation has also taken place. This may have derived from a concern with simplification and intelligibility for the audience, but the terms used to describe the relationship between the achievements of Asian and African Caribbean pupils and those of the ethnic majority carry potential explanatory implications which run counter to the interpretative policy of the Review. Indeed, a term is used to describe the performance of African Caribbean pupils, 'underachievement', which the authors of the Review specifically warn against. They did this on the grounds that it has been misinterpreted in the past as implying explanations on the basis of the lower ability, lesser effort, and/or the cultural characteristics of the pupils concerned. Furthermore, use of terms like 'outshining' and 'outperforming' are also not ones that were used in the Review or summaries of it, and these too can be taken to imply a different way of explaining ethnic differences in educational performance from that adopted in the Review: the competition rather than the distribution model.

Let us now move on to the remainder of the news reports dealing with the Review during the *Today* programme. These were as follows:

[7.00 a.m. headlines:]
New research on the performance of pupils from the ethnic minorities suggests Asian groups are doing well, Afro-Caribbeans are falling behind.

[7.00 a.m. news bulletin:]
The Schools' Inspectorate has published the results of research comparing the educational achievements of pupils drawn from the ethnic minorities. It says pupils from some Asian groups are performing better than white

children, while Afro-Caribbeans are falling behind. Here is our education correspondent, Sue Littlemore.

> SL: This study is described as the first major review of the achievement of ethnic minority pupils in over ten years. It draws on research which shows, by the age of 18, Asians have on average more GCSEs and A levels than any other ethnic group. Proportionately more Asians and African Caribbeans than whites stay on at school or college after age 16. But in general African Caribbeans, particularly boys, appear to be underachieving. There's evidence that as a group they show the slowest rate of improvement in GCSE results, and compared to white pupils they are six times more likely to be expelled. The report calls for more monitoring of the progress of ethnic minority groups and criticises schools which have failed to take account of the learning needs of pupils with different racial backgrounds.

[7.30 a.m. news summary:]
Research published by the Schools' Inspectorate shows that Asian pupils are passing more GCSEs and A levels than any other ethnic group. By contrast, Afro-Caribbean pupils seem to be underachieving in the classroom.

[8.00 a.m. news bulletin:]
The Schools' Inspectorate has published a report comparing the educational achievements of pupils drawn from the ethnic minorities. The study, the biggest of its kind for more than ten years, concludes that pupils from an Asian background, especially Indians, are passing more GCSEs and A levels than any other ethnic group. By contrast, the results achieved by Afro-Caribbeans show the slowest rate of improvement.

[8.30 a.m. news summary:]
A study from the Schools' Inspectorate concludes that pupils from an Asian background are passing more GCSEs and A levels than any other ethnic group. By contrast the results achieved by Afro-Caribbeans show the slowest rate of improvement.

In the 7.00 a.m. headlines we have a vaguer formulation than earlier ones. Asian groups are 'doing well', but we are not told here in what terms, though it is likely to be heard as comparative with other ethnic groups, and the meaning is specified in the bulletin that follows. African Caribbean pupils are described as 'falling behind', and here the image seems to be very much the competition model.

In the 7.00 a.m. news bulletin there is, as earlier, the introduction of a qualification: it is now *some* Asian pupils who are performing better. Moreover, their performance is compared not with their 'classmates' but with 'whites'. Where, before, the comparison was between Asians and all other pupils, now the comparison is explicitly between this ethnic minority and the 'white' majority. This is not a comparison that is made explicitly in the press release summary, or in the short summaries in the Review. Moreover, the *contrast* between Asian and African Caribbean performance now becomes linguistically marked through use of the word 'while'. At the same time, the image of a competition or race seems to be retained, with African Caribbean pupils once again being described as 'falling behind'.

The account provided by the education correspondent Sue Littlemore as part of this news bulletin is much fuller, more complex and detailed than what has been presented previously. It starts with some background about the Review. The correspondent then presents the high academic achievement of Asian pupils in fairly specific terms, referring to 'more GCSEs and A levels'.[16] And, this time, the comparison is with other ethnic groups (rather than with the majority of pupils, or specifically with 'whites'). Information about staying on rates after 16 is also provided. Here the contrast is drawn between Asians and African Caribbeans, on the one hand, and 'whites' on the other. In this contrast, African Caribbeans are on what we might call the positive rather than the negative side of the account. It is also striking that in the education correspondent's report the term 'African Caribbean', rather than 'Afro-Caribbean', is used, in line with usage in the Review and in recent research. However, she does also report that 'in general, African Caribbeans, particularly boys, appear to be underachieving'. Here, she uses a term which, as we saw, was rejected in the Review; however, in the next sentence she employs a formulation that is closer to the language of the Review's authors: 'slowest rate of improvement'. She also includes the finding about differences in exclusion rates, not used in any of the headlines or bulletins, though she deviates from the Review in using only the highest estimate (six times) and referring to exclusion as 'expulsion'.[17] Finally, she summarizes the practical recommendations of the Review which, as we noted, had not previously been mentioned.

The 7.30 a.m. news summary reformulates the first element of the contrast which was used in previous headlines and news reports in terms that are taken from the education correspondent's account, so that Asian pupils are described as 'passing more GCSEs and A levels'. At the same time, and in line with that report, African Caribbeans continue to be described as 'underachieving'.

---

16 In fact, the Review does not provide precise information about ethnic differences in A level performance, but it does give the strong impression that some groups of Asian pupils do better at this level compared to other ethnic groups.

17 It may be that this term is used because it is likely to be more intelligible and familiar to the audience.

The 8.00 a.m. news bulletin also draws on what the education correspondent has said, albeit to present much the same overall message as before. The background information about the 'Report' is included, and 'pupils from an Asian background, especially Indians' are described as 'passing more GCSEs and A levels than any other ethnic groups'. Furthermore, in describing the performance of 'Afro-Caribbeans' a formulation that is closer to that of the Review is employed: 'slowest rate of improvement'. The 8.30 a.m. news summary, while around half the length, keeps to much the same terms.

Several general points can be made about this coverage, in addition to those made about the opening 6.30 a.m. headline and news bulletin. First of all, in the headlines at 7.00 a.m. the Review is described as 'new research'. Neither here nor elsewhere is there any indication that what is being referred to is a *review* of a large amount of existing academic research on education. The only exception is in the report by Sue Littlemore, the education correspondent, who does describe it as a review (the first in over ten years). But even she does not indicate the academic character of the research reviewed, or the fact that the authors were located at the London Institute of Education. This tendency to represent the Review as an official report may arise from the assumption that members of the audience would not grasp the meaning of the distinctions involved. But neglect of the point that the source is a review may also stem from the fact that news reports focus on a quite narrowly defined time period, a matter of days. In these terms, the studies which the Review covers could not be news because they are too old. To have emphasized that the Review was a review might therefore have downgraded its news value. Indeed the education correspondent's use of 'review' in her report probably gave the impression to most listeners that the Review was directly reporting on the current state of ethnic differences in educational performance (reviewing them), rather than reviewing research that had taken place over the previous ten years.

A second point is that, looking over the different news reports, we can see the two findings dealing with the educational performance of Asian and African Caribbean pupils solidifying into a single story, in which their levels of achievement are explicitly contrasted. Along with the use of terms like 'outshining', 'outperforming', and 'underachieving', this may carry the explanatory implication for many listeners that this difference arises from the intrinsic characteristics of different ethnic groups, rather than from differential treatment within the education system of pupils with different ethnic backgrounds. At the same time, we should note that in the education correspondent's report the Review is presented as criticizing schools for not doing enough ethnic monitoring and for not taking account of 'the learning needs of pupils with different racial backgrounds'. This can be read as indicating that the explanation could lie in a different direction. It is perhaps also worth underlining that what explanatory conclusion listeners draw, if any, from these news headlines and reports will depend upon their existing knowledge of educational matters and their own tendencies to adopt one sort of explanation rather than another for differences in achievement, in general as well as specifically in relation to ethnicity.

Today programme items

I want to look next at the two items dealing with the Review which occurred in the body of the *Today* programme. Such items can take a number of forms. One format is a live or pre-recorded report from a correspondent. Where the report is live, it may involve an interview between presenter and correspondent. Alternatively, items may consist of an interview with one or more people who have some role in relation to the issue, an interest in it, or who are in a position to comment on it. The first *Today* item dealing with the Review consists of a live discussion between the presenter and one of the BBC's education correspondents, in fact the one who provided the report in the bulletin discussed above (Sue Littlemore). The other item, as announced in the headlines at 6.30 a.m., is an interview with two headteachers. I will look at each of these in turn.

Interview with the education correspondent

The first *Today* programme item happened at 6.38 a.m., after the opening headlines and news summary, and before the headline summary at 6.44 a.m. One of the *Today* presenters, James Naughtie, begins it:

> *JN*: Pupils from some ethnic minorities perform significantly better at school than those from other groups according to an Inspectors' report which is out today. Our Education Correspondent is Sue Littlemore. Sue, what does it say?

> *SL*: Well, the report shows a gap between the achievements of different ethnic minority groups in our schools and for example by the age of 18, it says, Asians have more GCSEs and A levels than any other group. If you are Chinese or Indian, proportionately, you are more likely to get to university than your white colleagues; and there are concerns about the performance of African Caribbeans pupils, particularly boys. They seem to be showing the slowest rate of improvement at GCSEs, and are much more likely, six times more likely, than their white classmates to be expelled.

In his introduction Naughtie uses a formulation that is less specific than the account in the headlines and news summary. What is left unspecified is both *which* groups are performing significantly better and whose performance this is being compared with. It may be that this lack of specificity was designed to lead into the presentation of more concrete information by the education correspondent. She certainly provides this, but it is framed very much in the same terms as the news items: as a contrast between the achievements of Asian pupils and the 'performance of African Caribbean pupils, particularly boys'. This contrast is described as a 'gap'. And, as before, it is presented against the background of comparison with white pupils. In some places, though, the formulation is closer to the Review than to the news headlines and bulletins. Here, the terms 'outshining/ outperforming' and 'underachieving/underperforming' are replaced by more specific descriptions, ones that do not carry strong explanatory implications.

It is also worth noting that the education correspondent's summary of the Review here, like her earlier pre-recorded account of the Review, reveals that she has read the body of it. Once again, she reports that 'by the age of 18 ... Asians have more GCSEs and A levels than any other group', and that 'if you are Chinese or Indian, proportionately, you are more likely to get to university than your white colleagues'. These points are not to be found in the press release or in any of the short summaries in the Review.[18]

The interview continues as follows:

> *JN*: Now this is the kind of finding that we saw ten years ago in the Swann Report, isn't it, so that not much has changed. What are the reasons that have been put forward for this difference?
>
> *SL*: The Report is saying that it is not necessarily well understood what the reasons are. And one of the main things it's calling for is <u>better</u> national monitoring of the picture. But for example there has been, in this report, some research amongst teachers who report that they find African Caribbean pupils extremely challenging and disruptive and Asian pupils tend to be, particularly Indians, well motivated and very conscientious.

Here, the presenter locates the education correspondent's summary of the findings of the Review by means of a chronological reference back to the Swann Report. And this leads into the suggestion that 'not much has changed'. The effect of this is to focus attention on the second of the two findings reported in the news bulletin: the fact that the level of African Caribbean pupils' achievement remains lower than that of other groups. And the presenter follows this by asking for the reasons 'that have been put forward for this difference'.

This question is ambiguous in two key respects. And, once again, it may have been designed to open the way for more specific information from the education correspondent. What the presenter says is uncertain, first of all, in terms of whether he is asking for the reasons put forward *in the Review* or those that are put forward more generally. Second, what he says is unspecific as regards the 'difference' being referred to. Is it the difference between the level of educational achievement of Asian and African Caribbean pupils, remembering that the first component of this difference *has* changed over the previous ten years? Or is he referring to the difference between the average performance of African

---

18 They *are* to be found in the executive summary, though not specific information about A level results.

Caribbean pupils and that of others more generally and in particular of white pupils?

The education correspondent's response to this is to present a point that, while not explicitly present in the Review, can be interpreted as implied by it, given that it places a great deal of emphasis on the complexity of the situation and the need for further research. Indeed, she goes on to mention one of the main recommendations of the Review – the need for greater ethnic monitoring. After this preface emphasizing the uncertainty of what is known, the education correspondent provides one 'reason for the difference', which she claims to draw from the Review. Here, first of all, we have the Review being described as reporting that teachers say that they 'find African Caribbean pupils extremely challenging and disruptive', and then it is reported that 'Asian pupils tend to be, particularly Indians, well motivated and very conscientious'. These formulations imply that the ethnic difference in educational achievement is to be explained in terms of different orientations towards school on the part of ethnic minority groups. This contrasts with the account in the Review where, as we saw in the previous chapter, teachers' claims about differences in the behaviour of different ethnic groups are treated as stereotypes and as themselves the cause of conflict, and thereby of ethnic differences in educational achievement.

The remainder of the interview is as follows:

> *JN*: Does it suggest there are sort of cultural reasons for this? The way the family operates, cultural background and so on?

> *SL*: Absolutely, and that is obviously going to be one factor and one explanation for that. But others will argue that those sorts of analyses are dangerous or at least unhelpful stereotyping which will lead to negative expectations which will also be part of the problem. And this report has found that in some areas like Tower Hamlets, in London, where they have targeted their Bangladeshi pupils and Birmingham, where they have targeted their African Caribbean pupils, they have been able to improve results. So one of the messages is that these things can change.

> *JN*: But it does require targeting and understanding what the characteristics of particular groups appear to be wherever they come from?

> *SL*: Absolutely. Another main message from this report is schools must not be, as it puts it, 'colour blind'. It must recognize the different learning needs of different ethnic minority groups and tackle them.

> *JN*: Sue Littlemore, thank you.

In some ways, the presenter's question here seems to repeat his previous one in more specific terms, as if he did not get the answer he was expecting: he asks about cultural differences between ethnic groups that might explain the different levels of achievement, and also mentions the role of the family. But, of course, the question also picks up from what the education correspondent has just said.[19] And she confirms this interpretation of what she has said, indicating that this is 'obviously going to be one factor and one explanation'.[20] Here the potential explanatory implications of terms such as 'outshining', 'outperforming', and 'underachievement' are made explicit, though she does not attribute these directly to the Review (except insofar as she is responding to a question about what the Review said). She goes on to present a contrary point of view which is implicitly attributed to the Review, highlighting that it suggests that the first explanation involves unhelpful or dangerous stereotyping which will lead to negative expectations and thereby be part of the problem. Here, the education correspondent seems to be picking up on the argument in the executive summary and the Review itself about the danger of analyses formulated in terms of 'underachievement'. And, reinforcing the point, she goes on to summarize 'one of the messages' of the Review, which is that things can be changed; and, in this context, this clearly means that things can be changed through the actions of schools. In the course of this, she refers to what we saw was the central practical recommendation of the Review, headlined in the press release: the need to abandon 'colour-blind' policies.

What we have here, then, is the provision of more detailed background information about the Review, through the medium of a simulated interview between the *Today* presenter and a journalist who specializes in educational matters. It is worth exploring something of the nature of media interviews in order to understand what is happening here.[21] Interviews are often designed to set out conflicting points of view. Where there are two interviewees, these are frequently selected so as to represent different views. And where there is only one interviewee, the interviewer often formulates questions that represent a different view from that of the person being interviewed, or even challenges the interviewee as if he or she held the contrary view. It seems likely that the aim in doing this is both to display the different views that are to be found on an issue, and to ask questions or make comments of a kind that the audience may well themselves be asking.

19 While it could be argued that she had already presented a cultural explanation for ethnic differences in educational achievement, it is worth noting that the difference in orientation to school she describes could be explained in other ways, for example as a reaction to 'racial' prejudice and discrimination.
20 We should note, though, that in this kind of staged interview between colleagues agreement is probably a very strong preference. As we shall see, there is a contrast in this respect with the second item, the interview with two headteachers, where disagreement was clearly the journalistic preference.
21 For useful discussion of the distinctive character of broadcast news interviews, see Heritage 1985, Clayman 1988 and 1992, Heritage and Greatbatch 1991, Greatbatch 1992, Clayman and

By contrast, other interviews with a single person are more designed to elicit background information. Here the concern is to find out what the audience might want to know, and to clarify anything in what is said that might be obscure to them. This is the usual format where the interviewee is not a lay person but a correspondent. Interestingly, though, what seems to happen in the example being discussed here is that the education correspondent herself displays some of the contrasting views to be found about the issue. Controversy is a sign of newsworthiness: what is being reported is not simply already known and accepted. So newsworthiness is not simply a matter of whether an audience finds it interesting; it may be possible to persuade them that it is interesting on the grounds that others disagree about it. Moreover, here, in doing this, an argument that is at the core of the Review is introduced.

What we have, as a result of the frame set up by the interviewer, is the presentation of an explanation for ethnic differences in educational achievement that is at odds with the one emphasized in the Review. And the education correspondent accepts the relevance of that frame, even though she subsequently inserts the rather different perspective presented in the Review. One might see this interview as offering a distorted account of the Review's message. Alternatively, it might be understood as an enactment of the kind of interchange that might be expected in public discussions of its findings. As we shall see, the second item on the *Today* programme comes even closer to the latter model.

Two headteachers

I want to look next at the other detailed discussion of the Review that occurred on the *Today* programme. As we saw, in the initial 6.30 a.m. headlines, an interview with two headteachers was promised. This occurred at 7.22 a.m. Here is the opening section:

> *JN*: Now why do pupils from <u>some</u> ethnic minorities perform better at school than those from others? An inspectors' report which is out today says for example that children from Indian families tend to be near the top, Afro-Caribbean pupils on the other hand often underperform. Well two head teachers join us now – Carlton Duncan [*CD*] of the George Dixon School which is in Edgbaston in Birmingham and William Atkinson [*WA*] of the Phoenix High School in Hammersmith in London.

Here, as elsewhere, the Review is described as an 'inspectors' report'. Furthermore, once again, the focus is on the contrasting performance of different ethnic

---

Heritage 2002. See also Myers 2004 on the production of 'public opinion' in these and other contexts.

minority groups, the contrast being formulated as between 'Indian' and 'Afro-Caribbean' pupils, with the latter being described as often 'underperforming'. This focus frames the subsequent discussion:[22]

> *JN*: Mr Duncan first of all, does the general finding here that there are significant differences between groups and that those need to be taken into account by schools strike you from your experience as being the truth?
>
> *CD*: Good morning to you. Yes, I believe this to be the case. I was a member of the Rampton and indeed the Swann Inquiry which reported over ten years ago, and indeed the findings which we are having now seem to tally somewhat with the findings then, so it's a concern which I have experienced for a long time, and which bears out now.
> [
> *JN*: Of course it also suggests – the point you are making there really is that nothing has changed. The points that were made in the Swann Inquiry have not been addressed and dealt with.
>
> *CD*: Well, the points which were made in the Swann Inquiry have been addressed by many schools, indeed by many local authorities and in some cases by central government. I have to say looking back over a period of ten years now, that I must be partly to be blamed, together with the others on the inquiry, who rigorously refused – defended any attempt to put part of the responsibility on the
> [
> *JN*: Well ...
> [
> *CD*: ... structure of the Afro-Caribbean family. We at that time felt that that was politically not acceptable.
>
> *JN*: And you now accept that that has got to be discussed more openly?
>
> *CD*: And I feel that that must now be a factor. We need to, as schools, and central government, make – give some sort of compensation for the absence of the extended family support which the Afro-Caribbean children do not appear to have and yet ...
> [
> *JN*: Can I bring in, let me bring in, Mr Atkinson, Mr Duncan
> =

22 In the extracts that follow, square brackets have been used to indicate utterances that begin before the other speaker has finished. An equals sign indicates that the utterance follows on immediately from a previous one.

CD:	Yes.
	=
JN:	to join in.

The presenter's first question is concerned with whether what the Review says matches this head's experience. It is thereby made clear that the authority of this speaker lies in his practical experience as a headteacher. On the basis of this experience, he is presumably being asked to provide an assessment of the validity of the Review's findings, and of what is taken to be its main recommendation: that differences between ethnic groups must be taken account of by schools. However, we should note the ambiguity here, as earlier. It is not clear whether 'the general finding that there are significant differences between groups' refers to ethnic differences in educational achievement or to socio-cultural differences between ethnic groups that might cause these, especially since the latter were referred to in the previous item on the *Today* programme devoted to the Review.

So, the question potentially ties together the findings and recommendations of the Review, albeit in a less than fully explicit manner. And, of course, it is perhaps to be expected that the emphasis in talking with headteachers would be as much on the remedy as on the problem. In his response, the first head indicates his agreement and suggests that the findings match those of the Rampton Committee and the Swann Inquiry, in which he was himself involved. By mentioning this involvement he indicates a further source of authority for his views, showing that he has long been concerned with this issue, and that his concern and expertise have been officially recognized. Note too that the tentativeness of his formulation, that the new findings 'seem to tally somewhat' with the findings of the previous inquiries, may suggest that he has not yet read the Review, or it may be a pointer to the fact that he is about to distance himself from the views of the Swann Committee.

The presenter then reformulates this as a lack of change and proffers an explanation for it in terms of the education system's failure to deal with the issue: the recommendations of the earlier inquiry have not been addressed. It is of some significance that what is involved here is not just explanation but also, potentially at least, the allocation of blame. Thus we can read what the presenter attributes to the first headteacher in his reformulation of what he had said as laying blame on the government, and/or on schools, for not implementing previous recommendations. And, of course, this – identifying a failure to act and who might be responsible – is a common focus of journalistic reportage.

In response, Mr Duncan denies this proffered explanation, and also explicitly addresses the question of blame. He suggests that it is he and other members of the earlier inquiry who are partly to blame for playing down what he now thinks is a key explanation for African Caribbean underachievement. They 'rigorously refused – defended any attempt to put part of the responsibility on the structure of the Afro-Caribbean family'. And he also explains this behaviour on the grounds that 'We at that time felt that that was politically not acceptable'. In short, what happens here is that in response to an attempt on the part of the interviewer to frame the issue in terms of a failure to act by the government and the education system, the interviewee points as part of the explanation to what he claims is a distinctive feature of the family backgrounds of African Caribbean pupils. And the failure of government policy to address this is partly to be blamed on the advice they received from the Swann Committee, of which he was a member.

Following this, the presenter turns to the other headteacher:

JN: Does what Mr Duncan is saying, himself from an Afro-Caribbean background, does that make you – does that ring true?

WA: In my experience, and I have been a head teacher in three secondary schools in and around London, Afro-Caribbean parents are just as supportive as parents from the indigenous population as far as schooling is concerned.

       =

JN: So you are a bit worried at that general approach to the problem. I mean, how would you explain it?

WA: Well, it is a very complex issue and the fact is we need to bear in mind that there are significant numbers of Afro-Caribbean boys who pass successfully through the system and go on to university. It was only a few weeks ago that we were reading in the national media that working class white boys were underperforming in a significant way.

        [

JN: But (everything) ...

             [

WA: There is an issue about underperformance which needs to be dealt with right across the system.

Here, the presenter asks the second head whether what the first head has said matches *his* experience. Again, this indicates the nature of the authority being attributed to this speaker: he is someone who has relevant practical experience. In the course of doing this, James Naughtie points out that the first headteacher is himself 'from an Afro-Caribbean background'. This, presumably, is for the benefit of the audience rather than for that of Mr Atkinson, who will know this. There could be two reasons for mentioning it. The intent may have been to discount the possible interpretation of what Mr Duncan had said as racist stereotyping, as amounting to the explaining away of the lower level of academic achievement on the part of African Caribbean pupils as a product of their deficiencies, in this case a deficiency of their families. The implication might be that, since Mr Duncan is African Caribbean himself, what he said cannot be racist in this sense. The second point is closely related: being African Caribbean himself, Mr Duncan has knowledge of the nature of African Caribbean families. Thus, this is a further indication of the first head's authority to speak on this issue. So what James Naughtie says here could be designed to prevent any immediate dismissal of what Mr Duncan has said, on grounds of either bias or ignorance.[23]

In his response, the second head underlines the basis of his own authority by indicating his experience as a head in several schools in London. While he offers evidence which can be read as running counter to the explanation that the first head had put forward, he does not present it as a disagreement. However, James Naughtie does formulate this as a contrast in view, albeit in a low key way, suggesting that the second head is 'a bit worried at that general approach'. And, without waiting for any acknowledgement, he goes on imme-diately to ask for the second head's explanation. Here, it seems the presenter is attempting to engineer a clarification of the nature of the disagreement by eliciting the second headteacher's own view about the issue.

In replying, the second head again downplays any conflict in view by empha-sizing the complexity of the issue, and elaborating on this by pointing out that some African Caribbean boys are successful while there has been much recent concern about the underachievement of white boys. The presenter tries to come in at that point, but the second head continues, proposing that under-performance is a problem 'right across the system'. Here he is suggesting that the problem does not relate specifically to ethnicity.

The way in which this interview is organized is fairly typical of the use of this format on the *Today* Programme. The presenter plays the role primarily of 'master of ceremonies': outlining the topic, eliciting points of view, asking for (or sometimes providing) clarification where he or she believes it to be necessary for the audience, and getting one interviewee to respond to the views of the other. As noted earlier, where two people are interviewed simultaneously, very often they have been selected on the expectation that they will have different views about the matter. And here the task of the presenter is to orchestrate the disagreement, one element of which is to maintain a more or less equal balance between the two sides, and thereby to sustain the disagreement for the period of the discussion without allowing it to get out of hand.[24]

It is perhaps as a result of this concern with orchestrating disagreement that the presenter attempts to interrupt both interviewees on several occasions, some-times successfully. Equally important, though, is likely to be his awareness of the brief span of time available. All items on the *Today* Programme operate within tightly scheduled time boundaries. Moreover, not only is the interviewer

---

23 It may also be designed to protect the BBC from accusations of racism, underlining that it was Mr Duncan who said this and that he cannot be racist because he is African Caribbean. It is striking that it is left implicit that the other interviewee is also African Caribbean.

24 On the ways in which interviewers seek to generate disagreement among interviewees in 'debate interviews', see Clayman 1992:176–8 and Greatbatch 1992.

(probably unlike the other participants) aware of the limited time available but he or she is responsible for shaping the item properly, and is accustomed to operating under these pressures as well as recognizing that lay interviewees (unlike correspondents) probably are not.

As already noted, underlying the surface issue of how 'the significant differences between groups' are to be explained is the question of who is to blame, who is responsible. I noted earlier that Mr Duncan had explicitly raised the question of blame, and one possible interpretation of what he said, implicitly acknowledged by the presenter's reference to him as 'from an Afro-Caribbean background', is that it is African Caribbeans themselves who are to blame for their lower level of average educational achievement, though Mr Duncan explicitly indicates that it is the responsibility of government and schools to compensate for the deficit. The explanation that the second head offers here effectively nullifies that possible conclusion by framing the problem as one of *general* underperformance. And the effect of this is, even more strongly, to move attention away from the distinctive features of ethnic groups back to the system itself, the implication being that this is where the cause and the blame lie.

On the basis of this, the presenter turns back to the first head:

> *JN*: Yes. Mr Duncan, does – Mr Atkinson there is clearly disturbed by the sort of approach that you are suggesting, really against your previous instincts, you might have to take now.
> *CD*: No, I cannot deny that Afro-Caribbean children, as do others, do significantly well in academic performances and so forth. But this tends to be where they have an extended family support which is so evident in for example the Asian family.

Here, the interviewer continues to try to orchestrate the display of contrasting views: he formulates the second head as 'clearly disturbed' by the first head's views (a significant upgrading from 'worried', and this despite the second head's implicit denial), and invites the latter to respond.[25] Mr. Duncan does so by acknowledging that some African Caribbean children are successful, but he indicates that this is compatible with his explanation: it occurs where they have the extended family support that he has referred to. The presenter then turns back to the second head to try to clarify his views, as these relate to what has been emphasized as the main finding of the Review: the contrast in educational performance between Asian and African Caribbean pupils.

> *JN*: Do you accept, Mr Atkinson, that there is a difference there, between the way the two groups generally perform?

25 It may be that there was non-verbal evidence that the second head was worried or concerned about what the first head was saying. However, there is nothing in what the second head says that indicates anything other than disagreement over the explanation.

WA: I think there is a real danger and I am not here speaking in opposition to what Mr Duncan is actually saying.

[

JN: No, I understand that.

[

WA: There is a real danger in <u>generalizing</u> about a complex issue and treating a large population, a community, Afro-Caribbean community or Asian community <u>as a whole</u>. There are tremendous differences between the communities and I think what we need is a detailed analysis of the situation on the ground that goes beyond simple statistical analysis. We need to find out exactly what is going on within the institution and within the communities that we are referring to.

=

JN: Mr Atkinson, Mr Duncan, head teachers both, thank you very much.

Again, here there is a potential ambiguity about whether what the presenter is referring to are outcome differences in educational achievement or differences in orientation towards school on the part of ethnic groups (though it seems likely to be interpreted as the latter). In response, Mr Atkinson begins by distancing himself from any direct challenge to what the first head has said, and the presenter accepts this. Such distancing could be a response to the orchestration of disagreement by the presenter and/or to a desire to maintain solidarity with the other speaker, perhaps both as fellow African Caribbeans and as fellow headteachers.[26] It also seems to link with what he goes on to say: the problem is a complex one, a statement also made in the Review. The implication is that to present it as simply a product of cultural differences between ethnic groups, or even in terms of a dispute between those who assert this and those who deny it, is too crude. Thus he goes on to argue that generalizations are dangerous, a statement that seems to confirm the presenter's attribution of worry and concern. Interestingly, what he calls for is an investigation that 'goes beyond simple statistical analysis'. This reinforces the suspicion that neither he nor the first head have yet had chance to read the Review, since as we saw the latter gives considerable emphasis to qualitative as well as to quantitative research on the topic. Moreover, the presenter perhaps does not know this either; certainly he makes no reference to it. It is also notable that the second head calls for more investigation not just of processes within the education system but also within the communities from which pupils come, thereby leaving open the question of where the explanation lies.

---

26 In fact, there seems to be a preference, within conversations generally, for agreement as against disagreement, probably related to a commitment to preserve face: see Pomerantz 1984 and Goffman 1972.

As a final point, it is worth noting the ways in which the journalists concerned chose to deal with this item on the *Today* programme, in terms of who was interviewed: a BBC education correspondent to start with, and then two head-teachers. This contrasts with how three other items dealing with research were dealt with on the same day. All of these, covering a conference about the Big Bang, the discovery of a new prime number, and a claim that pets can antic-ipate their owners' homecoming, were dealt with through interviews with the researchers.[27] The difference in treatment here may tell us something about how journalists perceive the distribution of authoritative knowledge on the issue cov-ered by the Review as compared with these other items: it is a matter on which teachers, and especially headteachers, have important knowledge, over and above what comes from research. It is relevant here that these headteachers were not interrogated about how schools were failing to deal appropriately with African Caribbean children. At the same time, these other research items did involve the interviewer in raising questions that listeners might want to ask, including for example the creationist reaction to Big Bang theory and the issue of whether the large amount of public money spent on the CERN accelerator can be justified. It is also striking that the treatment of each of these other items involved some humour, by contrast with coverage of the Review.

In the remainder of this chapter I will look, much more briefly, at other coverage of the Review on radio.

THE WORLD AT ONE

The other two main news programmes on BBC Radio 4 are *The World at One*, running from 1.00 p.m. to 1.30 p.m., and *PM*, running from 5.00 p.m. to 6.00 p.m. The Review was reported as part of the news at the beginning of *The World at One*. Here it is presented as fourth out of six items.[28] The main item is a combination of two of the stories that had been presented on the *Today* news, about the Conservative and Labour election campaigns and about a report from executives of large companies backing the single currency. The item dealing with the Review took the following form:

> The Education Minister, Cheryl Gillan, has published a ten-point plan to try to improve the performance of school children from the ethnic minori-ties. The announcement coincides with the publication of a report by the Schools' Inspectorate which suggests that while some Asian groups are doing

27 These were single items, and not mentioned in the headlines.
28 In terms of wordage it is possibly higher up the ranking, following items on the European Union and political campaigning, on Iraq, and on a cargo vessel on fire at sea, and before an item on Ireland and one on the England cricket selectors' decision to retain Michael Atherton as captain.

better than white children, Afro-Caribbeans are falling behind. Here's our Education Correspondent, Sue Littlemore.

SL: The report finds that over the last decade achievement among ethnic minorities has improved in many areas of the country but the gap between different groups continues to grow. In Brent in London, for example, Asians have been outperforming whites in GCSEs. African Caribbean pupils have shown the worst results. Nationally, compared with their white classmates, a higher proportion of Pakistanis are excluded from school. African Caribbeans are six times more likely to be expelled. The Government describes these findings as a real cause for concern and has announced a number of measures to tackle them. They include compiling inspection evidence on racial harassment and stereotyping, and improving the monitoring of ethnic minority progress.

Here the format is a brief outline by the newsreader, followed by a (probably pre-recorded) report from the same education correspondent who appeared on the *Today* programme. In the outline, the focus is now on the government's response to the Review: the story has moved on since the morning. Furthermore, the education correspondent's account is substantially different from that produced for the 7.00 a.m. news, though the first two-thirds of it cover much the same ground. Here, she seems to put together the first 'good news' item with the first 'bad news' item from the press release summary. But we have the same contrast format, this time presented in terms of the metaphor of a competition among three ethnic groups. Moreover, African Caribbean pupils are not just in third place, but are 'falling behind'. And it is striking that there is a direct reference to the item in the press release summary which I suggested earlier was the model for the BBC news headlines; and while this focuses on the situation in Brent it is likely to be heard as exemplifying the national situation. The Review's findings about the high level of exclusion of African Caribbean pupils is repeated, again quoting the maximum figure rather than the range. A new finding is also introduced: a higher proportion of Pakistani pupils are excluded than whites. This seems to have been derived from the body of the Review rather than from any of the summaries. Indeed, it does not appear in the written text of the Review, only in a figure based on OFSTED data. This shows the exclusion of Pakistani pupils at around 35 per thousand secondary school pupils, whereas the exclusion rate for whites is around 28 per thousand. However, 'Black African' and 'Black Other' groups show ratios of 62 and 66, while the 'Black Caribbean' rate is around 156 per thousand. Indian, Bangladeshi and Chinese students are shown as having lower exclusion rates than whites. Once more, the (necessarily) highly selective reporting of findings from the Review is illustrated.

The final part of the education correspondent's account relates to the government's response to the Review, and the measures it has proposed to deal with the problem. This can be heard as simultaneously underlining the importance of the Review and moving the focus away from it.

There was no further treatment of this item on the programme, and it was not included in the final news summary. Nor was it covered by the *PM* programme at 5.00 p.m.[29]

CONCLUSION

In this chapter I have looked in detail at the BBC radio coverage of the Review, in the *Today* programme and on the lunchtime *World at One* programme. I noted how the headlines select and reformulate two of the findings listed in the press release summary. Moreover, while initially these are presented separately, over the course of the news presentations in the *Today* programme, they quickly become structured into a single story in which the achievement levels of Asian and African Caribbean pupils are contrasted. Furthermore, terms are used to describe these achievement levels which could be taken as implying that the difference is to be explained by the distinctive features of the two ethnic groups, an explanation that is perhaps already suggested by the contrast structure of the story.

I also looked at the two items dealing with the Review on the *Today* programme itself. The first consisted of an interview between one of the *Today* presenters and a BBC education correspondent. This was designed to provide more detailed background information about the Review. Here too the same focus is adopted, but it is presented in more specific terms, along with information about other findings. However, the presenter frames the interview in terms of differences between ethnic groups as explanations for variation in educational achievement, and the education correspondent accepts this, while also indicating implicitly that the Review puts forward a different argument. In doing this, she notes that the explanation proffered by the presenter can be seen as itself part of the problem, as stereotyping ethnic groups. And she reports the view that the situation can be changed by action on the part of schools, referring to the Review's findings about the improvement of Bangladeshi pupils' educational performance in Tower Hamlets.

The second *Today* item on the Review differs in format but links back in content and orientation. I argued that this interview with two headteachers was orchestrated as a display of contrasting views by the presenter, and this despite a denial on the part of one of the heads that he was opposing what the other had said. The first head suggests that the lower level of average achievement of African Caribbean pupils stemmed from a lack of 'extended family support', which must be compensated for by government and schools. The second questioned this indirectly, and argued that the problem is complex, is not specifically about ethnicity, and requires a policy initiative directed at schools to deal with it.

29 I had been approached the previous day by a researcher on the *PM* programme to suggest possible contributors. But it seems that the item was not taken forward.

The message presented by the headlines used in the *Today* programme is relatively simple, and focuses on contrasting levels of achievement between ethnic groups, highlighting something that is not given emphasis in the Review: the relative success of some Asian groups, particularly Indian pupils. The fuller report, and the two items in the body of the *Today* programme, while having much the same focus, present a rather more complex message, one that indicates the scope for disagreement about the explanation for ethnic differences in educational achievement.

3   Television news coverage

The distinctive feature of television as a medium is, most obviously, its reliance on visual material. While a few news items are covered without this, generally speaking pictures of some kind are provided, if only as a backdrop to what the newsreader is saying, and these are often moving pictures. They may be drawn from a library archive of relevant material, sometimes clearly indicated as such, but often there is an attempt to cover stories via pre-arranged or live filming, whether simply of a correspondent speaking from an appropriate location or of relevant events. This is seen as providing 'actuality' (see Schlesinger 1987: 128–9). One of the problems that television journalists face is that providing accompanying film can be both expensive and difficult to arrange, particularly in the case of news items that relate to situations outside the usual run of locations covered by the media – those concerned with national politics – and where no video material is available from other sources. Filming relevant material may require several days' advance notice. This was available in the case of the Review, at least for the BBC, and as we shall see they shot relevant outside broadcast material for their items dealing with the Review. Channel 4 also provided such material, though this seemed to be produced live, on the day after the Review was released.

It is probably also the case that there is much more pressure on space in television news than either on radio or in the newspapers. As a result, specialist education correspondents must often work hard to persuade the news desk to include items, and – here, as elsewhere – there may be different perspectives on the part of these two groups of journalists about whether and how particular issues should be covered – with the availability of interesting film material being a consideration. What this points to is that, even more than in the case of radio, there is a complex process of selection going on. First of all, education journalists must select from among what comes to their notice that which is going to offer a good story; and questions about how this could be covered, about timing and resources, as well as the more general issue of what would be the top line, must be resolved as part of this. To some extent, at least, it seems that what are most likely to get selected are events about which there is prior warning, and where a press release is provided that gives a clear basis for what the top line or angle might be, and where there is scope for providing interesting visuals.

I have data from five television news programmes on the day after the publication of the Review: the lunchtime, the early and the late evening BBC news; the lunchtime ITN news; and the evening Channel 4 news. It was a major item on four of these, while the ITN news included only a very brief report. I will look at the BBC coverage first, and then at that of ITN and Channel 4.[1]

BBC TELEVISION COVERAGE

The headline dealing with the Review on the BBC lunchtime news was as follows: 'Some ethnic minority groups are doing well, especially Indian girls, but boys of African Caribbean origin are doing poorly in exams and are more likely apparently to be expelled from school.' These words were spoken by the newsreader in the studio.

The headline here is similar in some respects to the radio news headlines. Once again, the focus is on the findings of the Review rather than on its recommendations, and a contrast is drawn between the relative educational performance of two named ethnic minority groups. However, there are differences from the radio coverage. First, not only are the more successful pupils identified as Indian rather than Asian, but a direct gender contrast is introduced between Indian *girls* and African Caribbean *boys*.[2] Second, level of exclusions is mentioned as well as examination achievement, though the message may be much the same, exclusions being taken as a sign of educational failure.

As I noted in the previous chapter, in good news/bad news formats of the kind used here, the rhetorical weight may often fall on the second part, though it is possible that the effect is softened here slightly by use of the word 'apparently' to qualify the claim that African Caribbean boys are more likely to be excluded from school. It is also worth noting that the newsreader speaks against the background of a picture of an African Caribbean boy and male adult facing one another in a context which looks like a classroom.[3] The effect of this could be further to reinforce the bad news second part.

Once again, then, the focus in the headline is on a very small number of the findings reported in the Review, and the same contrast between ethnic minority groups is used, albeit perhaps with slightly more emphasis on the lower level of achievement of African Caribbean boys (without any indication that what is being referred to here is *average* level of educational performance in 16 plus examinations). However, the formulation does not imply a contest in the way that many of the radio news headline formulations do, and as a result there are

1 There may have been coverage on other news reports, and on other channels. The coverage here reflects what was successfully recorded at the time. Furthermore, I do not have information about the other items reported on these news programmes, or about the order in which they were covered.
2 It is not clear where this emphasis on Indian *girls* comes from, there is no claim in the Review specifically about this, as far as I know.
3 In fact, this picture comes from the volunteer project which is referred to later in the item.

no strong implications as to responsibility for the situation. In other words, the opening headline does not imply that the explanation for ethnic differences in educational performance is to be found in differences in the characteristics of ethnic groups. 'Doing well/doing poorly' is a much weaker formulation than 'outperforming' and 'underachieving', for example. These are terms that are often applied to patients suffering from some illness, and in that context there is no strong blame attribution involved, and any such attribution is at least as likely to go in the direction of medical staff as in that of the patient (and therefore, in the case being considered here, in the direction of schools or policymakers).

Following this opening section, there is a report by a different BBC education correspondent from the one involved in the *Today* programme: Mike Baker. This report opens with footage from a mentoring project for black pupils in Birmingham. The focus here, then, is on an attempted solution to one of the problems which the Review identifies, the one indicated in the opening headline. Selection of this project probably reflects, in part, the opportunity to present interesting visual material: to get away from a presentation that simply involves 'talking heads' in a studio, or reliance solely on textual summaries of the Review's findings.[4] The project is introduced via voice-over commentary from Baker:

> At KWESI, a mentoring project for black pupils in Birmingham, volunteers work with boys from 6 to 16, befriending, observing and advising them. It's hoped that providing successful adult role models will help overcome the underachievement of black boys.

Here, then, the focus on the lower level of achievement of African Caribbean boys is reinforced. Moreover, this is formulated as 'the underachievement of black boys'. The term 'underachievement' can suggest that the problem lies with the pupils; as we saw, it was specifically criticized and avoided by the Review's authors for this reason. Moreover, reference to the need for adult role models implies that the lower average level of achievement may be a result of family background. On the other hand, the use of colour rather than ethnic terminology could be taken to indicate that racism is a factor. It is worth noting too that the account presented here is implicitly attributed to the African Caribbean adult males who run the project, and it is not clear how this might influence interpretation of the message by audiences.

There follows a brief extract from an interview with one of the adult volunteers on the project, who outlines what he sees as the problem that the project is designed to deal with:

> Youngsters have grown up in a society that they feel they're not a part of, that they feel they don't really belong to and as a result of that over the

---

4 As noted earlier, the material was filmed a few days before the Review was published, on the basis of advance information about it provided by OFSTED to the BBC.

years they develop an alienation from the society where they don't feel that they're intrinsically a part of it and eventually that will impact on their level of achievement in school.

What is offered here is a rather different explanation from those aired in the radio coverage, and from what is implied in Mike Baker's initial commentary. The volunteer's account explicitly offers an explanation in terms of black boys' experience of the wider society. This is portrayed as generating a sense of alienation which, in turn, affects their level of school achievement. At the same time, it is striking that this account is studiously non-evaluative; certainly the boys themselves are not blamed, but nor are schools or the wider society in any explicit way. And, given the context of the mentoring project, the implication is that the problem can be tackled at local level, and the educational performance of African Caribbean boys thereby improved. While there is no specific reference to the Review in this part of the item, this message that change is possible matches one of its key themes, though in this case it is to be brought about by action outside the formal school system.

In the next section, the education correspondent provides a more detailed summary of the findings of the Review than was given in the opening headline:

Today's report shows not only that African Caribbean pupils have not shared fully in rising examination pass rates but in some areas their results are getting worse. [Here the picture focuses down on a single black boy.] They're also up to six times more likely to be excluded from school as other groups.

But some ethnic groups do very well. [The picture switches to Asian pupils answering questions in a school classroom.] Indian pupils achieve more highly than others of South Asian background and in many urban areas do better than white pupils. At secondary school Asian pupils make better progress than whites of the same social class.

Here we have the two elements of the story that were presented in the radio headlines and in the opening BBC television headline, but this time they are sequenced in reverse order, no doubt to provide a link from the KWESI project. Moreover, what is presented here verbally in terms of findings is very close to the formulations that can be found in the Review. In particular, the words used to describe African Caribbean pupils' achievement draws on the distribution rather than the competition model.[5] And some of the sentences are virtually direct quotations from the Review or the executive summary. However, the contrast

5 Interestingly, here the gender contrast is removed (except perhaps through the effect of the visuals).

between African Caribbean and Asian pupils, reinforced by the screen images, may well still carry the implication that the difference in average performance is something to do with the pupils, especially since the Asian pupils are shown competing to answer a teacher's questions.

It is also worth noting that the range of comparison is broadened here compared with the initial headline. Whereas, in the latter, the contrasting educational performance of African Caribbean and Indian pupils was foregrounded, here both groups are compared with a wider range: African Caribbean pupils are more likely to be excluded than other groups; Indian pupils are compared with others from a 'South Asian background'. Nevertheless, the overall structure of the summary of the findings of the Review provided by Mike Baker is still in terms of a contrast between highest and lowest achieving ethnic groups.

As we saw, the high levels of achievement of some Asian pupils was not a theme that was highlighted in the Review, though it was mentioned as a subordinate part of one of the summary items, and it was indicated in the body of the Review. Moreover, there is a sense in which the contrast between higher and lower achieving groups matches the overall good news/bad news format of the summaries provided in the Review and the press release.

The next part of the item features an extract from an interview with the lead author of the Review (the caption reads: 'Dr David Gillborn, report author'):

> *DG*: All ethnic minorities are not the same and the Indian community in particular has a different social class profile to other groups. Indian students are much more likely to come from a family with a kind of middle class family background and we've known for many years that there's a very strong relationship between social class and achievement in education.

This comment introduces an issue that is not highlighted in any of the summaries in the Review, and was not given attention in the radio coverage: there are differences between ethnic minority groups in Britain that are educationally relevant but independent of ethnicity, such as their social class profiles. And the speaker goes on to imply that the difference in level of performance between Indian and African Caribbean pupils may be a product of social class rather than of ethnicity, or more specifically that the reason why Indian pupils are doing so well is because a greater proportion of them come from middle-class families.

It is worth noting the rather different use of interviews here from the *Today* programme. As we noted, there was no interview with either author of the Review on the latter; indeed, they never emerged from behind the label 'the Schools' Inspectorate'. Even in this television interview the identity of the speaker is specified only in terms of authorship of the Review, plus the title 'Dr'. The latter implies an academic identity, but leaves open the possibility that he is a member of the inspectorate. Also noteworthy is that the radio interviews were live and much longer than this very brief extract from a pre-recorded interview. So, by contrast, this interview material is much more under editorial control here than the interview with the two headteachers, in the sense that the extract had probably been selected to make a point within the item, perhaps to indicate the complexity of the problem.

In the fourth section of the news item, the conclusions and recommendations of the Review are summarized, using both voice-over by Mike Baker and a list on the screen

> *MB*: The report urges more ethnic monitoring of school performance ['more ethnic monitoring' comes up as text], something the government has agreed to restart, and says that explicitly targeted action for ethnic minority groups does work ['targeted action works' comes up on the screen]. Instead they should target appropriate action to particular groups and so-called colour-blind policies where all pupils are treated the same should be dropped [on screen: 'drop "colour–blind" policies'] as they've failed to reduce inequality.

Here it is striking, first of all, that there is a very strong emphasis on a component of the Review and press release that was given relatively little mention in the radio coverage: the policy recommendations. Furthermore, also included here is a reference to the government's reaction to the Review, reflecting the fact that events had moved on over the course of the morning. This latter theme is continued with an extract from a pre-recorded interview with the then head of OFSTED:

> [Caption: Chris Woodhead, Chief Schools Inspector]
> *CW*: Schools do need to look at the issue of expectation, teacher stereotyping. I believe that they must do everything possible to understand the background of children from different ethnic groups have but without compromising their expectations for those children.

The focus here is on what schools need to do to remedy the problem highlighted by the Review that is central to this news item. In the process, however, a possible explanation for the lower average level of African Caribbean pupils' educational performance is indicated, in terms of the role of teachers' expectations and stereotypes. This is very much in line with a theme presented in the body of the Review, particularly that dealing with qualitative research. At the same time the proposed remedy seems to be complex, if not ambiguous: schools must take account of pupils' ethnic background but without lowering their expectations for those children. On the one hand, teachers are to expect that children from different ethnic communities will be different; on the other, they are not to have lower expectations of any ethnic group. As we saw, this complex message is to be found in the Review's conclusion.

The final segment of the item begins with further visual material from the KWESI project, but with a voice-over from the education correspondent that is not specifically about that project:

> *MB*: The government has responded by promising to restart ethnic monitoring, something it dropped in the past, and says it will look into what action can be taken. But Labour says the government should not be phasing out the special funding for teachers of pupils who do not have English as a first language.

The visual picture then changes to the correspondent standing outside the OFSTED building, with the nameplate in shot:

> This is not a simple picture: social class and gender are just as important factors as race. But the main focus of concern is why boys, either African Caribbean or white working class, so often are turned off school.

The initial focus here is on the government and Labour Party responses to the Review. This underlines its newsworthiness: it is something to which political parties feel it necessary to respond; it is a significant new element in the national political environment.

The education correspondent's summarizing conclusion underlines the complexity of the picture, picking up the point made earlier, by David Gillborn, that the effects of ethnicity/race are mixed up with those of social class. And both complexity and the role of social class are themes in the Review, albeit for the most part minor ones. However, in his final sentence Mike Baker goes on to identify the core issue in terms of gender. This implies a different explanation from the others already suggested, one which takes emphasis away from ethnicity or race, towards more general processes affecting boys.[6] This message is not to be found explicitly in the Review, though it links up with what was a rising theme in the media at the time concerning boys' underachievement.

This item was repeated on the 6.00 p.m. news, with some minor changes. For example, in the introduction Indian girls are now described as 'tending to outperform white children', while 'boys of African Caribbean origin' are described as 'generally doing less well'. Use of 'outperform' moves the message towards the competition model. Furthermore, here an explicit comparison with the white majority is introduced, and introduction of the word 'generally' perhaps gives the impression that all African Caribbean pupils are doing less well (though it could perhaps also suggest that some are doing better). The overall length of the item was reduced by around 30 seconds, largely by editing down the education correspondent's commentary.

6 This is an issue on which Mike Baker has written elsewhere: Baker 1994.

A rather different version of the item was included in the 9.00 p.m. news. Here the opening introduction took the following form:

> Black boys of African Caribbean origin are not sharing equally in the rise in educational standards according to a report from the Schools' Inspectorate. It shows that some ethnic minority groups are doing well, especially Indian pupils. But boys of African Caribbean origin are doing poorly in exams and are more likely to be expelled from school.

Here the initial focus is on the performance of African Caribbean boys compared with other groups: the order of mention has been reversed. Moreover, the formulation is that of the Review: 'not sharing equally'. The now familiar other element of the message, about the higher levels of achievement of Indian pupils, also appears, but here it has lost its gender-specific formulation; and it is followed by a repetition of the point about the poor performance of African Caribbean boys, this again being specified in terms of exam performance and exclusion from school.

The next section of the item has footage about a summer scheme in Birmingham called the University of the First Age. Once again, this seems to have been pre-recorded, and its use was designed specifically to add variety to the day's news bulletins, as well as to provide another angle on the issue. The education correspondent's commentary, Mike Baker again, reports that the scheme 'is designed to stop underachievement amongst inner-city pupils'. The commentary continues:

> Birmingham has led the way in ethnic monitoring. It found that African Caribbean pupils did best of all in tests at age 5 but by 16 they had fallen way behind. The innovative University of the First Age aims to halt that slide.

Here, the item implicitly picks up a key recommendation from the Review, and also foregrounds a finding that is to be found in the body of the Review (p. 13).

Once again, then, the focus is very much on the issue of the educational performance of African Caribbean pupils (not only boys), even though the project being discussed, unlike that included in the previous two bulletins, is not specifically aimed at these pupils but is for 'inner-city pupils' in general. Furthermore, the formulations used here do not seem to point in any particular explanatory direction, except that they do hint that local initiatives can have an effect – one of the messages of the Review.

There is then an extract from an interview, on camera, with one of the people involved in running this scheme:

> It's targeted at children aged 11–14 because that's the age group we find children tend to turn off school. And if we can turn them on to learning and work with the schools so that they see learning is something that's for them

and they feel successful in learning, then we'll keep them to their GCSE years and beyond.

Here, then, an explanation is offered for a general problem relating to inner-city children, that they 'tend to turn off school' around the ages of 11–14. The implication could be that the cause of this lies outside schools, that it is something to do with maturation, though there is a potential counter-implication that schools are not doing their job properly, since otherwise there might be no need for the University of the First Age. Again, here, the general stance is non-evaluative.

The picture then switches to the footage used in the previous bulletins, relating to the KWESI project, and the education correspondent's commentary continues as follows:

> Another Birmingham initiative, KWESI, involves volunteer adults acting as mentors and friends to black pupils who are falling behind. Today's report shows African Caribbean pupils aren't matching the academic achievement of other ethnic minorities and they also have a worse disciplinary record.

Interestingly, here the language used is open to the interpretation that the lower average level of educational achievement of African Caribbean pupils reflects something about them: they are 'falling behind', an implicit reference to the competition model. Similarly, 'they also have a worse disciplinary record' is a formulation using the metaphor of possession that largely cuts out the possibility that this is the result of discrimination on the part of teachers against these pupils. As we saw, by contrast, the latter is a message that can be derived from the Review.

There then follows an extract from an interview with the same KWESI adult volunteer as in the previous bulletins, but while the gist of what he says is the same, it is formulated differently:

> Youngsters feel that they're not part, not intrinsically a part, of the society, part of the mainstream. They feel they are on the margin of society. And this impacts on their sense of self worth and value and eventually this works itself out in the classroom.

The picture then switches to the same footage of Indian pupils in the classroom used in previous bulletins. And, while the education correspondent's commentary is formulated slightly differently, the central meaning is much the same:

> But Indian pupils are achieving better than other ethnic minorities and in many places are also ahead of white pupils.

Use of 'ahead' once again seems to involve the metaphor of a competition or race.

There then follows the interview extract with one of the authors of the Review, David Gillborn, in the same form as before, while the extract from the interview with Chris Woodhead, the Chief Inspector, is omitted. The picture then goes back to the KWESI project with a commentary by the education correspondent:

> The report urges the government to restart ethnic monitoring and today it agreed to do so. And schools are urged to abandon so-called colour-blind policies which ignore race. Instead, they're advised to target action at different groups.

As in the earlier bulletin, then, there is coverage here of the recommendations of the Review.

Finally, there is the concluding section with the education correspondent pictured outside the OFSTED building. This has exactly the same content as earlier.

The treatment of the Review on BBC television news tends to place the lower average level of achievement of African Caribbean pupils, especially boys, at the forefront. While, generally speaking, the formulations employed are close to those of the Review, there are places where they deviate, for example in using 'underachievement' and formulations like 'falling behind' or being 'ahead'. However, unlike the BBC radio coverage, the items include a brief extract from an interview with the lead author of the Review. This and the interview with one of the people involved in the KWESI project provide distinctive perspectives. While, by contrast with the interviews in the *Today* programme, there is less highlighting of differences in view that exist about the issue, the various formulations used in the commentary and the relationship between the interview extracts from two rather different projects do underline the point that is explicitly made about the complexity of the issue.

ITN AND CHANNEL 4 COVERAGE

The treatment of the Review on the lunchtime ITN news was very brief indeed. The presenter reported publication of the Review (it was pictured in the top left corner of the screen, above her shoulder, before the whole view switched to archive film of children, from different ethnic groups, leaving school). The news report continued: 'School Inspectors found growing numbers of African Caribbean youths were underachieving, and their results were getting worse, despite a general improvement in standards for other pupils.' This is a much starker message than any of the others we have examined. Not only are *growing numbers of* African Caribbean pupils described as 'underachieving', but it is suggested that their results are actually getting worse. Moreover, this is compared with 'a general improvement in standards for other pupils'. The formulation is to a large extent at odds with that employed in the Review, both in terms of its explanatory implications and because the qualification 'in some areas' has been dropped from the idea that the performance of these pupils has worsened. The term 'youths' may possibly also carry negative connotations arising from its frequent use in descriptions of street crime. One can speculate that many viewers will hear this report as indicating failure on the part of African Caribbean pupils, even though there is no explicit steer in any particular explanatory direction.

There was rather more coverage of the Review on the evening Channel 4 news; though even here it was dealt with as an item within the summary section, not as the top story of the day.[7] The item begins with the newsreader announcing a growing gap in educational achievement among ethnic minority groups 'according to a new report from the Office for Standards in Education', and it is added that 'the government have announced a ten point action plan to try and reverse the trend'. Here, the official source from which the Review comes is emphasized, and also the government's response. There is then a switch to film footage of pupils coming down a staircase in a school, with a voice-over referring to 'a school in Leicester where 90 per cent of pupils are from ethnic minorities'. The correspondent on location reports that at this school, 'OFSTED's conclusions have not come as a surprise'. And the commentary continues: 'What the staff here are <u>more</u> concerned with is finding solutions rather than just highlighting the problems, such as the emergence of what the OFSTED report describes as an underclass of African-Caribbean children.'

There is little detail about the findings of the Review presented here. Initially, the focus is on the government's response, and it then switches to the response of teachers in schools that include a high proportion of ethnic minority pupils. An opposition seems to be set up here between OFSTED and schools, with the former being portrayed as (merely) highlighting problems, whereas the latter are concerned with finding solutions. There is also a formulation of the problem using the term 'underclass' which is at odds with the spirit of the Review, and is falsely attributed to it.

This theme is developed in the next section of the report, which includes an extract from an interview with the headteacher at the school, who makes the following comment:

> We are looking to use this sort of research whereby it gives us some <u>specific</u> information that we can use then to build on. Where it just is reinforcing the worst stereotype, I think that is a very negative message both to those particular groups and in a way to the schools and maybe to the parents.

From this, the headteacher seems to be ambivalent towards the Review, with the balance of emphasis probably falling on the suggestion that it might 'reinforce the worst stereotype' and amount to 'a very negative message'. However, it may well be that this apparent ambivalence stems from the fact that the headteacher

---

7 However, this channel's summary items are much longer than those on other news programmes, reflecting the fact that the programme lasts an hour.

has not read the Review, and has not been briefed in any accurate detail about it. Nevertheless, we shall see in the next chapter that complaints against the Review for stereotyping some ethnic minority groups as underachieving did sometimes come from other quarters too, including well-informed ones.

The Channel 4 commentary continues:

> But the report suggests that there is only so much schools can do in raising educational standards among targeted groups and that the impact of other social factors cannot be ignored.

This summary is sharply at odds with the main import of the Review. It derives instead from some of the commentary provided by Chris Woodhead, the Chief Inspector of Schools. And a clip from him follows in which he says:

> Schools can and do make a difference but I think it would be blinkered in the extreme ... to pretend that the family background, the social class, the ethnic origin isn't also significant.

This is a complex statement in which both the sorts of explanation that emerged in the BBC coverage are present. The formulation is such, though, as to give emphasis to family background, social class and ethnic origin. Interestingly here the factor of social class, introduced into the BBC television coverage by one of the authors of the Review, is assimilated to explanations of children's performance in terms of extra-school factors. Here in effect, then, we have the Review being presented as placing the primary emphasis on social class and ethnic differences in family background. At the same time, the television report also indicates that at least some teachers and headteachers challenge this message, and the report goes on to indicate that some parents reject it as well:

> This suggestion [the statement from Woodhead] cuts little ice with some parents of African-Caribbean children, they blame the system, and OFSTED's report does draw attention to the potential for racial conflict in the classroom and widespread incidents of harassment.

Here, initially, the Review is positioned on the other side from 'some parents of African-Caribbean children' who 'blame the system', just as it has already been in relation to the teachers and headteacher of the school. However, the remainder of the sentence points to an important finding – about conflict and harassment – presented in the Review, and one that goes some way to realigning its position in this report. Furthermore, this is a finding that is given little attention in other television coverage, or on the radio, though it should be said that the focus here could be on conflict and harassment *among pupils*, rather than between teachers and ethnic minority pupils, which also forms part of the message of the Review.

In the next section of the item, the commentary begins by reporting that 'In Leicester there is a campaign for separate schools'. There is then an interview extract with an African Caribbean parent, a member of the African-Caribbean Support Group. He says:

> If you see your children coming out with nothing in terms of their future well-being, social and life skills, you are going to get frustrated and disappointed with the system that in a sense is not performing effectively and you would want alternatives to make it better for your child.

Here, the emphasis is not on family background but on the school system. However, as in the case of one of the headteachers interviewed on the *Today* programme, Mr Atkinson, the implied explanation is overall ineffectiveness, rather than discrimination against African Caribbean pupils, though that could be read into it.

The final summing-up by the commentator is as follows:

> The government admits that there is a real cause for concern about ethnic underachievement. It plans to monitor ethnic standards more closely and review methods for dealing with classroom racism. But reversing such a trend will not happen overnight.

Here, then, there is a return to the issue of the government's response. Further-more, it is implied that 'classroom racism' may be the source of the problem.

There are several general points of interest here. First of all, it is striking, by comparison with the BBC coverage, that in the ITN and Channel 4 reports there is no mention at all of the relatively high achievement of some South Asian pupils. Second, as elsewhere, there is no recognition that what is involved is a *review* of *academic research*. And not only is the Review identified with OFSTED, but interpretation of its message is strongly shaped by that identification. A third point, following on from this, is that in the Channel 4 report an opposition is set up between OFSTED/the Review, on the one hand, and schools/African Caribbean parents, on the other. Moreover, the formulation of this contrast is such as to put the former in a negative light. The findings of the Review are described as being 'no surprise' to staff in the school, and these staff are presented as being 'more concerned with finding solutions' than 'highlighting the problems'. Finally, the only summary provided of the content of the Review attributes to it a claim about 'the emergence of ... an underclass of African-Caribbean children'. While this can be recognized as a formulation of the finding that these pupils have the lowest average level of educational achievement, that their performance is worsening in some areas, and that they experience a higher rate of exclusions, it departs sharply from the Review in the terminology used, and thereby probably in the message given. Moreover, later in the report the message of the Review seems to be assimilated to a statement by the Chief Inspector of Schools which carries a message that is at odds with the spirit of the Review. At the same time, in the course of the item, the role of conflict and harassment in schools is indicated as reported in the Review, there is mention of 'classroom racism', and we are offered the perspectives not just of a headteacher who criticizes stereotyping but also of an African Caribbean parent who blames the education system for failing children from his community.

CONCLUSION

In this chapter, I looked first of all at the BBC television coverage of the Review, from the lunchtime news onwards. These reports began by contrasting the relatively high level of average performance by some Asian groups with the lower average level of achievement of African Caribbean pupils, especially boys. However, they focused primarily on the latter, using pre-filmed material to illustrate initiatives designed to tackle the problem. The language used mixed the distribution model employed in the Review with the discourse of the competition metaphor. The items included the views of someone involved in a mentoring project who portrayed society as alienating African Caribbean boys, and an extract from an interview with one of the authors of the Review. There was also coverage of the Review's recommendations. However, in the closing commentary by the education correspondent, the issue seemed to be assimilated to that of boys' underachievement generally, which was not part of the Review's message.

The lunchtime news coverage on ITN was very brief, and it focused exclusively on the 'underachievement' of African Caribbean pupils, suggesting that their results were 'getting worse'. There was no mention of the educational performance of other ethnic minority groups, and the language used probably tended to imply an explanation of African Caribbean 'underachievement' in terms of the distinctive ethnic characteristics of the pupils themselves and their home backgrounds.

The Channel 4 news coverage in the evening was almost as long as each of the BBC items. Here the focus was initially on the government's response, and subsequently very much on the critical, or even negative, reactions of a headteacher and ethnic minority parents to what were portrayed as the findings of the Review. The Review is criticized for highlighting problems rather than looking for solutions, for possibly reinforcing stereotypes, and for neglecting the fact that the education system fails African Caribbean pupils. The account of its findings uses the term 'underclass', and the Review is largely assimilated to part of the Chief Inspector's comments which stressed the role of family background. There is also little coverage of the recommendations of the Review. However, the item does note that the Review points to 'the potential for racial conflict in the classroom and widespread incidents of harassment'. And this is an aspect of the Review's findings that was largely absent from other television coverage.

4 The Review in the press: national, ethnic minority and local newspaper coverage

Publication of *Recent Research on the Achievements of Ethnic Minority Pupils* was very widely reported in the national press and in ethnic minority newspapers, and there was also considerable coverage in the local press. In addition, it was reported in some specialist education publications: *The Times Education Supplement* and in *Guardian Education*. In this chapter, I will focus first of all on *where* in each publication the Review was covered and on the *amount* of coverage given to it. These features will be used to assess the prominence assigned to the story. The rest of the chapter will be concerned with the *way* the Review was presented: in the headlines, and then in the reports themselves. I will look at variation in how it was described as a source; in the balance of emphasis given, respectively, to its findings and to the government's and others' reactions to it. Finally, in relation to the Review's findings and recommendations, I will look at how these were formulated in newspaper reports, in particular at implied explanations for ethnic educational inequality and indications of where praise, blame and remedy (if required) might lie.

THE LOCATION AND EXTENT OF COVERAGE

The approach taken here will be a fairly simplistic one, assuming that, broadly speaking, the nearer the front page an item is reported and/or the more space it is given, the higher the news value it is has been accorded. As we will see, these measures are not unproblematic, and do not always vary closely together, but they are a rough guide.[1]

The first newspaper reports appeared on the Sunday before the Review's publication date: in *The Sunday Times* and in the *Independent on Sunday*. The account in *The Sunday Times* was 733 words in length, and appeared on page 5. It took up around a third of the page (50 per cent of the space devoted to news rather

1 I have not adopted the more sophisticated, structuralist form of analysis offered by Kress and van Leeuwen 1998, since this seems to me rather speculative, in relation to both production and reception.

than adverts), included a photograph of an Asian pupil, and was located in the top left corner. In the *Independent on Sunday* the report appeared on the front page and was 324 words in length. It was a relatively short report, but was located just below the middle of the page, immediately under the main headline story. There was also further brief mention of the Review in an item on page 8, reporting a reduction in the number of specialist teachers employed to work with children for whom English is a second language.[2]

Turning to the national dailies, *The Sun* published a very brief report on the Monday, but all of the others carried the story on the day after the Review appeared (Friday 6 September 1996). The coverage is summarized in Table 4.1.

There is no simple match between the three measures of prominence included in Table 4.1, each of which is problematic in itself.[3] Nevertheless, these three measures give us a rough sense of the level of, and variation in, priority given to the story about the Review by national newspapers. *The Independent* assigned the story the highest prominence on all three measures. *The Guardian* was next, followed by *The Daily Telegraph*. By contrast, while *The Sun* put the story on page 2, the amount of wordage is small even by tabloid standards.

Not surprisingly, the Review was covered in the two main education supplements, both of which are tabloid in format.[4] *The Times Educational Supplement* included two articles in its 6 September issue. The first was on page 3, took up around a quarter of the page, and was 413 words in length. The second was on page 13, took up the whole page, and was 1,327 words long. There was also an editorial on the issue, and a smaller piece the following week about some of the reaction to the Review (this was on page 12 and took up about an eighth of a tabloid page). *Guardian Education* covered the story on Tuesday 10 September.[5] Three articles appeared on page 4, taking up around a tabloid page and a half (including photos and a chart), and these were 1,717 words in length overall.

---

2 This piece was headlined 'English language teaching jobs lost', and concerned failure to fund the replacement of specialist language teachers in Tower Hamlets. It notes that the Review 'praises Tower Hamlets' work in teaching English to ethnic-minority children, saying that Bangladeshi children who achieve lower scores than their white classmates at GCSE were surpassing them after they became fluent in English'.

3 The problem with the first measure – position of the report in terms of pages – is that while inclusion on the front page certainly indicates high priority, it is less clear that subsequent pages represent a linear decline in prominence. Moreover, the length and internal textual organization of newspapers differs considerably, as regards where home and international news is placed, where television listings occur, and so on. The problem with the second measure is that assessments of space on the page are very dependent not just on page size but also on the amount of advertising, headline sizes, use of pictures, and so on. Furthermore, judgement of size of headlines is also relative to the practice of a particular newspaper. Finally, wordage does not take proper account of the presence of photographs and charts, and is again very much relative to the newspaper concerned.

4 There was no coverage in the education sections of *The Daily Telegraph* and *The Independent.*

5 It is only published on Tuesdays.

Table 4.1 Coverage of the story in national daily newspapers by rank order in wordage

Newspaper	Position of report	Space on page	No. of words
The Independent	Front page	Around ¾ of news space, some 15% of the broadsheet page, including cartoon	417
	Page 3	Full-page article, including photos, and a summary box	1,484
	Page 17 of tabloid supplement	Suzanne Moore column	1,018
The Guardian	Page 5	Full page: three articles, including photos and charts	1,617
The Daily Telegraph	Page 4	Nearly half a broadsheet page, including photograph and three charts	660
The Times	Page 6	Top left of page, around an 1/8 of a broadsheet page, including photo	584
Daily Mail	Page 12	Top of page, large headline, story is roughly ¼ of a page, and around ½ of news space	432
Daily Express	Page 21	Just less than ¼ of page, though around ½ of news space	377
Daily Star	Page 8	Over ¼ of tabloid page, with large headlines, including photos	295
Daily Mirror	Page 11	Small piece at the top left of the page	140
The Sun	Page 2	Small box, with text printed in bold, on the left-hand side of the top half of the page	71

The ethnic minority press also covered the story over a period of two months following publication of the Review.[6] This time spread reflects the fact that these publications are weekly or monthly, and that some included follow-up items. I have focused here on publications that are in English and that deal with UK news. There was considerable variation in the coverage given to the story, and this is summarized in Table 4.2.

6 For an outline history of the ethnic minority press in Britain, see Benjamin 1995.

Table 4.2 Coverage of the Review in the ethnic minority press, by rank order in terms of wordage

Newspaper	Position of report	Space on page	No. of words
The Voice 10.9.96	Page 5	Around ¾ of a tabloid page (nearly all the news space), large headlines at top of page, including 3 charts from the Review	723
	Page 8 editorial	Most of column on left hand side of page, over ⅛ of page	404
17.9.96	Page 11 Tony Sewell's column starts from the Review and criticizes some aspects of it	Over ½ a page, and most of non-advertising space	552
24.9.96	Page 8	All the news space on a tabloid page, around 9/10 of the page (including photographs), with large headlines at the top	872
The Muslim News 24.10.96	Page 4	Around ⅓ of a tabloid page	855
Eastern Eye 6.9.96	Page 4, but part of a larger item spanning pp. 4 and 5	A little under ½ a tabloid page	638
	Editorial	Small item, middle of three editorial comments	125
The Weekly Journal September–October 1996	Page 13	Whole-page editorial	77
		Article by Carlton Duncan.	516
	Page 24	Brief item, around a 1/10 of the page.	144
Caribbean Times 12.9.96	Page 5	Just less than ¼ of a tabloid page, with headline at the top of the page	589
Asian Times 5.9.96	Page 2	Roughly ⅓ of a tabloid page (nearly half the news space)	534
The Weekly Gleaner	Page 2	Around ⅛ of a tabloid page (less than a third of the news space)	194
India Weekly 6.9.96	Page 3	Small item, in bottom right-hand corner	72

Judgements about level of prominence here are even more difficult than in the case of national newspapers, notably because format varies even more across these newspapers. Nevertheless, in broad terms, *The Voice* has the highest level of coverage, and *The Weekly Gleaner* and *India Weekly* the lowest. It is more difficult to discriminate among the remaining newspapers in terms of the relative importance they assigned to publication of the Review.

Items dealing with the Review also appeared in many local newspapers, including *The Birmingham Post*, the *Birmingham Evening Mail*, the *Bradford Telegraph & Argus*, the *Derby Evening Telegraph*, *The Leicester Mercury*, the *London Evening Standard*, the *Manchester Evening News*, the *Oldham Evening Chronicle*, *South London Press*, *The Western Mail*, the *Wolverhampton Express and Star*, and the *Yorkshire Evening Post* and *Yorkshire Post*.[7] Here too coverage varied, but generally speaking it was limited to a smallish item on an inside page, and in one case, that of the *Yorkshire Post*, there was an editorial.

In summary, there was widespread coverage of the Review in different types of newspaper, as well as some variation in the prominence given to the story even within each category of newspaper. This variation can be explained, in part, in terms of journalists' judgements about the likely level of reader interest in the Review, and in the issues surrounding it. *The Independent* and *The Guardian* probably had the highest level of coverage among the national dailies because substantial portions of their readership work within the education system.[8] And the same is even more obviously true for the education supplements. However, the relatively high level of coverage in *The Daily Telegraph*, along with *The Sun*'s placing of the story on page 2, are more difficult to explain in these terms. Other factors affecting variation in coverage might include the differential level of pressure on space in each newspaper on the day concerned, given their varying news priorities, and whether the Review had links with previous stories carried by that particular newspaper.

Likely interest on the part of readers probably explains the relatively high level of coverage in much of the ethnic minority press too: their audiences can be assumed to have considerable interest in ethnic variation in school achievement. However, this factor does not explain the differing coverage across these newspapers. This may reflect differences in the age structure of readerships and in the extent to which these publications are concerned with British news versus news about the Indian subcontinent or the West Indies.

Variation in the prominence and amount of newspaper coverage of the Review is certainly one factor relevant to its likely impact on readers. Equally important, though, is the way in which the story was presented. As we shall see, there

---

7 For useful discussion of various aspects of the British local media in recent times, see Franklin and Murphy 1998. To some extent coverage here did seem to correspond to areas where ethnic minority groups are particularly concentrated.

8 Lacey and Longman (1997: 81) draw on MORI data to show the issues of most and least concern to readers of different British national newspapers. Both *Guardian* and *Independent* readers listed education as a topic of high concern.

were considerable differences in this respect, even among newspapers allocating roughly the same amount of space; and sometimes even among those dealing with similar readerships. Of particular importance in terms of impact on how readers respond to the Review are likely to be the headlines, so I will look at these first.

HEADLINES

Headlines serve a number of functions. They are in large part designed to attract the attention of the reader, but they also provide a framework in terms of which the report below them can be, and probably will be, read (van Dijk 1991: 50–1). In some cases, there was more than one headline to stories dealing with the Review; and secondary headlines were sometimes combined with by-lines, sometimes not. Occasionally, it was not clear which was the main headline, in that the top headline was in smaller print than the lower one. For example, there are four headlines dealing with the issue in *The Guardian*. The first one – 'Tory attacks on "loony left" programmes are reversed' – is right at the top of the page, but is in a smaller font size than the others (though it is printed in white on a black background).[9] The next headline, which also applies to the whole story – 'Ministers in school anti-racist drive' – is again at the top of the page, just below the first one, and is in much larger print. Then there are two other headlines, appearing further down the page, relating to stories about the issue of ethnic minority achievement in particular schools, which are in a smaller font than the second headline, but larger than the first.

   I will look initially at what the headlines focus on, then at the selection of particular findings for inclusion, and finally at the ways in which these are formulated and how this varies across newspapers.

Headline focus

A broad distinction can be drawn between those headlines that were concerned with the Review and those that focused on the government's, or others', reaction to its publication and/or which addressed the issue more generally. Table 4.3 indicates the pattern among national newspapers in this respect. As can be seen, the headlines in most national newspapers focused on the Review, but some of those giving the story highest prominence were in the other category.

   The two educational supplements differed in their focus. The main headline in *Guardian Education* concerned the government's response to the Review, though the secondary headline does refer to one of the Review's findings: 'Alarming evidence of underachievement among some ethnic minorities is shaking up

9 In journalistic parlance, this is referred to as a 'strap'.

Table 4.3 Emphasis in national press headlines on the Review versus on reactions to it[a]

Main focus on the Review	Main focus on reactions to the Review and the issue more generally
The Sunday Times	The Times
Independent on Sunday	The Guardian
Daily Mail	The Daily Express
The Daily Telegraph	The Independent
The Sun	
The Daily Mirror	
The Independent	

Note

a It was impossible to classify the *Daily Star* headlines ('Black to the Drawing Board: Kids turning to crime because they hate Sir'). There were two headlines in *The Independent* falling into different categories.

thinking in Whitehall and town hall.' By contrast, the headlines and secondary headlines to both articles included in *The Times Educational Supplement* focused on the Review itself.

All the reports in the ethnic minority press concentrated on the findings of the Review (though the *Caribbean Times*' and *Muslim News*' headlines are hard to classify: 'Are black boys really the problem?' and 'Ethnicity Matters', respectively).

The pattern in the local press was fairly similar to that in national newspapers. Once again, most newspapers focused on the findings, but there was a minority whose main concern was reaction to the Review (see Table 4.4).

Table 4.4 Emphasis in local press headlines on the Review or on reaction to it

Focus on the Review	Focus on reaction to the Review
The Birmingham Post	Birmingham Evening Mail
Bradford Telegraph & Argus	Derby Evening Telegraph
	The Leicester Mercury
London Evening Standard	Yorkshire Post
Manchester Evening News	
Oldham Evening Chronicle	
South London Press	
The Western Mail	
Wolverhampton Express and Star	
Yorkshire Evening Post	

Selection of findings for inclusion in headlines

I want to look next at the headlines focusing on the Review in order to document which of its findings are most frequently referred to. Table 4.5 provides
information about the incidence of various findings, and also of falsely reported
findings, in the Sunday and daily national newspapers. Here what we might
refer to as a failure story, concerning the lower average level of achievement of
African Caribbean pupils, is the most common finding headlined, being the focus
in four newspapers. By contrast, the 'success' story given some prominence on
the radio and television, of high levels of achievement by some Asian pupils,
is the topic in only two newspaper headlines. The Review's recommendation of
more ethnic monitoring is given the same level of coverage as the performance of
Asian pupils, with the growing gap in performance levels coming next. There are
also two headlines which present 'findings' which are not present in the Review.
One of these is concerned explicitly with the educational performance of African
Caribbean pupils, and the other relates to it implicitly.[10]

Headlines in *The Times Educational Supplement* focused on the widening gap
in performance among ethnic groups, on 'teachers creating conflict with their
African-Caribbean pupils', and on 'black children still get a raw deal'. The second
headline in *Guardian Education* focused on 'underachievement', but without
indicating which ethnic minorities were involved. In these specialist publications,
even more than in the Sunday and daily press, the emphasis was on failure;
however, explicitly or by implication, this failure was on the part of teachers and
policies rather than of ethnic groups.

Coverage of findings in ethnic minority press headlines was more focused,
with just three findings represented, and one finding not in the Review reported
(see Table 4.6). Here, by contrast with the national newspapers and education
supplements, the most commonly reported finding relates to the success of some
Asian pupils. However, this was only the main theme in those newspapers aimed
at an Asian readership. Publications serving African Caribbean readers focused
on the lower level of performance of African Caribbean pupils. There was a
sharp differentiation here.[11] One of the Asian newspapers highlighted variations

10 The formulation of the findings in the headlines is, of course, often rather different from in the
    Review. Moreover, while there is a difference between accurate and inaccurate reporting, the
    line between them is fuzzy. This makes identifying findings reported in the media that are not
    found in the Review very much a matter of judgement. In the case of the *Independent on Sunday*
    what is involved is an elaboration on one of the Review's findings that is not only not present in
    the Review but runs against part of what might be taken to be one element of its message: the
    possibility of improving the situation. In the case of the *Daily Star*, it is hard to see the headline
    as anything other than simply inaccurate as an account of the Review. It would be possible to
    see one of the *Independent*'s headlines – 'Teachers to be monitored for racial harassment' – as
    inaccurate, but I judged this to be close enough to the spirit of the Review.
11 There were some explicit signs of this targeting, for example the comment at the end of the
    Asian Times report: 'However, the overall picture painted by the report is encouraging towards

Table 4.5 Incidence of findings in the headlines of national newspapers[a]

Research findings	Main headline	Secondary headline
1 Lower than average performance of African Caribbean pupils	*The Daily Telegraph* *The Independent* *The Times* *The Independent on Sunday* *The Sun*	*Daily Mail*
2 Asian/Indian pupils achieving at higher levels, on average, than other groups	*The Sunday Times*	
3 More detailed ethnic monitoring recommended	*The Express* *The Independent*	
4 Growing gap in performance between pupils from different ethnic groups	*Independent on Sunday*	*Daily Mail*
5 African Caribbean boys more likely to be excluded than others	*Daily Mirror*	
6 Teachers have low expectations of African Caribbean pupils	*The Daily Telegraph*	
Findings not in the Review reported in headlines		
African Caribbean pupils locked in a cycle of failure	*Independent on Sunday*	
'Kids turning to crime because they hate Sir'		*Daily Star*

Note

a Some headlines referred to more than one finding. Headlines from the *Guardian* and the *Daily Star* could not be classified, the first because it focused on government reaction, the second because it was obscure in meaning.

in performance within the Asian category, suggesting that Pakistani pupils face prejudice.

In the case of the local press, quite a few headlines focused on national or local policy or were difficult to categorize.[12] Nevertheless, Table 4.7 indicates the relative focus on different findings from the Review here. Even more than elsewhere, it is the lower level of performance of African Caribbean pupils which gets the most coverage in headlines. Only one newspaper leads on the higher than average performance of 'Asian' pupils. A couple of other newspapers highlight findings not represented in the national and ethnic minority press. Finally, the second most common 'finding' reported relates to the discovery or presence of an

all Asians, with a growing increase in academic achievements reported for each of the southern Asian groups'. And the headline in *The Voice* was 'Our Kids are Still Missing Out'.

12 See Appendix 1 for a listing of all the newspaper headlines.

Table 4.6 Incidence of findings in the headlines of ethnic minority newspapers[a]

Research findings	Main headline	Secondary headline
1 Asian/Indian pupils achieving at higher levels, on average, than other groups	*Eastern Eye* *Asian Times* *India Weekly*	*Eastern Eye*
2 Lower than average performance of African Caribbean pupils	*The Voice* *The Weekly Gleaner*	*The Voice*
3 Growing gap in performance between pupils from different ethnic groups	*Asian Times*	
Findings not in the Review reported in headlines		
Pakistani students face university places prejudice [While the Review reports that 'Black Caribbean and Pakistani applicants continued to be significantly less likely to have been admitted to university', there is no statement that this results from prejudice. However, the report quotes from an interview with the lead author of the Review, David Gillborn, in support.]		*Asian Times*

Note

a Headlines in the *Muslim News*, *The Weekly Journal* and the *Caribbean Times* could not be categorized. As with the national press, in some cases more than one finding was reported in the same headline, and the formulation of the findings in the headlines is often rather different from in the Review.

'underclass', something that does not appear in the Review and can be interpreted as running counter to its spirit.

The predominant emphasis in newspaper headlines, then, aside from those aimed primarily at an Asian readership, was on the lower average level of educational performance of African Caribbean pupils. Nevertheless, there was considerable variation across newspapers in what was presented in headlines as the key issues arising from the Review.

Headline formulation

I want to look next at how the headlines were formulated, and thereby at what message we might expect readers to take from them. Of course, this is not a straightforward matter. What constitutes the effective message of a headline for an audience depends upon their interpretation of it. No more than, indeed

Table 4.7 Incidence of findings in the headlines of local newspapers[a]

Finding	Main headline	Secondary headline	Editorial
Lower average achievement of African Caribbean pupils	*Manchester Evening News, Oldham Evening Chronicle, South London Press, The Western Mail*	*South London Press*	
High average level of performance of some Asian pupils	*Wolverhampton Express and Star*		
Stereotyping	*The Leicester Mercury*		
Colour-blind policies have failed	*London Evening Standard*		
Findings not in the Review reported in headlines			
Emergence of an ethnic underclass in education	*The Birmingham Post, Oldham Evening Chronicle, Yorkshire Evening Post*		*Yorkshire Post*

Note

a Headlines in the *Birmingham Evening Mail, Bradford Telegraph & Argus, Derby Evening Telegraph, Yorkshire Evening Post,* and *Yorkshire Post* could not be categorized.

perhaps less than, any other kind of text can headlines be treated as having fixed, semantically given, meanings. While, like all communications, they are designed for an audience, and while audiences usually interpret communications in terms of what they take to have been the intended message, there is always some scope for misinterpretation, or shall we say for *variations* in interpretation.[13]

Moreover, sometimes headlines play on ambiguities, and as I have already noted there are some whose message is unclear, or at least very abstract, when read separately from the reports underneath them. This reflects the fact that

13 The reason why variation from intended message may not be misinterpretation is that any message is open to being used to draw further inferences, and it is often not clear whether or not those inferences were intended as part of the message. While it is often fairly straightforward to identify what the central core of the message was, there will usually be a penumbra surrounding this, shading into inferences about the significance of the message that were fairly clearly not part of what was intended. I am retaining the distinction between meaning (or message) and significance (Hirsch 1967) here, as do Fenton *et al.* (1998), but emphasizing that the boundary between the two is not clear-cut.

headlines are frequently designed to puzzle in order to encourage readers to give attention to the news item, and in mass circulation tabloids they are occasionally designed to entertain through puns and other devices. The headline in the *Daily Star* was 'Black to the Drawing Board', and the obscurity of this was reduced very little by the sub-headline 'Kids turning to crime because they hate Sir'. The main headline makes little sense even in the context of the report, and the second focuses on an aspect that is only mentioned at the beginning and end of the report, and that has little relation to the Review.[14]

The two headlines in the *Daily Mirror* were 'Class Chaos: Probe on expelled blacks'. The first of these, involving heavy alliteration, does not give much indication of the topic. Even if 'class' is interpreted as 'school class', it is not clear what sort of chaos is involved. The second headline does mention one of the findings of the Review, relating to exclusion levels, and employs a racial/ethnic label, though only the by-line, which refers to the author as education correspondent, indicates that what is being referred to is exclusion from school. Given this, the message is still obscure, even taking both headlines into account. Above all, there is no clear story implied in these two headlines. The 'expulsions' may be read as resulting from the chaos, but it is not clear who has caused the chaos even if the reference to a probe perhaps suggests that it was not black pupils.

An even more opaque headline, where there is also no reference to education, appeared in *The Muslim News*. It read: 'Ethnicity matters'. Only retrospectively, in the context of the report, can this be given some sense.[15] Another difficult-to-interpret headline occurred in *The Leicester Mercury* (6 September). It read: 'School pupils: "Don't fall into stereotyping trap"'. This makes clear that the report is about pupils in school, and it may be that the reference to ethnic minority pupils can be inferred from the word 'stereotyping', though this is a very weak implication. Moreover, this headline might seem to involve an injunction to pupils not to fall into the stereotyping trap, whereas in fact it becomes clear from the report that the injunction is directed at teachers.

Despite problems of interpretation in some cases, as with radio and television coverage, it is possible to identify implicit models in many of the headlines. There are at least three such models: the distribution, competition, and discrimination models. These conceptualize differently the process by which variations in educational outcomes occur, and as a result they offer different implicit explanations for varying levels of educational outcome across ethnic groups. In addition, they hint at who (if anyone) deserves praise or blame, whether or not there is a problem that needs to be remedied, and, if so, whose responsibility it is.

As we saw, the distribution metaphor was predominant in the Review. It represents education as a good that is in some sense distributed across groups or

---

14 This may reflect the many hands that usually go into producing newspaper reports: see Bell 1991: 34–6, and also Eason 1988: 206.
15 At the same time, the Review was mentioned in the opening sentence of the report, and this publication provides a lengthy account covering many of its findings.

individuals. In these terms, any inequalities in educational achievement among ethnic groups, where one or more ethnic minorities achieve at a lower than average level, are seen as mal-distribution. Furthermore, even where there is no indication that someone is to blame for this, the metaphor tends to imply that teachers, schools, the education system or the government have a responsibility to rectify the situation, since they are in charge of the distribution.

By contrast, the competition metaphor, which was prevalent in radio and television coverage, portrays educational performance in terms of a team competition, with ethnic groups competing, rather in the manner that children in a class might compete, to achieve the highest level of performance. This model can be taken to imply the allocation of praise or blame to ethnic groups (the pupils themselves or parent communities) according to their relative performance. And, unless otherwise indicated, where there is a lack of success it is implied that the responsibility falls on the group itself to remedy the situation, if remedy is possible. In pure form, this model does not imply any social problem that requires a public policy intervention to correct it.

Finally, the discrimination model has a much more specific focus, and can stand alone or be used to qualify either of the other two models. It points to the occurrence of forms of action that disadvantage some ethnic groups as against others in relation to educational performance. Given that these actions are internal to the education system, there is a strong implication that those in authority within that system are to blame for inequalities, through acts of commission or through omission, and that they are also responsible for eliminating them.

I will now look at the extent and ways in which each of these models appears in the headlines.

The distribution model

There are only two headlines that seem to rely on this model, even though it was central to the Review and also to the summaries of its findings presented on the cover and in the press release. The by-line to the second article in *The Times Educational Supplement* dealing with the Review read as follows: 'Reva Klein looks at the background to a new report that shows black children still get a raw deal from the education system'. The phrase 'raw deal' implies an unequal *distribution* of education. And while it does not necessarily suggest that someone is to blame, the language used does imply a responsibility to do something about it on the part of 'the education system' – in other words, teachers, schools, and/or the government.

The Voice's headline carries similar implications: 'Our kids are still missing out: Report highlights lack of progress in tackling Afro-Caribbean performance in schools', and the message was reinforced by the title to an editorial: 'Standing up for our children's schooling'. The phrase 'missing out' carries much the same implication as 'raw deal'. And, interestingly, what is involved here is a largely negative denial of responsibility: it is certainly not 'the kids' who are responsible. It is not made obvious who *is* responsible, but there are some hints. These are provided by the contrast between the 'us' referred to in the main headline and the agent who has not made progress in dealing with 'our kids' performance in schools'. In other words, there is a weak implication here that it is a failure of government or of the larger society generally; and this implication might well have been stronger for readers of *The Voice*.

A less clear example that could perhaps be placed in this category is the headline in the *South London Press*: 'Black kids suffer: Gap widening between Afro-Caribbean children and other ethnic groups'. To 'suffer' is a passive act, grammatically speaking, so that once again it is clear who is *not* to blame. Unequal distribution is one source of suffering, but there are others; indeed, one can suffer from natural disasters. So, the term does not necessarily imply culpable action on the part of any agent. However, it does leave open this possibility. At the very least, the word probably implies that there is a problem that some agency has the responsibility to remedy.

An example where the causal narrative implied is even more uncertain, but clearly runs in the same direction as the distribution metaphor, is the *Evening Standard*'s headline: 'Colour-blind policies "are failing pupils from ethnic minorities"'. That it is the 'policies' that are failing, not the pupils, is made very clear here, even though it is not indicated *how* they are failing ethnic minority pupils.

The competition model

This model was almost universally implied in those headlines that focused on the success of some Asian pupils. The headline in *The Sunday Times*, appearing before the Review was published, read: 'Indian pupils outclass all other groups'.[16] The headline in *The Sun*, published the next day, was: 'Asian pupils top whites in classroom'. The words 'outclass' and 'top' are both used as active verbs here, and they carry a strong implication of competition. As we saw, this finding was the most commonly reported in the Asian press. The headline to a very short report in the *India Weekly* was 'Indian students excel in Britain'; in the *Asian Times* the main headline was 'Indians ahead as academic race gap widens'; while that in the *Eastern Eye* was: 'Top of the Class. New education report puts Asian students ahead again'. In the local press, the *Wolverhampton Express and Star* had: 'Asian pupils top the exam tables'.[17]

In all these headlines (with the possible exception of that in the *India Weekly*) ethnic groups are portrayed as competing with one another in terms of educational performance. And this was also true of some reports which focused on

---

16 *The Sunday Times* story is perhaps particularly important because it seems to have been a source used by other journalists: it is mentioned explicitly in the *India Weekly* report.

17 *The Asian Times* headline is notable for an ambiguity in the meaning of the term 'race', as referring to ethnic variation, to a competition, or to both. It is worth noting that the sense of the word 'top' seems rather less active in the *Wolverhampton Express and Star* headline than it was in *The Sun*'s headline.

the educational performance of African Caribbean pupils. Thus the *Manchester Evening News* reported that: 'Afro-Caribbeans do worse at school'.[18] The headline in *The Western Mail* carries the same message even more strongly: 'African Caribbean youths trail badly'. These are active constructions, and the image presented is a comparative, and probably a competitive, one.

As already noted, what is particularly significant about the competition metaphor, in this context, is that, unless otherwise stated, there is no implication of a problem requiring remedy by anyone other than those who are doing badly. In none of these headlines is there any indication that the competition is unfair; and, without this, the message communicated is probably that it *is* fair. There is a sharp contrast here with the other two models.

Most of the other headlines concerned with the performance of African Caribbean pupils do not rely explicitly on the competition model, but sometimes they are open to much the same interpretation. The headline in *The Weekly Gleaner* was: 'Underachievement of black boys'. This can be read as a simple presentation of descriptive fact: black boys achieve at a lower average level than the majority of pupils. Of course, it is also likely to be read as carrying a negative evaluation – that this underachievement is a bad thing – a reading that is especially likely on the part of an African Caribbean readership. However, there is no indication of cause here, or of who is to blame. Black pupils are described in passive terms, grammatically speaking. But there is the possibility that the term 'underachievement' will be taken to imply that the blame lies with *them*. We saw that 'underachievement' is a term that the authors of the Review specifically warned against, on the grounds that it is often taken to attribute responsibility to pupils themselves, their families or their ethnic group as a whole; or to imply a fixed incapacity on the part of one or more of these. It is also worth noting the gendered character of this headline. It taps into another educational achievement theme emerging at the time in the mass media, picked up in BBC television coverage – boys' underachievement relative to girls – and this too is one that often involves the competition model. Over and above this, it may be that formulating the problem as one relating to black *boys* carries the implication that the problem lies with the boys themselves, rather than with parents, teachers, the government, or even their families. After all, if black girls are not underachieving, and this seems to be implied, then why cannot black boys do better?[19]

Some other headlines dealing with the lower level of performance of African Caribbean pupils adopted concepts that are similar in character to 'underachievement', referring to a 'cycle of failure' or to the emergence of an 'underclass' and sometimes these were combined with the competition metaphor. The headline

---

18 In fact, this headline is ambiguous: it could mean African Caribbeans do worse than before rather than, or as well as, that they do worse than other groups.

19 This seems to be implied because if both sexes had been underachieving there would have been no need to be gender-specific – an implication based on Grice's maxim relating to quantity (Grice 1978).

in the *Independent on Sunday* read: 'Black pupils falling behind at school in "cycle of failure" '.[20] 'Falling behind' can be read as implying some sort of race, while 'cycle of failure' suggests processes that perpetuate this failure. Moreover, it is the black pupils who are 'in' the cycle of failure; no one else seems to be implicated, except perhaps their families and communities.

Much the same idea is probably implied by the notion of an 'underclass' which was used by several newspapers, even though (like 'cycle of failure') it was not present in the Review, and runs counter to the spirit of that document. Thus the headline in the *Daily Mail* was: 'The ethnic underclass: Black pupils "falling behind whites and Asians in school performance" '.[21] 'Falling behind' implies a race, and assigns responsibility to 'black pupils' for not 'keeping up'. What is less obvious is what work the term 'underclass' does. But perhaps it suggests an element of inevitability, in line with the passive construction of 'falling behind'. There are, of course, two main possible causes of failure in a competition, aside from unfairness: those who are failing have not tried hard enough, or they are simply not as capable, in relevant respects beyond their control, as those against whom they are competing. Use of the term 'underclass' could imply either interpretation.

None of the ethnic minority newspapers used the concept of underclass, but many local newspapers did. The headline in *The Birmingham Post* was 'Report highlights ethnic under-class in schools'; that in the *Oldham Evening Chronicle* was: 'Afro-Caribbean "underclass" in education'; and the *Yorkshire Evening Post*'s headline read ' "Underclass" in the classroom'.[22] In all but one of these examples we have the use of invented quotations to present a message that is at odds with the spirit of the Review.

There is probably more semantic steer built into the term 'underclass' than into either 'underachievement' or 'cycle of failure', since it marks off an ethnic group as having distinct characteristics, and these are likely to be seen as explaining their lower level of educational performance. There is also an evaluation built into 'underclass', with the idea that what is being referred to is a class that occupies the bottom of a ranking, 'below' the normal run of people. Furthermore, of course, underclass theories in the academic literature, which are referred to explicitly in the editorial in one of these newspapers (the *Yorkshire Post*), do treat the underclass as a causal factor, not just as a product of social structural forces. Certainly, there is no indication of responsibility on the part of the education system in any of these headlines.

Some of the headlines concerned with the government's reaction to the Review also seemed to carry a message similar to that of the competition model. Thus *The Times* reported that 'Ministers act to help failing black pupils', while the *Daily Express* announced 'Race checks to help our black pupils work better'.

20 The quotation marks here are spurious; this concept is not used in the Review.
21 Here, again, the quotation is an invented one.
22 The *Yorkshire Post* used the following headline for an editorial: 'Bottom of the underclass'.

The implications for responsibility built into these two headlines are quite complex. On the one hand, the terms 'failing' and 'work better' imply something like the competition metaphor (though what is involved may be an absolute rather than a comparative measure), and therefore could be assigning responsibility to the pupils. On the other hand, the fact that ministers are acting to 'help' might be taken to imply that help is deserved; and therefore that the competition is not fair. Yet this is not made explicit, and the implication could equally be that help is needed because without help 'black pupils' are not capable of competing successfully. In this sense, being given help can be stigmatizing, or could even imply that the action is unfair on others. Furthermore, the reference in the *Daily Express* headline to 'our black pupils' could be read as carrying paternalistic connotations of an imperialistic kind. It is unclear who the 'our' refers to here, but the newspaper's readership ('us') clearly forms the core. It is also possible that for this newspaper's audience any sort of 'race check' is in itself illegitimate. We have to acknowledge that these headlines are open to alternative interpretations, but they may be less ambiguous for the readers of the newspapers concerned than I have suggested.

The discrimination model

The third model does not involve a metaphor but instead carries a direct reference to the role of discrimination in producing inequalities. A clear example is provided by the headline and by-line of the first report in *The Times Educational Supplement*. This reads: 'Ethnic gap growing in many areas. Frances Rafferty on the major report that finds white teachers creating conflict with their African-Caribbean pupils'. Here the implication is that the Review blames the 'ethnic gap' on teachers 'creating conflict' with African Caribbean pupils. One of the headlines in the *Independent*, on the front page, also refers to a form of discrimination: 'Teachers to be monitored for racial harassment'. It might reasonably be inferred that if teachers are to be monitored in this way, there must be at least some reasonable suspicion of harassment on their part; and, of course, harassment is the sort of thing that could cause poor educational performance.

The headlines in both the *TES* and *The Independent* suggest that what is involved is direct discriminatory action on the part of education system personnel – their 'creating conflict' or engaging in 'racial harassment' is portrayed as the cause of the ethnic differences in educational achievement the Review reports. Usage of both these phrases often involves strong attributions of agency, and perhaps even of intention. In semantic terms, what is 'created' is normally what is intended, and harassment is something that is done knowingly. At the same time, we should note that both words have come to be used in looser ways that do not necessarily imply intention. Someone may be described as 'creating mayhem' without this having been his or her intention. And, in the context of 'sexual harassment', the term 'harassment' is sometimes employed in ways that do not depend on intention, or even conscious recognition: those engaging in harassment may regard what they are doing as, for example, 'joking around', and therefore as tolerable. In the same way, perhaps, teachers might be engaged in 'racial harassment' without intentionally doing so, and even without accepting the validity of that description of their behaviour. They too might see themselves as 'just joking', or as simply dealing with unacceptable behaviour in the classroom in an effective way. All that said, it seems likely that readers will infer from these headlines that direct discriminatory action is operating.[23]

A succinct and direct attribution of responsibility in the same direction, this time in the form of an invented quotation, is to be found in *The Daily Telegraph* headline: 'West Indians "fail because teachers expect them to" '. A very specific form of discrimination, one mentioned explicitly in the Review, is highlighted here: differential expectations on the part of teachers. So, while the quotation is spurious, it does capture the gist of an important strand in the Review's argument. At the same time, we should note that the use of quotation marks here may serve to distance the newspaper from the finding, perhaps even thereby weakening readers' acceptance of it.

Part of the *Daily Star* report also implies the discrimination model: 'Race watchdogs blamed the racist attitude of some teachers for the poor performance of black youths'. I am presuming, and assuming that readers will too, that the 'race watchdogs' mentioned here are the authors of the Review, or its sponsoring organization, though, as we shall see later, the report goes on to quote a spokesman from the Commission for Racial Equality. It is striking that this is the only explicit attribution to the Review of a charge of racism on the part of teachers.

There are a number of other headlines that imply discrimination in some form, but in less clear or specific ways. An example is *The Guardian*'s: 'Ministers in school anti-racist drive'. There is no necessary implication here that racism actually operates in schools, though this is likely to be inferred. There is also no indication of the nature of the problem: for example it could be racism on the part of pupils, and this is a topic that is covered in the Review (though it is not referred to in the Guardian report).[24] The headline to the 'Observer' column in *The Voice*

---

23 To the extent that this is true, these headlines could be interpreted as misrepresenting the Review, in that the latter suggests that teachers *inadvertently* discriminate against some ethnic minority pupils.

24 Interestingly, the other *Guardian* headlines suggested that positive moves on the part of schools could improve educational performance: ' "Do well" imperatives boost Asian children. Bradford. Martin Wainwright visits a girls' high school at which cynicism about education is nowhere to be found', and 'Where ethnic mix proves no barrier to success. Liverpool. Headteacher relies on happy atmosphere and effective monitoring to provide encouragement, writes David Ward'. Much the same is true of a headline in *The Weekly Journal* above an article by a headteacher which discusses the issues raised by the review: 'Change the School Menu. ... headmaster of the George Dixon School in Birmingham Carlton Duncan presses home the importance of putting more colour in the curriculum'. Interestingly, as we have seen, elsewhere (on the *Today* Programme)

also hints at the discrimination model in rather general terms: 'Schooled in doing badly'. *The Leicester Mercury* headline is more specific in its reference but not very clear in its meaning, as I noted earlier: 'School pupils: "Don't fall into stereotyping trap"'.

Finally, it is worth mentioning an interesting case of dual headlines which combine the competition metaphor with the discrimination model. The *Asian Times* headlines read: 'Indians ahead as academic race gap widens; Pakistani students face University places prejudice'. This combination of different models, implying discrepant causal and blame implications, probably reflects the newspaper's orientation towards two ethnic groups among its readers whose fortunes, as reported in the Review, are rather different. Furthermore, there is a sense in which a similar asymmetry is to be found across all the newspapers: the educational performance of Indian pupils is always represented in terms of the competition metaphor, whereas the achievement level of African Caribbean and other groups is sometimes represented by one of the other two. Indeed, as we saw in Chapter 2, there is a sense in which this asymmetry is to be found in the message of the Review itself, where the term 'achievement' is retained, but 'under-achievement' avoided.

Finally, it is worth noting that there are a number of headlines which, rather than implying a particular model, deny a specific causal and/or blame attribution, or question the existence of the phenomenon that the three models are intended to explain. The headline in the *Caribbean Times* read: 'Are black boys really the problem?' It is not clear to whom the claim questioned here is being attributed, but the headline could be read as countering the implications of the competition metaphor. Interestingly, in more specific terms, this question can be seen as a response to *The Weekly Gleaner*'s headline: 'Underachievement of black boys'. Indeed, it even shares the latter's reference to gender. While neither the Review nor the government's reaction to it carried any implication that it was black boys who were the problem, this attribution of responsibility is well known to be influential among certain parts of the general public, and perhaps even within the African Caribbean community. The *Caribbean Times* headline is probably designed to deny or at least question this.

The headlines to a follow-up article in *The Voice* also raised questions, but this time about the factual component of the problem identified in the Review. These headlines read as follows: 'Exam figures that miss the mark. Official statistics say that black pupils fail at school. But is that a true picture? This is the success story that government figures don't show'. What we have here is not just a questioning of whether it is something about black pupils which leads to their lower average level of performance, but an insistence that in fact, on the contrary, they are relatively successful. Interestingly, the competition metaphor seems to

Duncan identified the problem as lying, in part at least, in the African Caribbean family structure.

be accepted here, but the facts of relative performance among ethnic groups – as presented in the rest of the media coverage, including the *Voice*'s own previous coverage, and in the Review itself – are challenged.[25]

Variation in use of the three models across newspapers

I have analysed the headlines in some detail, looking at the models that seem to be implied in many of them, and at the implications these may carry regarding praise or blame and responsibility to act. It is now worth looking at the distribution of reliance on these different models across newspapers (see Table 4.8). We can

Table 4.8 Newspapers' use of the three models in headlines[a]

Competition model	Distribution model	Discrimination model
The Sunday Times Independent on Sunday		
Daily Mail The Sun The Times		The Daily Telegraph The Guardian The Independent
	The Times Educational Supplement	The Times Educational Supplement
The Asia Weekly Eastern Eye The Weekly Gleaner	The Voice	The Voice
The Birmingham Post Manchester Evening News Oldham Evening Chronicle The Western Mail Wolverhampton Express and Star Yorkshire Evening Post	South London Press London Evening Standard	The Leicester Mercury
Total number of headlines = 14	Total number of headlines = 4	Total number of headlines = 6

Note

a Newspapers have been omitted where no clear model could be discerned.

25 A similar line of argument was implied by the headline to a follow-up article that appeared in *The Times Educational Supplement* a week after the first report on the Review. The headline here

see the predominance of the competition metaphor here, notably in newspapers with the highest circulations. The distribution model is relatively rare: it appears in none of the national Sunday or daily newspapers, in only one ethnic minority newspaper, and in only a couple of local newspapers. However, its presentation in *The Times Educational Supplement* may have maximized its impact on teachers. The discrimination model is to be found in the headlines of three national dailies, all broadsheets, two of which are generally judged to be left of Centre in political terms. At the same time, this model only appears in one ethnic minority newspaper (in fact the same one as the distribution model), and in only one local newspaper.

THE REPORTS BELOW THE HEADLINES

As noted earlier, headlines are likely to be very significant in attracting the attention of readers, sometimes in giving them the gist of the message, and in framing their reading of the report that follows underneath. However, headlines would not have entirely determined what message readers drew from newspaper coverage of the Review; the character of the reports below them could have had a significant independent impact. In looking at the body of the reports I will focus first on variation in the balance of coverage between the Review itself and on other matters, including reactions to it. I will then look at how the Review is presented as a source in newspaper reports, and at other sources of comment on it that are reported or quoted. Finally, I will assess the implications of the accounts provided, in terms of causation and responsibility.

The balance of focus in newspaper reports

There was considerable variation in the extent to which newspaper reports focused on the Review itself or on related matters. This can be documented crudely in quantitative terms by the number of words, and percentage of the report, devoted to each. Table 4.9 gives the results of this analysis.

As regards the national newspapers, in terms of percentage coverage of the Review, we have three (*The Sun*, *The Daily Telegraph* and *The Mirror*) in a top band, allocating almost twice as much space to the Review as to other matters (though in the case of *The Sun* and *The Mirror* the reports were extremely short). The *Daily Mail* is in the middle, with all the remaining newspapers in the 32 per cent to 20 per cent range. There is a sharp contrast between the two education supplements, with *TES* focusing on the Review while *Guardian Education* is preoccupied with reaction to the Review and with other matters. There is a more even distribution across the ethnic minority press, though it involves the same

was 'Black sociologist attacks race "doom and gloom"'. However, on its own, this headline does not present a clear message.

Table 4.9 The allocation of wordage in news reports to the Review as against reactions to it or the issue more generally (rank order in terms of percentages)[a]

Newspaper	Percentage of report	No. of words
Broadsheet dailies		
The Daily Telegraph	88	580
The Independent	28	388
The Times	24	115
Daily Express	22	84
The Guardian	20	106
Tabloid dailies		
The Sun	100	65
The Daily Mirror	88	113
Daily Mail	48	207
Daily Star	32	87
Education supplements		
The Times Educational Supplement	100	1740
Guardian Education	34	126
Ethnic minority press		
India Weekly	100	67
Muslim Times	100	855
The Weekly Journal	90	737
The Weekly Gleaner	78	152
Eastern Eye	53	623
Asian Times	53	285
The Voice	31	221
Caribbean Times	29	173
Local Press		
Bradford Telegraph & Argus	100	238
Manchester Evening News	100	168
Oldham Evening Chronicle	100	199
The Western Mail	100	263
Yorkshire Evening Post	100	169
London Evening Standard	79	191
The Birmingham Post	61	222
Wolverhampton Express and Star	60	268
Birmingham Evening Mail	36	225
Derby Evening Telegraph	26	50
South London Press	20	314
The Leicester Mercury	17	276
Yorkshire Post	16	742

Note

a In those cases (for example, *The Independent*) where there was more than one report in a newspaper, I have combined the results for each article. The distinction between those parts of a report that focused on the Review and those that concerned reaction to it were not always easy to make. For example, in *The Weekly Journal* I have included the article by Carlton Duncan which is a commentary on the issue in general not just on the Review, and in *The Asian Times* report I have included a portion that relates to an interview that the journalist carried out with one of the authors of the Review, David Gillborn. Note too that some reports included charts and/or pictures, and summary tables of findings. The last of these was included in the wordage, but the rest were not.

sort of range in variation. The local press shows an even wider variation than the other categories in terms of the percentage of coverage given to the Review, but again a fairly even distribution across the spectrum.

The Review as source

While presenting what the Review said, newspaper reports are also simultaneously engaged in implicitly justifying the newsworthiness of what is being reported to their readers, indicating why they should read it. And, in the case of the Review, one way in which they do this is by how they identify the source. This can be significant for how readers respond to news reports, affecting what credence they attach to it as well as how much attention they give it. Furthermore, the ways in which the source of a news story is represented also tells us something about how journalists relate to their sources.

A preliminary point to be made is that there are ambiguities about what 'source' means. In one sense, for its readers, the newspaper itself is the source. But what I have in mind here is the sources on which journalists rely and how they present them to readers. Even so, there is still an important area of uncertainty in this case, over whether the source is the Review itself, as a document, or the people or organizations cited as having produced it.[26] Below I will look at how both are represented.

Very often, the Review is presented as a 'report', so that neither its character as a *review*, nor as a review of *research*, is indicated.[27] Indeed, this designation does not give much information at all about the character of the source, though there is perhaps an implicit attribution of expertise to those 'reporting' and/or an associated assumption that reports are from official agencies of some kind, so that institutional authority may be implied. The latter is reinforced in some newspapers by references to the Review as 'a *government* report' (emphasis added), as in *The Independent on Sunday*. A very similar, though less frequently used, description of the Review is as a 'study'; and this too is sometimes attributed to the government, as in the case of *The Sunday Times*. Along the same lines, *The Leicester Mercury* refers to the Review as a 'survey', while *The Bradford Telegraph & Argus* describes it both as a 'national study' and as a 'nationwide survey'. Like 'report', the terms 'study' and 'survey' probably indicate that some investigation has been carried out; and where there is an attribution to the government, some institutional authority is explicitly implied. 'National' and

26 This is compounded where reports cite extracts from interviews with David Gillborn, the Review's lead author, or with Chris Woodhead, the head of OFSTED.
27 References to the Review as a 'report' are already found in some headlines: citations of a 'major report' and a 'new report' in *The Times Educational Supplement*, of a 'new education report' in *Eastern Eye*, and just of a 'report' in *The Voice* and in *The Birmingham Post*. Evans (1995) has noted the tendency in the United States for the terms 'science' and 'research' not to be applied to the work of social scientists in the way they are to that of natural scientists, and how this downplays its authority. Whether something similar is operating here is hard to tell.

'nationwide' indicate the scope of the Review, suggesting that it is not restricted to a particular locality (though it is not clear which national unit is involved), and they may also add to the authority of what is presented.[28]

In a few cases the Review was explicitly described as a review. One example is the *Muslim Times*, another is the *Asian Times*, which described it as 'the first major review of performances of ethnic groups at school since the Swann report ...'. Of course, whether such a term, on its own, carries any meaning for readers distinct from 'report', 'study' or 'survey' is questionable. And, as with these other terms, in some cases 'review' was given official weight, notably in the phrase 'government inspectors reviewing trends', which appears in the *Manchester Evening News*, the *Oldham Evening Chronicle*, *The Western Mail* and the *Yorkshire Evening Post*.[29] However, some newspapers referred to the Review explicitly as based on research, sometimes suggesting that it involved primary research (which to a degree it did).[30] Thus *The Times Educational Supplement* describes it as 'the most far-reaching research review on its subject since Swann'. And the *Eastern Eye*, while initially referring to 'a Government study', later described the Review as 'the research from the Institute of Education in London'. The *Muslim Times* and *The Weekly Gleaner* also indicate that the Review is based on research, while the *Birmingham Evening Mail* refers to it as the product of 'a ten-year study', and the *London Evening Standard* as 'a study of several major reports on academic performance of ethnic pupils'. Some newspapers also quoted the title of the Review, which clearly indicates its status as a research review.[31] Without using the term 'review' specifically, the *Daily Mail* provides a fairly accurate account, to the effect that: 'the inspectors analysed trends in the education of ethnic minorities, bringing together research for the first time since the 1985 Swann Report'. And the reports in the *Oldham Evening Chronicle* and *The Western Mail* do much the same.

As already indicated, this first meaning of 'source' cannot be completely separated from the second one that I identified: the question of who produced the Review. There is considerable variation in attribution here, not only across newspapers but sometimes even within the same news report. There are three very common attributions, all of which characterize the source as official, governmental or quasi-governmental. As noted, some newspapers attribute

28 In fact, the Review is concerned only with England and Wales; it is not intended to apply to other parts of the UK, though of course the findings may apply there too. Furthermore, some of the data discussed in the Review do relate to particular localities rather than to national aggregates.

29 In fact, the reports in most of these latter newspapers were very similar. This may reflect reliance on a common source, for example a news agency like the Press Association, or sharing of reports across local newspapers owned by the same chain.

30 In a later report, also published by OFSTED, one of the authors has produced a more detailed piece of primary research on similar data: see Gillborn and Mirza 2000.

31 *Muslim News*, *Guardian Education* and *The Times Educational Supplement* provided the full publication details of the Review, most newspapers did not.

the Review to the government (*Independent on Sunday, Sunday Times, Asian Times, Asia Weekly, Eastern Eye, The Voice, Birmingham Evening Mail, The Birmingham Post* and *Bradford Telegraph & Argus*). Other newspapers described it as produced by 'Government inspectors' (*Daily Mail, Manchester Evening News, Oldham Evening Chronicle, The Weekly Gleaner, The Western Mail, Wolverhampton Express and Star* and *Yorkshire Evening Post*). Third, it was often attributed to OFSTED or to some approximate synonym: 'an education standards watchdog' (*Daily Mail*); 'the school inspection body' (*The Independent*); 'school inspectors' (*The Times*); or, in one case, to 'race watchdogs' (*Daily Star*).

Only in a few cases was the Review identified as the work of academics. The sole attribution in *The Sun* was: 'says the Institute of Education', though what meaning this would have for its readers is unclear. More informatively, *The Weekly Journal* refers to 'a new report carried out by two professors at London University's Institute of Education'. Other newspapers mentioning the authors or their institutional affiliation did so after already using one of the 'official' designations. Thus, having referred to 'a government study', *The Sunday Times* later cited the authors as researchers 'from the Institute of Education in London'. The *Eastern Eye, The Daily Telegraph, The Independent*, the *Muslim Times* and *The Times Educational Supplement* do the same, sometimes referring to the authors as 'academics' and/or giving their names and titles.

Only two publications, apart from *The Sun* and *The Weekly Journal*, presented the Review, initially and consistently throughout, as a product of academic research. In the *Muslim News* it is described as 'the result of research carried out by the Institute of Education (London University) and commissioned by OFSTED'. And the second article in *The Times Educational Supplement* describes it as 'the most far-reaching research review' and cites the authors as 'Dr David Gillborn and Professor Caroline Gipps, both of London University's Institute of Education'.

Some tentative conclusions can be drawn from these various descriptions of the source. One is that most of the newspapers do not draw any sharp distinction between reports in general and research reviews in particular, perhaps reflecting journalists' judgements about the low salience of this distinction for their readers. The term 'report' is probably more general in meaning than 'review', so that what may be assumed is that there is no need to provide detailed information about the exact nature of the source, in this respect; or at least not in the opening sections of newspaper reports.

A second conclusion is that, for most of the newspapers, what made the Review especially newsworthy was that it came from a government agency, if not from the government itself. And, of course, as we saw earlier, some of the newspaper reports focused primarily on the government's announcement of policy in response to publication of the Review, and on political reaction to this. It might reasonably be inferred that the publication of academic research relevant to an important social issue, even in the form of a review of ten years' work on the topic, is not judged to be newsworthy in itself. This Review almost certainly came to be reported so widely, and with such prominence, largely because it was sponsored by a government agency and because the government felt it necessary to make a policy announcement in response to it.

It might be tempting to conclude that much coverage of the Review misrepresented its nature as a source. However, description of it as a 'report' is not in itself a misrepresentation; it simply lacks detail about the specific character of the Review, about what *kind* of a report it is. Moreover, what is relevant detail is a matter of judgement, and what is appropriate will vary across contexts. Most of the journalists have either not recognized the specific character of the Review or have not regarded this as important information, or perhaps as intelligible information, for their readers. It seems clear that, for most of the newspapers, it made little difference whether the Review was a product of the inspection process, of primary research, or involved the collation of research findings from many studies.[32]

In much the same way, description of the Review as produced by OFSTED or even by the government should not be judged as simply misleading. As Bakhtin, Goffman and others have noted, authorship is not as straightforward a matter as might initially be thought.[33] While Gillborn and Gipps wrote the Review, they did so in negotiation with OFSTED, and the fact that it was sponsored by the latter organization means that, in an important sense, the Review was speaking on behalf of it. After all, OFSTED organized the press conference, and far from issuing a disclaimer, the organization publicly endorsed its findings. Furthermore, since OFSTED is a government agency, it is not entirely inaccurate to describe the Review as a 'government report'.[34] And, again, while the government issued a policy statement in response to it, this did not challenge the Review's findings, but was more or less in line with its recommendations. Moreover, this could be regarded as rather surprising given that what was recommended was likely to generate opposition on the Conservative back benches, and to be viewed and portrayed by many as a 'U-turn'. *The Guardian* reported the government's announcement very much in these terms, and from the other end of the political spectrum the *Daily Express* concentrated on Conservative back-bench opposition to the policy announcement.

---

32 Smith 2000 has noted the tendency for OFSTED to present information from its inspections as if this were a product of research.

33 The person who mouths the words, or even the person who formulates them, is not necessarily the person who is speaking. A spokesperson speaks on behalf of someone else, whereas a speechwriter produces words for another agent to use. Note too that agents who can make statements are not limited to individual people; they may be organizations: here someone is authorized to speak on behalf of an agency, though they themselves may also be seen as embodying that agency, as when the Prime Minister presents government policy. Furthermore, people sometimes cite what others have said while distancing themselves from the saying of it (for example, to avoid libel actions). For Goffman's arguments along these lines, see Goffman 1981, especially ch. 3. See also Levinson 1988. Bakhtin draws attention to the extent to which we use, report, quote, or allude to others' words in what we say and write: see Todorov 1984.

34 OFSTED is a 'non-ministerial government department', according to its web-site: <http://www.ofsted.gov.uk/howwework/>

Crucial to how the source of the Review is represented is the issue of its authority. In terms of institutional authority, the government and OFSTED almost certainly score more highly in the public realm than do 'academic researchers based at the London Institute of Education'. At the same time, one of the reports describes the Review as 'independent', having initially labelled it as a 'government report'. Here and in other newspaper accounts where the academic authors are mentioned, and/or where the term 'research' is used, there is some ambiguity about the nature of the Review's authority: about whether it is institutional or intellectual in character. A further complication is that the authors' association with a university introduces an element of institutional authority that may be seen as at least partially independent of the government.

There is a possible tension here, of course. On the one hand, material from government sources is generally treated as of high newsworthiness. On the other hand, it is often subjected to scepticism, implicitly or explicitly, by the media – at least partly because of the suspicion that government sources serve their own interests.[35] In these terms, those who are independent of government gain potential authority, especially if they have a claim to expertise that is institutionally validated. In the case of the Review, the government, while having considerable information at its command, is certainly likely to be viewed as at least potentially untrustworthy since it is implicated in the situation being described. OFSTED might be regarded as more independent, but perhaps not completely independent since it is a governmental agency. Thus the Review's authorship by academic researchers having a specified institutional affiliation might be seen as giving it independent intellectual authority. Furthermore, since the overall message is endorsed by both OFSTED and the government, this could be regarded as making the Review an especially authoritative source.

Other sources in newspaper reports about the Review

In most newspaper reports there were other sources cited besides the Review.[36] What is important about this for my purposes here is that it presents the Review, or its authors, alongside other voices that are also being given authority of some kind to speak about the issue of ethnic inequalities in educational achievement. In fact, these other voices were rarely reported as speaking about the Review itself, but sometimes what they said had a bearing on its message and how this was likely to be received by readers.[37]

---

35 This is a dilemma that can be traced back right to the beginning of newspapers (see Allan 1999: ch. 1).
36 Exceptions include *The Independent on Sunday*, *The Sun* and *The Mirror*.
37 It is worth noting that in two reports there are quotations from interviews with David Gillborn, one of the Review's authors, elaborating on the findings and their policy implications. There are also a couple of newspaper reports that refer to other pieces of research in commenting on the Review. For example, *Guardian Education* refers to 'A recent study of black parents in Leicester'.

I noted earlier that some reports focused primarily on the government's reaction to publication of the Review and many newspapers included quotations from the government minister (though this was not possible for the two Sunday newspapers, whose reports preceded the government's press release). Here, for example, is an extract from *The Guardian* report:

> Cheryl Gillan, the Education Minister, said the Government would pursue a range of initiatives in schools in collaboration with the Commission for Racial Equality, including ethnic monitoring and schemes to tackle racial stereotyping. 'Some ethnic minority pupils do extremely well but others achieve less than they could. This is a real cause for concern. The Government takes it very seriously and is determined to tackle it.'

Here and elsewhere the comments quoted from the government minister supported the Review's findings and/or recommendations.

The second most frequently quoted additional source was the Chief Inspector of Schools, and the comments reported from him were sometimes quite extensive. *The Times* offered a relatively brief account of his views: 'Chris Woodhead, the Chief Inspector of Schools, said "Schools can and do make a difference. But it would be blinkered to pretend that family background and social class and ethnic origin are not also important".' The *Daily Mail* provided a rather longer account:

> Chief schools inspector Chris Woodhead cited black youngsters' average examination scores in the Labour-run borough of Camden in North London to illustrate how far they had fallen behind. Their average score fell from 25.5 in 1993 to 23.8 in 1994. In the same period, the average for pupils as a whole rose from 27.2 to 30.1. The statistical gap is equivalent to nearly five GCSEs per pupil. Asian pupils in London, however, were generally achieving significantly more than ten years ago, as were Indians in Birmingham. Mr. Woodhead called the figures 'disturbing' and said it was vital that the Government, and education authorities, started analysing exam results by ethnic origin. He said gender and social class were also important factors in pupils' success, but he was not reneging on his view about the 'central importance' of what happened within schools. 'Schools can and do make a difference,' he declared.

A rather different account of Woodhead's views is given in the *South London Press*:

> He dismissed claims that male black pupils were 'Teenage Tysons' terrorising teachers as unhelpful and without foundation. He said a whole range of socio-economic reasons was responsible for some of the 'disturbing' findings. He called on schools and teachers to concentrate on recommendations in the report. ... Welcoming the report Mr. Woodhead said, 'This

review shows that ethnicity is an important factor to be considered when new agendas are debated or targets are being set. In a complex educational area such as this, where so many factors and influences come into play, there are no quick and easy answers as to what produces high and low achievement. Schools are expected to have procedures in place to monitor achievement by different ethnic groups and failure to do this would be regarded as a significant weakness.'

The implications of the Chief Inspector's commentary for the reception of the Review are rather more complicated than those of quotations from the government minister. For one thing, given that the Review is often attributed to OFSTED, he could be seen as speaking on behalf of it; but since it was produced by academics associated with the London Institute of Education he could equally be viewed as giving OFSTED's perspective on it. Furthermore while, to a large extent, his comments reinforce the Review's key findings and recommendations, there are elements, notably the reference to the role of 'family background', which can be read as signalling a different message. As we saw in the previous chapter, this touches on an ambiguity in the Review, where the issue of economic background or social class is highlighted in some places, but very much within a framework that stresses the role of the education system. By contrast, Woodhead's comments could be taken to imply that while schools play an important role in ensuring fairness in terms of the performance of ethnic minority groups, there is a limit to their effect because variation in achievement levels also reflects differences in home background.

Many newspapers also quoted other sorts of commentator. Some of these represented agencies that could be regarded as having a legitimate voice on the issue. The *Daily Star* quoted one such voice: it reported that 'Chris Myant, of the Commission for Racial Equality, said: "A mutual distrust has developed between black boys and their teachers ... and tens of thousands face a trouble-torn future".' In the next paragraph, under the sub-heading 'Angels', he was quoted further: 'I'm not saying all teachers are racist and all black kids are little angels – but many have low expectations of young black males which become self fulfilling.' And, at the end of the report, after a summary of the Review's findings, there was also the following: 'Mr. Myant said many black youths from poor homes had no role models because fathers and elder brothers were often unemployed. This created a high degree of apathy, resentment and trouble.'

Here, while the first part of what is said supports a key element of the Review's message, and reinforces the discrimination model that appears early on in the *Star*'s report, the latter part appeals to home background as an explanation for lower levels of educational achievement on the part of some ethnic minorities. Indeed, there are echoes here of the concept of underclass. *The Independent* quoted another representative of the Commission for Racial Equality, this time its chairman, and he too introduced more or less the same explanatory account: 'Mr. Ouseley believes that, for many of those pupils, life on the streets is more exciting than going to school. It was important for parents and schools to find positive role models – adults who had made a success of a law-abiding lifestyle – to compete with the lure of the street gangs and the drug dealers.'[38]

Others quoted in newspaper reports included members of parliament and headteachers.[39] The inside page article in *The Independent* had the following:

> Bernie Grant, Labour MP for Tottenham, believes there is much that can be done and he is blunt in his analysis of why black teenagers are falling by the wayside. 'I think the schools are failing them and they can't cope with them,' he said. 'Other people suffer from social factors such as bad housing.'

> Mr. Grant cited the case of a girl he met recently in a north London school. Until a year ago she had lived in Barbados, where she was considered a below average pupil. Here, she was above average for black pupils, because the teachers' expectations were so low.

> She and the other black teenagers at the school were in danger of having their actions misinterpreted. 'I think they tend to talk back more, probably because of the feeling that they are discriminated against,' Mr. Grant said. But while schools are now bound to find themselves in the spotlight as the search for more information on discrimination and racial harassment continues, they cannot work in a vacuum.

> Carlton Duncan, the black head of George Dixon school in Handsworth, Birmingham, believes that the presence or absence of a strong, supportive family is crucial.

> 'African-Caribbeans who have come into this country have never been able to set up the extended family arrangements which lend additional support,' he said. 'If you take the Asians, they have managed to bring over their aunts, uncles and grandparents.'

> But he, too, believes that school has a crucial part to play in stopping up the gaps. His own school has set up a 'mentoring' scheme for teenagers who are likely to go off the rails, using local volunteers. As a result, the number of temporary exclusions has fallen from 40 a year three years ago to 11 last year. 'We needed to see what role the family could take, and if the

---

38 Unfortunately, it is not possible to compare these newspaper reports with what the spokespersons actually said.

39 There were also sometimes quotations from representatives of the teaching unions, notably in *The Guardian*. In addition, *Guardian Education* included an article by the Director of Education for Tower Hamlets.

family wasn't up to it, how schools and local authorities could compensate,' he said.[40]

Both the commentators quoted here offer accounts that support some elements of the Review's findings, though that from Carlton Duncan presents an alternative explanation as well, similar to the one he offered on the *Today* programme, and to what was indicated in other newspapers by the representatives of the Commission for Racial Equality and the Chief Inspector.

Some commentators quoted by newspapers focused on the government's announced policy, though this occasionally implied an attitude towards the Review's recommendations. Following a brief outline of the findings of the Review, the *Daily Express* report reads as follows:

> Tory backbencher and former headmaster Harry Greenway said: 'It is right to have the desire to be fair to all, but the way to achieve that fairness is to give everyone equal treatment – not picking out groups for special treatment. It can create serious inequalities and that is the road to disaster.'

This represents a direct challenge the Review's conclusions about 'colour-blind' policies, though it should be noted that it is doubtful whether this commentator, or any of the others, would have had time to read the Review before providing their comments.

Not surprisingly, commentators quoted by ethnic minority newspapers tended to come from their respective communities. Here is an extract from the report in *Caribbean Times*:

> Tommy Ellis, of the Black Community Education Support Group in Bristol, said: 'It is nothing new, which is upsetting. As a group, our focus has switched to where we can make some difference which is with parents.'
> ...
> Steven Morgan, a 24-year old PhD student at Queen Mary and Westfield University, claimed he had to overcome 'discouragement from teachers' before becoming an academic success story.
> ...
> Mr. Ellis fears that the real number of 'exclusions' may be far higher with pupils left outside classroom doors but within the school grounds.
>
> He said: 'There is a real crisis and I am not at all surprised that some parents are calling for black schools to teach our young. "The problem is

---

40 In this report the views of different authorities are orchestrated in a somewhat similar way to the interview with the two headteachers on the *Today* programme, in which Carlton Duncan also participated. Quotations from him also appeared in *The Times*, and he wrote an article on the issue for *The Weekly Journal*.

that teachers don't see children as children. They see white children and black children and as soon as you attach the black there is a problem. A few teachers have racist attitudes, but even more white teachers are afraid to discipline black children because they are afraid of being called racist. We see some of these excluded, problem children at our Saturday schools but they do not misbehave.' ...

Muhammed Al-Faisal, cofounder of the Rosa Parks School of Education, in east London, said that responsibility should be borne by men in the community. 'They should sacrifice £10,000-a-month of their nightclubbing budget to help us buy land and capital equipment to build schools that will prepare our children for the 21st Century.' Mary Francis, a parent governor whose teenage daughter, Yvonne, went to the Lewis Lynch High School in Barbados for two months as a comparative exercise, said: 'As West Indian parents we are too laid back, period. We have to be more pushy and meet the school half-way. That means going to parents' meetings, challenging the teachers and asking them what is going wrong. You can just walk into the school and make an appointment. There must be an increase in black teachers because, having been a nurse, I know that some black people only tell the whole story to other black people.'

The report in *The Voice* also drew on commentators from the African Caribbean community. It quoted Liz Rasekoala of the African Caribbean Network for Science and Technology as believing that:

Ofsted is "playing political games with the needs of Black children" by producing such a damning report and not forcing schools to follow its recommendations. "Ofsted have written this report, including various things that Black people should be very worried about. ... Ofsted need to be personally introducing ethnic monitoring and encourage role models in its inspection guidelines so that schools are forced to do it. It has to be a statutory requirement. School heads and local education authorities, even if they would like to follow Ofsted's recommendations, will not do it unless it is a statutory requirement."

The predominant emphasis of the commentators quoted in African Caribbean newspapers is on school and education system factors, and is therefore in line with the spirit of the Review, even when the latter is criticized.[41] By contrast, in the Asian press, where commentators were quoted they tended to reinforce the emphasis on pupil characteristics or home and community background in explaining the success of some Asian pupils. This was true, for example, of the

41 We saw the same ambiguity, arising from the Review being identified with OFSTED, in the case of the Channel 4 news report.

report in the *Eastern Eye*, which quoted a headteacher and an Asian pupil who had also been quoted in *The Sunday Times*:

> The pattern was highlighted by Small Heath Comprehensive, Birmingham, where over 96 per cent of pupils are Asian.
>
> The number of pupils there gaining five or more GCSEs at grade A to C has soared from just 7 per cent to an amazing 30 per cent in one year.
>
> 'They feel they have to be better qualified to succeed than their White counterparts', said head teacher Cecil Knight, whose pupils come mainly from Pakistani and Bengali backgrounds. 'I think they have more determination to achieve high standards from their parents.
>
> 'It has been ingrained in them whereas other cultures do not place so much emphasis on education so they lack the same incentives.'
> . . .
> Bright spark Jakira Khanam, 16, who left Small Heath Comprehensive in Birmingham with nine GCSEs, including two A stars, five As and two Bs, feels the reason behind this success is the attitude of Asian parents.
>
> 'There have been changes in attitudes among Asian families. Where once girls saw little value in education they are now as ambitious as the boys,' she explained.
>
> 'Asian parents have always thought that the girl's place was in the home but are gradually accepting that in Western society we need to get an education possibly a career.'
> . . .
> 'Asians have definitely made it to the top class,' added Jakira. 'They are really making the difference for once.'

Not surprisingly, the local press tended to draw on responses from local education authorities, teachers and others in the local area, though they sometimes included comments from national figures, especially the Chief Inspector. Here, for example, is part of *The Leicester Mercury*'s report:

> Leicestershire education director Mrs. Jackie Strong said although County Hall collected a wide range of data on ethnicity for the Government she felt it was of 'limited usefulness'.
>
> She said: 'I am much more concerned with the factors which affect everyone, such as good teaching, a good school ethos and support from families. We do live in a multicultural society, and I would rather see it as such than an amalgam of different cultures.'

Headteacher of Leicester's Rushy Mead School Mr Steve White said: 'I think all research is useful, but I am worried about some groups being stereotyped as under-achievers. "I agree that research is needed, on gender as well as ethnicity, but I do not like these sweeping generalizations. "When you talk about school exclusions we do not have many at Rushey Mead, but where we have there have not been proportionally any more African-Caribbean pupils than whites or Asians.'

Mrs. Freda Hussein, principal of Moat Community College, in Highfields, Leicester, said: 'I think although this sort of monitoring can be useful internally, we must be careful not to label or stereotype. "For the last three years my African-Caribbean children have achieved GCSE results which are above the national average.'

Here, again, it is likely that the commentators have not been able to read the Review, or even summaries of it. However, while they make criticisms of it, what they say is for the most part not at odds with its spirit.

Only in two cases did newspapers include voices that were explicitly and knowledgeably critical of the Review itself (rather than, for example, of OFSTED or of the government). In a follow-up article in *The Times Educational Supplement*, a sociologist, Heidi Mirza, was quoted as challenging what she saw as the gloomy message of the Review.[42] She was also quoted in a follow-up article in *The Voice*, the whole of which was aimed at questioning what it claimed was a misleading picture of the educational performance of African Caribbean pupils presented by the Review.

Inclusion of findings in newspaper reports

In this section and the next I will look in more detail at exactly how the message of the Review was presented in newspaper reports. I will begin by examining the selections made by newspaper journalists from the many findings reported in the Review.

National and Sunday newspapers

The three most commonly reported findings were that African Caribbean pupils had a lower than average level of educational performance, that they were more likely to be excluded, and that there is a growing gap in performance among ethnic groups. The high average level of performance of some Asian groups was the fourth most commonly reported finding, followed by the fact that there is conflict

---

42 The source for this was a paper given at the British Association for the Advancement of Science. The published version of this is Mirza 1998.

between white teachers and African Caribbean pupils and that 'teachers could create and amplify conflict' with this group. After this comes the finding that teachers had low expectations of African Caribbean pupils, and then, with three mentions each, the finding that achievement depends on social class/economic background and that colour-blind policies have failed. In addition, there are some 25 findings from the Review that are mentioned twice, or more usually just once, in newspaper reports.[43]

In general, then, the main emphasis was on what I referred to earlier as the failure story, or at least problem story, of a lower average level of African Caribbean achievement, and the increasing gap between this and the performance of other ethnic groups, rather than on the success story of the high and increasing levels of achievement of some Asian groups.

There were also a number of 'findings' reported in the newspapers that were not present in the Review. The most common one offered an explanation for the relative success of Indian pupils in terms of their personal characteristics and/or home background, a second involved reference to the existence of an 'underclass'.

Education supplements

The two education supplements to national newspapers that covered the story differed sharply in the number of findings from the Review that they included. Those mentioned in *Guardian Education* were comparatively few: underachievement among some ethnic minorities (in the sub-headline), improvement in achievement by many ethnic minority children, 'Indian pupils ... are reaching levels of success consistently above their white counterparts in several cities',[44] 'in the London Borough of Tower Hamlets children from poor Bangladeshi families have made "dramatic" progress', 'African Caribbean children – particularly boys – are not sharing in this general improvement', 'the appalling rate of expulsions from schools – six times that of their white peers'. There is also a quotation from the Review to end the article: 'One of the clearest findings of this review is that if ethnic diversity is ignored, if differences in educational achievement and experience are not examined, then considerable injustices will be sanctioned and enormous potential wasted.' This can be read as a formulation of the Review's conclusion that 'colour-blind' policies have failed.

By contrast, the two articles that appeared in the *TES* cover a very much larger number of findings from the Review, providing a fairly comprehensive account. These will be analysed in detail in a subsequent section.

---

43 The frequency with which different findings were included in national newspapers reports is indicated in Appendix 2.
44 This could be misleading since it obscures the fact that what is involved here is an average.

Ethnic minority newspapers

There is a significant difference from the national press here, with the relatively high level of educational achievement of some Asian groups being jointly the most frequently mentioned finding, along with the higher level of exclusions of African Caribbean boys. The lower average level of performance of African Caribbean pupils comes joint third alongside three other findings.[45]

However, these results conceal much greater diversity in reporting among these newspapers than was present in the national press. As we found with headlines, there is a clear ethnic divide in the frequency with which findings are reported, as indicated in Tables 4.10 and 4.11.

There are also some 'findings' that appear in the ethnic minority newspapers that were not present in the Review. The main one of these, included in two newspapers serving Asian communities, is the same as in the national papers: Indian pupils are 'better behaved in the classroom'.

Local newspapers

The pattern in the local press was similar to that in the national newspapers, except that the incidence of the top two findings was reversed: the higher exclusion

Table 4.10 Most commonly reported findings in Asian newspapers

1	Asian/Indian pupils achieving at higher levels, on average, than other groups	4
	Eastern Eye × 6, *Asian Times* × 2, *Asia Weekly* × 2, *Muslim News*	
2a	Bangladeshi pupils suffer the greatest level of poverty and are the least fluent in English	2
	Asian Times, Muslim News	
2b	Indians are more likely to stay on at school after the age of 16	2
	Eastern Eye, Asia Weekly	
2c	Colour-blind policy has failed	
Muslim News: 'To end with a positive note, one of the clearest findings of this review is that if ethnic diversity is ignored, if differences in educational achievement and experience are not examined, then considerable injustices will be sanctioned and enormous potential wasted.'		1

---

45 See Appendix 3 for the frequencies with which various findings are reported in the ethnic minority press.

Table 4.11 Most commonly reported findings in African Caribbean newspapers

1a	Lower than average performance of African Caribbean pupils	3
	The Weekly Gleaner × 2, *Caribbean Times, The Voice*	
1b	African Caribbean boys more likely to be excluded than others	3
	The Weekly Gleaner, Caribbean Times × 2, *The Voice* × 2,	
1c	Growing gap in performance between pupils from different ethnic groups	3
	The Weekly Gleaner × 2, *Caribbean Times, The Voice*	
1d	Conflict between white teachers and African Caribbean pupils	3
	The Weekly Gleaner, Caribbean Times, The Voice	
5	General rates of educational achievement have improved over the past 10 years	2
	The Weekly Gleaner, The Weekly Journal	
6	'Colour-blind' policies have failed	
	The Voice	1

rates for African Caribbean pupils was mentioned more frequently than their lower average academic performance.[46] A feature of the local press coverage was repetition of a small number of findings in more or less the same words across a number of publications: as already noted, this perhaps reflected their reliance on an agency report. There is also a problem in interpreting some of these reports because of the imprecise formulations used. There are quite a few that might reasonably be judged to misrepresent the Review, the most common being the reference to an underclass.

IMPLICIT CAUSAL NARRATIVES

Even more than with the broadcast media, in the case of newspapers we have communications which are structured so that a central message is first presented, followed by layers of further detail. It is important to take account of this layering if we are to make any judgements about the 'impact' of the newspaper reports on audiences. In this section I want to look at the order in which findings from the Review are presented and how they are combined, to one degree or another, into at least implicit causal narratives about ethnic variation in educational outcomes.

The three models of educational processes referred to earlier – the distribution, competition, and discrimination models – involve varying causal narratives

46 See Appendix 4 for the frequencies with which various findings are reported in the local press.

concerning how differences in educational outcome are produced. And, as we saw, these carry implications for whom, if anyone, deserves praise or blame, and for whether or not there is a problem that needs remedying and who is responsible for dealing with it. These can be reduced to two main causal narratives. Where, unqualified at least, the competition model implies that educational achievement is a product of the personal and social characteristics of pupils, of their families, and/or of their ethnic communities, the distribution and discrimination models both imply that the differences in achievement concerned are determined largely by the actions of teachers, schools and/or policymakers, or are their responsibility. And we can find significant variation across the newspaper reports in terms of the extent to which they give support to one or other of these causal narratives.

So, in this section, I want to look at how the inclusion of particular findings, the prominence they are given, and the formulations used in newspaper reports point to one or other of these two contrasting accounts.[47]

Causal narratives in the national newspapers

Table 4.12 indicates the pattern of variation in national newspapers. It is worth looking in more detail at the coverage provided at each end of this spectrum. I will compare two tabloid and then two broadsheet newspapers for this purpose.

In the case of *The Sun*, what we have is a very short report whose headline and opening paragraph focuses on the finding that 'Asian pupils' have 'topped' or 'outclassed' whites in examinations. Here we have phrasing that is a relatively pure case of the competition model. The second sentence-length paragraph falsely attributes a finding to the Review that explicitly provides an explanation: 'the reason is greater discipline at home, says the Institute of Education'. Furthermore,

Table 4.12 The balance of causal implication in national newspaper reports

Prime explanatory factor implied or indicated
Home background and/or pupil characteristics   *The Sun, The Sunday Times*
Mixed but tending towards emphasis on home background and/or pupil characteristics   *The Daily Express, Daily Mail*
Mixed but tending towards emphasis on teachers/schools/Government   *The Times, Independent on Sunday*

Teachers/schools/government
                 The Guardian, The Daily Telegraph, The Independent,
                                    The Daily Mirror

---

47 Detailed information about the sequencing of findings found in national newspapers is presented in Appendix 5.

this is an explanation that is in line with the causal narrative implied by the competition model. In the third sentence-length paragraph the lower level of achievement of African Caribbean pupils is reported, and this is also done in a way that potentially implies the competition model: African Caribbean boys are described as 'falling further behind'. The overall message here is quite clear.

The *Daily Mirror*'s report, slightly longer, is very different in focus. Both the main headline, 'Probe on expelled blacks' and the bulk of the report are concerned with the fact that African Caribbean pupils are more likely to be excluded from school than other pupils. Moreover, this is presented as something that is being investigated: it is the subject of a 'probe'. This, in itself, implies that the exclusion rate does not simply reflect differences in the behaviour of the pupils concerned; otherwise, presumably, there would be no need for investigation. Furthermore, the Review is then reported as saying that teachers may 'jump the gun in clashes with black pupils, because they have low expectations of them and think they will cause trouble'. This is a reformulation of two key findings of the Review, and it can be read as pointing to an explanation for differential exclusion rates. The next sentence-length paragraph reports the higher level of performance of Indian pupils in terms that are fairly neutral in causal terms: they 'performed better', and immediately following this is a paragraph reporting that OFSTED has 'pledged an inquiry into the expulsion figures', reinforcing the main thrust of the report. There is then a brief bullet point reporting 'the near-doubling of GCSE pass rates by Bangladeshi youngsters in east London, helped by extra teaching support', followed by a very short paragraph about cuts in funding for support staff. Here, too, then, the role of teachers is emphasized, this time in positive terms. The causal narrative consistently implied throughout this report is one in which ethnic differences in educational achievement are a product, in large part, of the activities of teachers and/or of the government.

In looking at the broadsheet press, I will compare *The Sunday Times* report with that in *The Guardian*. The former's headline reports that 'Indian pupils outclass all other groups', and the opening paragraph describes Indians as 'the most highly qualified students in British schools and colleges', reporting that a 'government study' warns of a 'growing gulf between the country's best and worst-performing ethnic groups'. 'Outclass' and 'best and worst-performing' can be read as belonging to the lexicon of the competition model, and are very likely to be read that way in this context. The next paragraph reinforces the same message, describing Indian pupils not only as 'more likely to stay on in education after the age of 16' but also as 'better behaved'. African Caribbean boys are then described as not 'matching' the advances made by Asians, as 'falling further behind', and as 'far more likely to be expelled or suspended from school'. Taken together, these three formulations again imply the competition model. The recommendations of the Review are formulated as advocating 'more detailed monitoring of how ethnic minorities perform to ensure poor achievers are identified and helped'. While this could be read as indicating that the competition is unfair, hence the need for help, there is little to encourage this interpretation here. In the next paragraph, continuing the theme, there is a reference to some experts fearing the 'danger of a black underclass'.[48] More detail is given about the findings of the Review, and there is then the following sentence-length paragraph: 'Education-ists believe that among Asians the cultural commitment to education and family support helps them to shine.' This reinforcement of the competition model, and of the causal narrative associated with it, is supported by information from a school in Birmingham, along with quotations from its headteacher and one of its Asian pupils. Later there is a further reference to 'variations in standards of behaviour', and to the Review's finding of an 'unusually high degree of conflict between white teachers and Afro-Caribbeans'. The context can be read as imply-ing that this reflects the behaviour of pupils rather than discrimination on the part of teachers. While the report ends with a reference to exceptional performance on the part of some black pupils, and by suggesting that 'the situation is too varied to speak of underachievement', the consistent message is of a causal relation-ship between pupils' home and community background and their performance in schools, with any blame, or at least responsibility, lying with pupils and/or their parents – though it is open to others to assist them. In summary, the strong implication in this report is that levels of educational performance, both positive and negative, reflect the characteristics of pupils and their home and community backgrounds.

By contrast, *The Guardian* focuses initially on what is portrayed as a reversal of 'more than a decade of attacks on "loony left" classroom policies', the gov-ernment instructing schools 'to adopt anti-racist and multi-cultural programmes to help students from ethnic minorities'. The second sentence-length paragraph of the report is concerned with the contrasting responses of 'Tory backbenchers' and teachers. In the third paragraph the Review is reported as saying that 'Colour-blind policies had failed to tackle inequalities, and the performance of African and [*sic*] Caribbean pupils – six times more likely to be expelled than their white peers – was of particular concern.[49] Some of the findings of the Review are then introduced: the 'dramatic improvement in exam results among some minority groups such as Bangladeshi children in inner London'; that the gap between highest and lowest achieving groups is growing; that Asian pupils are the most likely to be bullied; and that there is 'an unusually high degree of conflict between white teachers and African-Caribbean pupils'. The report then returns to the gov-ernment's policy response and other reactions to the Review's findings. The other two reports on the same page of *The Guardian* look at the issue of ethnicity in the context of two schools visited by reporters. Their headlines and the body of the reports carry the message that the problem is being successfully dealt with by some schools. Throughout, then, the coverage carries a consistent message that the issue is a matter for action on the part of teachers, schools and government to tackle inequalities.

48 And the remainder of this paragraph gives the impression that the experts referred to here are the authors of the Review.
49 'African and Caribbean' here should probably read 'African Caribbean'.

It is widely recognized that the different British national newspapers have characteristic editorial positions, and that this influences the selection and presentation of the news that appears in them (see Curran and Seaton 1991). This is closely linked to their market niches, in that particular newspapers develop links with audiences who have distinctive political and social attitudes. Lacey and Longman provide a detailed analysis of the 'cultures of understanding' associated with various British national newspapers, drawing on data about readership collected by MORI in 1990–92.[50] They see these diffuse and overlapping cultures as having 'at their core an array of beliefs and ways of looking at the world that need to be sustained by interpreting and presenting (or suppressing) world and domestic events in ways that do not disturb their central "myths" '. In these terms, 'the job of the newspaper becomes that of defending and maintaining the myths of the culture of understanding of its readers, enticing into readership similarly minded individuals and deriding the myths of opposing groups' (Lacey and Longman 1997: 76).[51] To some degree, at least, this may be the way in which newspapers currently function.

There is a fairly clear pattern of reporting the Review in line with the political orientations of national newspapers. The three that emphasize the background characteristics of pupils are generally recognized to be on the political Right, whereas three of the four newspapers that seem to emphasize the role of teachers, schools and government are on the Centre–Left. At the same time, there are some mixed cases, and exceptions.

An obvious anomaly is the position of *The Daily Telegraph*, and it is perhaps worth looking at this case in more detail. As we saw earlier, *The Telegraph* uses a headline that focuses on two findings of the Review, and moreover ones which carry a clear causal implication: 'West Indians "fail because teachers expect them to" '.[52] While the quotation is spurious, it is in line with the spirit of the Review; and, while the word 'fail' could imply the competition metaphor, in the context of the rest of the headline it does not. Furthermore, the message of the headline is repeated in the opening paragraph of the item, albeit in a slightly

---

50 See also Bell 1991: 109. The concept of 'culture of understanding' is close to what Hall *et al.* (1978: 61) refer to as the 'public idioms' of different newspapers. Lacey and Longman argue that these 'cultures of understanding' are stratified by social class; and they identify three broad groups of newspapers that primarily serve different segments of the British social class system: with the *Mirror*, *Star* and *Sun* serving the bottom half of the social class scale, the *Mail* and *Express* an overlapping middle segment, and *The Guardian*, *Independent*, *Telegraph* and *The Times* the top half of the scale.

51 There is an important connection here with what Carey (1989: ch. 1, see especially pp. 20–1) refers to as the 'ritual view of communication'.

52 This headline is partially offset by the large picture whose caption is 'Success story: Indian schoolchildren perform better at GCSE than any other ethnic group in the country, including whites'. The fact that 'West Indians' is preferred to 'African-Caribbeans', which is used in the Review, or even to 'Afro-Caribbean', perhaps reflects the character of the newspaper and perceptions of its readers: they are older, more conservative, and do not change language with fashion.

downgraded form and without the quotation marks: 'Children from a West Indian background are doing less well than other ethnic groups in Britain's schools, partly because teachers expect them to do badly.' A little later it is reported that 'Ofsted warns that a disproportionately high number of black children have been expelled from school, and says schools with so-called "colour-blind" policies are only allowing inequality of opportunity to persist.' The formulation here is again very much in line with an emphasis on the role of schools in generating inequalities, and on the responsibility of governments to intervene to prevent this. The finding about conflict between white teachers and pupils is included, and by means of a quotation: 'Teachers may, the report says, play "an active (though unintended) part" in creating conflict with West Indian pupils, "thereby reducing black young people's opportunity to achieve".' It is also reported that the Review states: 'Social class remains more important than ethnic background in determining children's achievements, and gender is also important.' What we have here, then, is a report that carries a causal narrative that is similar to that implied in the Review, and matches other newspapers at this end of the spectrum; for instance, there is a very close parallel to the gist of the message presented in *The Independent*.

Yet, of course, there is little doubt about the political orientation of *The Telegraph*. Its editor, writing in 1996, described it as 'Tory', commenting that this means 'that when the Conservative government forgets its Toryism, trouble starts'. 'Being Tory', he goes on, '*The Telegraph* has no illusions about the per-fectibility of man' (Moore 1996). Drawing on MORI data, Lacey and Longman note that *The Telegraph* has the oldest age profile of readers, and the highest imbalance towards male readers. And it may be that its coverage of the Review reflects one aspect of a rather old-fashioned conception of the role of newspapers, in terms of being primarily concerned with providing the facts about news events. This is suggested by the comments of another member of *The Telegraph*'s staff:

> ... one of the great virtues of the *Daily Telegraph* is that we do have this attitude that we report bombs, bullets and how many dead, how many people were displaced by this dam, how many people are starving in this rainforest, who was shot yesterday, instead of abstracts, and that is the way that we talk to our readers, who are dismissive of things that are not concrete, because they are busy business men, they are farmers, who deal in specifics, that's the kind of readership we have. A lot of hard headed people who you have to talk to in largely factual terms, and you will get through to in talking in factual terms. (Interview, March 1992, Charles Clover, Environment Correspondent, *Daily Telegraph*; quoted in Lacey and Longman 1997: 85)

The treatment given to the Review in *The Telegraph* perhaps also stems from the fact that the issue concerned is not one-dimensional, in terms of the political orientations of newspapers. Of course, at its heart is the question of attitudes towards ethnic minority groups; and expressed attitudes on this issue on the part of right-wing newspapers have changed in recent times, not least because of their need to compete for ethnic minority readers, paralleling a similar change within mainstream political parties. But, in the case of the Review, this issue is conflated with at least two others. First, there is the question of attitude towards the party in government at the time. The Conservative government's explicit support for the Review and its findings would probably have had some effect on how newspapers broadly in support of that government would report the Review. Perhaps more importantly, the teaching profession is implicated in the story, and some newspapers on the political Right had a history of criticizing teachers and the state education system generally. Indeed, by 1996 they were probably a more publicly acceptable target for criticism than ethnic minorities.[53] For this reason, focusing on the role of teachers in 'partly' generating ethnic inequalities in education may not have been at odds with the political line of *The Telegraph*. All this, though, can be no more than speculation.

A rather different kind of exception to the general pattern is represented by the *Daily Mail*. In Table 4.12 I located this in the mixed category but towards the end of the spectrum that emphasizes the role of the background characteristics of pupils. Yet, while this is true of the headline and opening paragraph, it is not an accurate representation of the rest of the report. The *Mail*'s headlines were: 'The ethnic underclass: Black pupils "falling behind whites and Asians in school performance"', and the report starts as follows: 'An educational "underclass" with increasing numbers of African-Caribbean youngsters was revealed yesterday. They are falling drastically behind whites and Asians in both examinations and school attendance.'[54] Here, then, the concept of underclass is foregrounded, with its connection to explanations for low educational achievement in terms of social background rather than school factors; and, in this context, the term 'falling behind' very much suggests the competition metaphor. Indeed, this implication is underlined by the false attribution to the Review of the claim that African Caribbean pupils are falling behind in *school attendance* as well as in examination performance. After all, while school or examination performance can never be completely under the control of pupils, attendance at school to a large extent is. And not being at school might reasonably be interpreted as self-inflicted damage to school achievement, as well as indicating low motivation.[55]

53 For an account of the campaigns of the right-wing press on education, see Alexander 1997: Part II.
54 We should note that in the second headline 'falling behind whites and Asians in school performance' is presented in quotation marks. So too is the word 'underclass' in the opening sentence of the report. Both are spurious attributions to the Review.
55 Presumably, what the *Daily Mail* report is referring to here is the finding about school exclusions.

However, what follows this opening paragraph is very different in its message, and it is worth quoting at length:

> Government inspectors found that black youngsters had not shared in the generally improving rates of achievement over the last ten years. In some areas, their performance worsened.
>
> The inspectors analysed trends in the education of ethnic minorities, bringing together research for the first time since the 1985 Swann Report. The findings, for the Office for Standards in Education, showed that for all ethnic groups, achievement at age 16 depended on economic background and that girls tend to do better than boys.
>
> Paradoxically, the report records dramatic increases in the examination performance of some ethnic minorities, especially Indians, even in poor areas.
>
> But, in many education authorities, the achievements of African-Caribbean youngsters, particularly boys, were 'significantly lower than other groups'. They were between three and six times more likely to be excluded from school than whites of the same sex.
>
> Blaming teachers for some of the problems, the 83-page report highlights the 'unusually high degree of conflict between white teachers and African-Caribbean pupils'.
>
> Despite their best intentions, there was evidence that teachers' actions could create and amplify conflict.

What is interesting about *these* paragraphs is how close they are in content, and even in language, to the Review itself. For example, the phrase 'not sharing in the generally improving rates of achievement' comes more or less intact from the press release or from the Review, and implies the distribution metaphor. Also, there is a reference to the significance of 'economic background', and this is an issue that is only dealt with in the executive summary and in the body of the Review (though it is formulated there in terms of 'social class'). The quotation about the achievement of African Caribbean pupils, especially boys, being significantly lower than other groups is accurate (it is from page 2 of the executive summary). The details about exclusions also come from inside the Review; and it is striking that unlike many other media reports this one includes the range '3 to 6 times', not just the highest figure. Finally, the statement that teachers' actions could create and amplify conflict with African Caribbean pupils is close to the wording in the executive summary.

Here, then, within a single newspaper report, we have two rather different accounts of the Review, carrying different messages. Once again, the conflicting formulations in this report are likely to stem from the fact that, like most newspaper stories, it was written by more than one person: the author of the headline and the first paragraph, probably a sub-editor, had perhaps not read the Review, while the author of the subsequent text clearly had. This may also reflect uneven commitment to the political orientation of a newspaper on the part of various levels of its staff, or different conceptions of what the task of such a report should be. Whatever the explanation, rather different messages could be derived from this one newspaper report by readers, though we should remember that it is headlines and opening paragraphs that are likely to have maximum impact.

Clearly the political orientation of newspapers will often have an effect on how reports about research findings are formulated, but as we have seen, this can be complex, since the issues concerned may involve conflicting tendencies. Furthermore, the influence of political orientation may be reduced by a commitment to reporting the facts. Finally, there is likely to be some contingency involved in how the report gets put together given the fact that several journalists are involved and that it is produced under pressure of deadlines.

Causal narratives in the education supplements

In quite different ways, the reports in both *The Times Educational Supplement* and *Guardian Education* imply narratives that emphasize the role of teachers, schools and government policy, either in causing ethnic variation in educational achievement or at least being responsible for remedying it.

As we saw earlier, the *TES* headlines, particularly the secondary headlines that are built into by-lines, give a clear steer towards the distribution and discrimination models. The reports themselves provide straightforwardly factual accounts of the findings, ones that operate within the Review's good news/bad news framework, and the formulations are largely within the terms of the distribution model employed by the Review. Thus the opening paragraph of the news report about the Review contrasts improved examination results on the part of ethnic minority pupils with an increase in the gap between highest- and lowest-achieving groups. The next emphasizes the role of social class, and the dramatic improvement in performance of 'certain disadvantaged groups, such as Bangladeshi pupils in the London borough of Tower Hamlets'. In the next paragraph African Caribbean pupils are described as 'not achieving the same level of success as other groups' and as in some areas 'falling further behind their peers'. However, any implication of a competition model is downplayed both by what has come before, particularly in the by-line, and by subsequent references to discrimination in acceptance by universities, to 'widespread racial harassment ... which is not always recognised by teachers'. Also, there is a quotation from the Review which repeats the theme of the by-line: 'despite their best intentions, teachers' actions can create and amplify conflict'. In addition, the final paragraph emphasizes the need for a change in policy, away from colour-blind approaches, on the part of schools.

The report on the Review in the Analysis section of *TES* is longer than the news report. However, it carries much the same message. Both the headline and the by-line carry implications along the lines of the distribution or discrimination models: 'Inequality "as bad as ever": Reva Klein looks at the background to a new report that shows black children still get a raw deal from the education system'. Moreover, as I noted earlier, while the quotation in the headline is spurious, it captures the spirit of the Review. This report formulates the performance of African Caribbean pupils via a quote that employs the language of the distribution model, reporting that they 'have not shared equally in the increasing rates of general achievement'. And the Review's challenge to the concept of 'under-achievement' is also mentioned. Furthermore, the authors are presented as having 'demonstrated the fallacy' of assuming that African Caribbean pupils are 'somehow incapable of achieving academically'. The Review is also cited as reporting how 'several studies since the 1970s have shown that black pupils are more likely to be criticized, punished and derided for their "bad attitude" than pupils of any other ethnic group'. And a further quotation from the Review reinforces this point. The report then continues: 'If the stereotype of the misbehaving, under-achieving black pupil is still entrenched, so, too, are the preconceptions about south Asian children.' The emphasis in this report is consistently on the role of teachers and schools in generating ethnic inequalities in educational achievement, notably through differential expectations.

At the same time, it is worth repeating that the *TES* carried an article the following week that reported a challenge to the findings of the Review, along similar lines to the follow-up article carried by *The Voice*. Below the headline 'Black sociologist attacks race "doom and gloom" ', there is a report about a conference presentation by 'prominent black sociologist' 'Dr Heidi Mirza, head of sociology at South Bank University', in which she criticized the Review and other 'commentators who blame racism for black underachievement'. She is reported as complaining about the likely demoralizing effect of the Review on black pupils and families, and insisting on the need to emphasize those areas where there had been improved performance. However, what is being criticized here, primarily, is not the causal narrative put forward by the Review (no alternative is reported), but what are taken to be the likely consequences of emphasizing the continuing lower level of performance of African Caribbean pupils.

Guardian Education adopts a line that is very similar to the coverage that had appeared in the main newspaper the previous week. The focus in the headlines is on what is represented as a change in government policy, responding to evidence of previous failure: 'About face on race: Alarming evidence of under-achievement among some ethnic minorities is shaking up thinking in Whitehall and town hall'. However, the opening paragraph of the report sets up a good news/bad news format, in terms of 'grounds for hope and anxiety in just about equal measure'. The next paragraph outlines positive developments, in terms of general improvement in examination results, the high average level achievement of Indian pupils, and the dramatic improvement of Bangladeshi pupils in Tower Hamlets. The next paragraph formulates the situation of African Caribbean children very much in the same terms as the Review, as 'not sharing in this general improvement'. And the finding about exclusions is reported as 'the appalling rate of expulsions from schools'. Interestingly, this then leads into presentation of the concept of an underclass, though without using that term: 'the prospect of an alienated, underqualified group emerging'. This 'frightening' prospect is deemed to have prompted 'the Government and Ofsted into taking the issue seriously after a decade of trying to ignore it'. Given the overall context, and the background assumptions of many *Guardian* readers, this allusion to an underclass is unlikely to imply or to be taken to suggest that ethnic background is the key factor determining educational achievement. The remainder of the article is about the government's policy announcement. There are also two other articles in *Guardian Education* dealing with the issue, each focusing on particular areas: Tower Hamlets and Leicester. The first, written by the Director of Education for the borough, emphasizes the possibility of substantial improvement if the right policies are adopted and resourced. The other article reports a black parent's view that teachers have failed her son, and that a policy of segregated schooling is the only solution; and, on the basis of research from Leicester University, it is argued that her views are widespread among black families. Black community groups are reported as complaining that 'ethnic Asians are gaining resources in Leicester at the expense of African Caribbeans'. There is then a response from 'a senior policy officer for Leicestershire County Council' denying inequality in resource allocation.

The overall effect of the *Guardian Education* reports, then, like those in the *TES*, is to portray the problem of lower average levels of performance on the part of some ethnic minorities as one that is system-generated, or at least as a responsibility of the education system, rather than having as its source ethnic differences in home or community background.

Ethnic minority newspaper narratives

Looking at the ethnic minority press, we find much the same spread as with the national newspapers. Here, though, as we saw with headlines, the critical factor seems to be which ethnic minority is being served. The pattern is documented in Table 4.13. The two newspapers that emphasize home background, or the characteristics of pupils themselves, are among those that took the relatively high average level of performance of some Asian groups as their main theme; and they are also among those that have Asian communities as their main readership. The *Asian Times* represents a partial exception, reflecting in its report, as in its headlines, the different average levels of educational performance of Indian and Pakistani pupils. At the other end of the spectrum are those newspapers that primarily serve the African Caribbean community or the Pakistani and Bangladeshi communities, and these emphasize the role of teachers, schools, and/or the government.

Another partial exception to this pattern is *The Weekly Gleaner*. The latter's brief report focuses on the performance of African Caribbean pupils, formulating

Table 4.13 The balance of causal implication in ethnic minority
newspaper reports

Prime explanatory factor implied or indicated	*Newspaper*
Fairly strong emphasis on home background/pupils	*Eastern Eye, India Weekly*
Mixed or balanced accounts	*The Weekly Gleaner, Asian Times*
Teachers/schools/government	*Caribbean Times, The Voice, Muslim News*

this as 'underachievement' in its headline. In the body of the report, there is the statement that the Review 'does not entirely blame black pupils for their low success rate in education', suggesting that it 'also partly blames teachers for the alienation that exists between them and black pupils, highlighting particularly the "unusually high degree of conflict between white teachers and African-Caribbean pupils"'. What is presented here is an account of some of the findings of the Review, but formulated in a way that maintains a balance between alternative causal narratives.[56]

The main factor shaping the nature of reports here, then, seems to be the likely differential concerns of the readerships of these newspapers. This is combined with the asymmetry that tends to operate in some press reports between how the relative success of some Asian pupils and the lower average level of performance of other groups, notably African Caribbeans, are represented.

Causal narratives in the local press

The local press is too diverse to provide a clear overall account, but I will look at two contrasting examples, and then at a more complicated case. The *Yorkshire Evening Post* has the headline ' "Underclass" in the classroom'. And its report begins: 'The emergence of an educational "underclass" with growing numbers of African-Caribbean youths – particularly boys – is highlighted in a report published today.' However, in the next sentence-length paragraph the formulation used is very much in line with that favoured by the Review, reporting that African Caribbean pupils 'had not shared in generally improving rates of achievement'. Here we seem to have a wavering message, similar to that of the *Daily Mail*, but one which on balance probably implies that ethnic home and community background is crucial.

By contrast, the *South London Press* offers an account that focuses entirely on the role of the education system and government policy. The headlines were

---

56 There is a parallel here with the commentary offered by Carlton Duncan in some of the newspapers.

'Black kids suffer: Gap widening between Afro-Caribbean children and other ethnic pupils'. And the opening paragraph, in bold, read: 'Black youngsters are being failed by schools leaving them falling behind in the classroom, according to a new report'. The finding about exclusions is formulated in terms of 'a disproportionately high number of black pupils' being excluded. There is coverage of Chris Woodhead's comments, as head of OFSTED, the main emphasis of which is on the responsibility of schools: 'Schools are expected to have procedures in place to monitor achievement by different ethnic groups and failure to do this would be regarded as a significant weakness.' The remainder of the report outlines the response from the government. Here the message is very clear, and is close to the spirit of the Review.

A more complicated case is that of the *London Evening Standard*. Following the opening headline 'Colour-blind policies "are failing pupils from ethnic minorities"', the first three paragraphs of this report are as follows:

> THOUSANDS of schoolchildren are being left on the educational scrapheap because politically-correct schools are failing to tackle the problems faced by children from ethnic minorities.

> 'Colour-blind' policies in schools have resulted in the social, economic and language difficulties of youngsters from some backgrounds being ignored. Experts are particularly concerned about Afro-Caribbean boys, who achieve the lowest examination results and are more likely to be expelled than other pupils.

> They have accused teachers of ignoring differences in racial lifestyles and of holding the misguided view that pupils should not be singled out for special treatment.

The first paragraph foregrounds one of the central messages of the Review in a way that no other newspaper or media report does, and in much more graphic terms than the Review itself. At the same time, use of the term 'politically-correct' gives an inflection to the finding that could be at odds with the Review, which certainly does not present political correctness as the problem.

The second paragraph suggests that it is 'colour-blind' policies that have been the cause of the differences in educational performance among ethnic groups. At one level, this could be a misreading of the Review, since its argument seems to be that those policies have not succeeded in eliminating barriers within the system to higher achievement on the part of ethnic minority pupils. However, at a deeper level it matches the spirit of the Review, which argues that schools have not adapted to the needs of different kinds of pupils, and that had they done this the reported differences in educational achievement would not have occurred.

The third paragraph continues with the same analysis. But, picking up from the reference to 'social, economic and language difficulties of youngsters from some backgrounds' in the previous paragraph, the formulation used suggests a kind of action on the part of schools that is probably not what the authors of the Review had in mind – 'singling out' ethnic minority pupils for special treatment – or at least is not the main part of it. What seems to be indicated here is the provision of compensatory support rather than restructuring the education system to achieve justice.

CONCLUSION

In this chapter, I have looked at how the Review was reported in the newspapers: the national Sundays and dailies, the weekly education supplements, the ethnic minority press, and some local newspapers. I examined the prominence given to reports about the Review, and looked at the way the issue was presented: in the headlines, and then in the reports themselves. Attention was paid to how the Review was described as a source, and to the balance of emphasis given, respectively, to its findings and to the government's and others' reactions to it. In relation to the Review's findings and recommendations, I looked at how these were formulated in newspaper reports, in particular at implied explanations for ethnic educational inequality and their implications for where blame and/or remedy might lie. In the next chapter I will try to draw together my analysis of media reports of the Review, in order to reach some more general conclusions.

5 Conclusion: a case of media distortion?

In this book I have examined the way in which one research publication, a review of research findings about ethnic inequalities in educational achievement, was represented in the mass media. Against the background of media reporting of social science generally, this is a relatively unusual case, in that the findings received wide and prominent coverage, and were treated for their news value rather than being used to inform a story about some other event. This contrasted with the very low level of media coverage, at best, given to the various studies on which the Review draws. At the same time, it seems unlikely that the Review was reported primarily because it provided new knowledge that demanded dissemination, or because of the intrinsic interest of its findings, as in the case of some discoveries in natural science or in medicine. I have suggested that the reason why the Review was afforded such media attention is because it was sponsored by OFSTED, an organization having both a high public profile and a very efficient dissemination procedure, *and* because the government responded to publication of the Review. So the substantial attention it received reflects the widely documented news values on which many media organizations operate, in which the activities of governmental agencies and governments are given high importance.[1]

As I noted in the Introduction, being reported in the media is a first requirement that must be met if research findings are to play their part in discursive democracy, in the manner sometimes envisaged by social scientists and others. A second requirement is that they are reported accurately. And this latter concern has set the framework for my analysis of coverage of the Review on radio, television and in the newspapers. We have seen that there was a high level of selectivity and considerable reformulation involved in media reports of the Review's findings. What I want to do in this chapter is to consider whether this amounts to systematic inaccuracy or distortion.

---

1 It is also significant that the Review came out some time before the news value of racism in the public services had been boosted by the inquiry into the police's handling of the murder of Stephen Lawrence, with its widely reported finding that there was institutionalized racism within the Metropolitan Police (Macpherson 1999).

My main aim in earlier chapters has been to identify differences between the content of the Review as a news source and media reports about it, especially those that could be interpreted as misrepresentation. In the Introduction I noted that social scientists have often complained that their work is distorted by the media. And there was a similar complaint in the case of this review. Its lead author, David Gillborn, described much newspaper coverage of it as striking 'a particularly alarmist and/or depressing note, casting Black children as "failures" and even presenting "underclass" analyses as if they were quoting an official source'. He protests that such accounts run 'directly contrary to the review which, while highlighting inequalities in attainment, explicitly critiqued the notion of "under-achievement" ...' (Gillborn 1998: 5). And he concludes: 'Much of the coverage bears only passing resemblance to the review: some is misleading, some is nothing more than an excuse to repeat chosen racist myths' (ibid.: 7).

It is important to note that what is involved here is not just a charge of inaccurate reporting but rather one of media *bias*. And, as we saw in the Introduction, this fits with much sociological work on the media, which has pointed to various forms of institutional bias as shaping the representations of the world provided in the newspapers and on radio and television, not least in their treatment of ethnic minorities. It is important to underline, however, that the differences between source and media reports that I have documented in this book do not *in themselves* constitute bias. For this judgement to be established several conditions must be met. First, the differences identified must be evaluated as inaccuracies. Second, they must all, or mostly, be in a single direction: for instance, underplaying or exaggerating specific types of inequality in a way that privileges a particular overall conclusion. Third, some convincing account must be provided of a systematic process that generated this pattern of inaccuracies. In short, the errors have to take a consistent direction that is shown to be the product of a governing orientation – conscious, unconscious, or institutional – on the part of journalists or media outlets. It is worth mentioning that these three requirements are the basic elements of the concept of ideology, in its usual interpretation.[2] In the next sections, I will summarize what I found in comparing media reports with the Review as source so as to examine the evidence for claims of ideological bias in media reports about it.

ACCURACY

Using the term 'accuracy' implies that the criterion setting the framework for description here is truth, interpreted as correspondence with the source. And truth-as-correspondence is directly implied as a standard when it is claimed that

2 For varying accounts of the concept of ideology, see Lichtheim 1967; Barth 1976; Centre for Contemporary Cultural Studies 1977; Larrain 1979; Thompson 1984; Eagleton 1991; Freeden 2003.

much of the newspaper coverage 'bears only passing resemblance' to the Review (Gillborn 1998: 7). Of course, questions can be raised about whether truth is a viable concept. Some of these derive from fundamental philosophical issues about that concept. Indeed, as we saw in the Introduction, partly as a result of such doubts, sociological research has tended to shift away from a focus on distortion in media reports to a more social constructionist approach, in which any contrast between true and false accounts is suspended or abandoned (see Golding and Elliott 1979: ch. 1; Berkowitz 1997).

The rationale for this trend is captured in an early and very influential study by Fishman, who writes that 'It is not useful to think of news as either distorting or reflecting reality, because "realities" are made and news is part of the system that makes them' (Fishman 1980: 12). In this way, social constructionists underline the fact that all accounts *inevitably* involve selection and formulation: journalists cannot but pay attention to *some* events rather than *others*; and, necessarily, they actively *make* sense of those events rather than simply reporting 'what happened'. This is because source material can always be formulated in multiple ways; and all of these are *accounts* of the world rather than simply *displays of the world itself*.[3] On this basis, it is sometimes denied that a correspondence between account and reality could ever be established convincingly, because we never have direct access to reality. Equally, it may be denied that a linguistic description can ever 'correspond' to a non-linguistic reality because they differ in their very character. Or, alternatively, it may be denied that there is any non-linguistic reality.

There are undoubtedly some difficult philosophical problems involved here, though in my view they do not undermine the concept of truth as correspondence; indeed I do not see how we could abandon this as a regulative idea either in doing research or in everyday life (Hammersley 2004b).[4] Moreover, to some extent at least, the case of the Review avoids these problems because what is to be represented here is itself a text. So, it would have been possible, in principle, for media reports to have reproduced, if not the whole Review, at least one or other of the short summaries provided within it or in the press release, in a way that an event in the world could never be reproduced. Second, in an important sense, the Review *can* be compared directly with media reports about it, in order to check the extent to which it 'corresponds'. In this case the source or referent is not epistemologically inaccessible. Third, given that the Review was already in linguistic form, no correspondence between linguistic and non-linguistic material seems to be involved here. For these reasons, we can address the question of whether the media accounts accurately reported what the Review

---

3 It should be noted, though, that this shift in approach has not led to the disappearance of terms such as 'distortion', 'myth' and 'ideology' from media analysis. Instead, these terms have often continued to be used alongside and within the emerging constructionist approach.

4 For a recent discussion of the philosophical issues, see Williams 2002. See also Blackburn and Simmons 1999: Introduction. It is, of course, true that there are always multiple true, though not incompatible, accounts of any phenomenon.

says in a way that involves fewer problems than there would be in many other cases.

Nevertheless, answering that question is by no means straightforward or uncontroversial. First of all, it would be a mistake to treat the message of the Review as uniquely tied to the words used in it, or even to those that are employed to describe it in the various summaries provided. This would be to assume that literal reproduction of a source is necessary and/or sufficient to preserve its message, in the sense of communicating this intact to a new audience. Such an approach treats communication as if it involved the sender encoding a message by means of syntactic and semantic rules, and the receiver decoding it using the same set of rules, so that the message is preserved.[5] But this is not a convincing theory of most human communication (see Sperber and Wilson 1986). Signs never entirely determine meaning: understanding requires us to interpret *acts of communication*; this must be done *in context*; and interpretation usually takes place on the basis of only *partially shared* cultural *resources* rather than exhaustive sets of rules.[6] This means that the same text cannot be assumed to communicate the same message across different audiences, or even to the same audience on different occasions. Thus, aside from the practical constraints under which they work, even for journalists to communicate to their readers the message of a textual source effectively would usually require not only selection but also some reformulation. Up to a point, then, the social constructionist critique has force.[7]

On the basis of this interpretative theory of communication, what is demanded of media reports for them to be accurate is that they represent the Review in such a way as to make its central message accessible to the target audience;[8] this message being independent of the particular formulations used in the Review or the press release, even though not independent of *all* verbal formulation. Given this, a necessary first step towards answering the question of how accurately the media reports captured the message of the Review is to identify what that message was.[9]

---

5 This is the model of communication built into information theory (Shannon and Weaver 1949), and also into some forms of structuralism: see Leach 1976: pp. 11–12.

6 Some writers would wish to restrict usage of the term 'interpretation' to a conscious, deliberative process. I am using the term here in a broader sense to include what, equally anachronistically for some, is often referred to as unconscious inference.

7 Nevertheless, I am relying on a moderate version of communication as interpretation here, one which retains the idea that an intended message is embodied in most communicative texts, and that this can be distinguished from the motivation and significance of the communication (see Hirsch 1967).

8 We should not assume, of course, that journalists have a very accurate, or necessarily a complimentary, view of their audiences: see Schlesinger 1987: ch. 5.

9 In effect, I have had to do this throughout the study, and in doing so I have drawn on my background knowledge of the relevant research field, and on many close readings of the text of the Review. What I want to do in this Conclusion, however, is to try to construct the Review's message from the point of view of a journalist approaching it under the constraints characteristic of that occupation.

If we look at the summaries provided in the Review and in the press release, we find a message consisting of a series of research findings, very few of which found their way into headlines and only some of which were included in media reports. In relation to these, we must consider whether the degree and kind of selectivity involved amounts to inaccuracy. First of all, we need to consider whether the various points included in the summaries, and in the Review more generally, are independent items, such that omission or downgrading of one does not affect the meaning of the others. There are some grounds for making this assumption. They *do* seem to be largely independent if looked at in terms of their intrinsic content. And this would seem to legitimate the kind of selectivity employed in many of the media headlines and reports. Of course, this is not to deny that these items can be combined to make stories that link them together: for example the growing gap in the performance of ethnic minority groups can be linked to African Caribbean pupils not sharing equally in the overall improvement that has taken place, and so on. And we saw that media reports did often construct narratives of this kind, with varying degrees of explicitness. However, this is not done within the summaries provided in the Review.

At the same time, as noted in Chapter 1, the summaries in the Conclusion, on the back cover, and in the press release *were* structured in terms of a good news/bad news format. While this involves formal rather than substantive links among the listed items, we might nevertheless argue that it amounts to an overall message: to the effect that the situation has improved in some respects but in others remains a cause for concern. And if we interpret the message of the Review as unitary in this way, then the selectivity displayed in many of the news reports, and especially in the headlines, does indeed involve some inaccuracy.

Only a few media reports followed this good news/bad news format in their headlines. As we saw, this was true of most headlines on the *Today* programme, and of the opening headline statements on BBC television news, though in both cases this involved selecting a finding that was not included as one of the main components of the short summaries – that in some areas some Asian groups had a higher level of achievement than all other groups – and contrasting this with the bad news about the continuing lower level of achievement of African Caribbean pupils. At the same time, *within* media reports, generally speaking, both 'bad' and 'good' news items were included, albeit being accorded varying salience. The main exceptions were among ethnic minority newspapers, some of which concentrated entirely on the higher average level of achievement of some Asian groups or on the continuing lower level of performance of African Caribbean pupils.

Of course, not just selection but also reformulation was involved in the media reports. Here, too, interpretation and judgement are required in assessing accuracy. That said, there are some examples of what would be judged as inaccuracy from almost any perspective: the *Daily Mail* reported that the Review shows African Caribbean pupils to have a lower level of school *attendance* than other groups, while *The Sun* claimed that the Review explains the higher than average achievement of some Asian pupils in terms of 'greater discipline at home'.

Another clear case of inaccuracy, more substantial in character, is that of the *Daily Star*, where the very few findings reported from the Review are swamped by other claims, to the point where, in terms of the headlines and the opening paragraphs, it is difficult to recognize the story as relating to the Review at all. Its message is presented as claiming that African Caribbean pupils are turning to crime because of conflict with teachers.

There are some other examples that are not quite so clear. One is the claim, in *The Sunday Times* and repeated in *India Weekly*, that the Review reports that Indian pupils 'are better behaved and are achieving better examination results than their white counterparts'. The Review does not state that these pupils are 'better behaved', though it does suggest that teachers see them in this way. Moreover, the evidence about their relative, average level of examination performance is declared to vary according to area, and it is made clear that recent national data are not available. Given this, the claim that Indian pupils are achieving better examination results than whites across the board, or that they are 'outshining' their classmates – as also reported in the *Today* programme headlines or in the *Eastern Eye* – is misleading. Moreover, the *Today* programme example illustrates another respect in which many media reports could be evaluated as reporting the findings of the Review inaccurately. This concerns the use of global ethnic categories, most notably 'Asian', which could give a misleading impression, covering over significant differences in educational performance among sub-groups.

Also significant is the use of quotation marks in newspaper headlines and reports to enclose words and phrases that do not actually appear in the Review. It seems likely that this is a device designed to circumvent the extra wordage that reported speech would require. And in some cases the 'quotation' may capture the gist of a key finding from the Review, or one of its messages. An example is one of the two headlines in *The Times Educational Supplement*: 'Race inequality "as bad as ever"'. Other cases seem more likely to involve inaccuracy in content or implication, for example the use of 'underclass' in the *Daily Mail* headline, in the Channel 4 report, and in the headlines used by some of the local newspapers. However, as I argued in Chapter 4, whether or not inaccuracy is involved here is a matter of judgement: much depends on what the term 'underclass' is taken to mean.

Identifying other potential inaccuracies or misrepresentations relies on even more complex and uncertain interpretative judgements. The most common discrepancy I identified in earlier chapters concerned implied explanations for ethnic differences in educational achievement, and associated attributions of responsibility. As we saw, many media reports presented causal narratives that were close to what I called the competition model, rather than to either the distribution or discrimination models. In other words, these media reports could be taken to imply that the lower level of average educational achievement on the part of some groups, notably African Caribbean pupils, reflected their characteristics, or those of their homes and local communities. And this is very much at odds with most of the formulations in the Review, and with the declared intentions of its authors.

However, in terms of the interpretation of the Review's message I have outlined up to now, this shift in causal narrative does not amount to inaccuracy. After all, on this reading, the message consisted of specific items reporting various kinds of difference, improvement and occasional worsening in the educational outcomes achieved by ethnic groups, perhaps along with the overall point that there has been some improvement but that there were also continuing problems. There was nothing in the short summaries of the Review to highlight the significance of the particular formulations used by its authors, nor was there any criticism there of the term 'underachievement'. This only appeared in the executive summary, and in the main body of the Review. Given this, it is not clear that portrayal of the findings in language reflecting the competition model can reasonably be treated as inaccuracy.

There is, however, a second, very different, interpretation of the message of the Review, one which *does* make the issue of causal narrative central. On this reading, there is a single overall conclusion, to which all else is subordinated. This is the one encapsulated in the press release headline: that 'colour-blind' policies have failed. This message links closely to the authors' rejection of the term 'underachievement', and to their interpretative policy of treating lower levels of achievement on the part of ethnic minority groups as indicating the operation of discrimination within the education system, or at least as cause for concern. As noted in Chapter 1, the whole Review is organized in terms of this interpretative policy, even though it is not made explicit in the short summaries.[10]

In the context of this alternative message structure, most of the selections and reformulations used by the media could be interpreted as representing serious inaccuracy: few reports are organized in terms of this central theme. The only clear example is the report in the *Evening Standard*, whose headline was: 'Colour-blind policies "are failing pupils from ethnic minorities" '. Instead, most reports are organized around one or other of the specific findings about the performance of ethnic minority pupils, or around reactions to the Review. Indeed, the conclusion that 'colour-blind' policies have failed is not even mentioned in many reports. Furthermore, as just noted, the reporting of specific findings often involved formulations that tended to carry explanatory implications, and associated attributions of responsibility, which run counter to this second interpretation of the Review's message.

To summarize, then, selection and reformulation do not, in themselves, indicate inaccuracy. Judgement of whether inaccuracy is present depends on

---

10 In the case of the press release, the link between its headline and the summary of the content of the Review it provides is largely implicit, though it is true to say that the failure of colour-blind policies is mentioned again towards the end, and given some elaboration. In an interview four years after the publication of the Review, David Gillborn claimed that the main message of the Review was that the situation is getting worse, and that there are things we can do to make things better (David Gillborn, personal communication). This is quite close to the message that 'colour-blind' policies have failed.

interpretation of the central message of the Review. And that message is open to somewhat different readings. If we interpret it as consisting of the set of findings and recommendations included in the brief summaries and in the press release summary, and especially if we assume that each of these findings can be treated as relatively independent from the others, then for the most part the items selected by the media as headlines do not involve substantial inaccuracy. Furthermore, from this point of view, the reformulation of the Review's findings by the media in ways that open up the implication that ethnic inequalities in educational achievement are a product of the features of ethnic groups themselves, relying on the competition model, should not be read as inaccuracy – since explanation of the inequalities was not explicitly part of the message. By contrast, if we take the second interpretation of the Review's main message, presented in the headline of the press release as well as elsewhere, then it could reasonably be argued that serious inaccuracy is involved, in terms both of selection and reformulation, in most if not all of the media coverage.

There is a general point here, then, about the scope for different interpretations of the message of a source, especially a long and complex text such as the Review. This is a particular problem where what is being reported is a *review* of research rather than a single study. Relevant here is the fact that reviews often have a complex structure consisting of multiple findings, sometimes with no single overarching message. And it is certainly true that the main body of the Review consists of a very large number of knowledge claims, that the executive summary contains 68 bullet points, and that even the brief summaries involve lists of findings. As we have seen, the news media selected just a few of these to be headlined, and did not always include in their reports even all the points contained in the short summaries. They also varied in the emphasis they gave to the particular findings presented.

There is also an issue that is specific to this particular review. The authors' discussion of problems with the concept of underachievement indicates a concern on their part with how readers might interpret the ethnic inequalities reported, in particular that they will judge the lower level of achievement of African Caribbean pupils as reflecting the characteristics of that ethnic group. One aspect of the authors' response to this concern seems to have been to emphasize the *achievements* of ethnic minority pupils. This is done most obviously in the Review's title, but also in the initial parts of the short summaries in the Review, which are copied in the press release summary.[11] At the same time, the authors wanted to emphasize that there is still cause for concern, even while avoiding the term 'underachievement'. This terminological strategy – emphasis on achievement, but avoidance of the term 'underachievement' – makes for a particularly complex message; one which probably invites reformulation by the media in their attempt to present brief and clear headlines, and accounts

---

11 The word 'achievement' may have been taken into the title from the original tender specification put out by OFSTED (David Gillborn, personal communication).

that are immediately intelligible to their audiences.[12] Much the same applies to their associated use of the distribution metaphor in formulating inequalities in educational achievement.

There is also some ambiguity built into the core of the second interpretation of the Review's message I identified, concerning the failure of 'colour-blind' policies. The problem here, I suggest, is that most people would assume that children should be treated the same irrespective of their ethnic identities, and that to treat them differently on this basis amounts to racism. In these terms, 'colour-blind' policies, to the extent that the term is understood at all, would seem obviously correct, and this creates a puzzle regarding how they could be judged to have failed. Moreover, there is not much explication in the Review of the authors' argument on this issue: that teachers need to take account of ethnic differences in such a way as to ensure that curriculum content, pedagogical practice, and institutional procedures do not disadvantage ethnic minorities unfairly.[13]

SYSTEMATIC INACCURACIES AND UNDERLYING MECHANISMS

I suggested earlier in this chapter that, in the task of identifying bias in news reports, documenting specific inaccuracies is only the first step. Equally important is that the inaccuracies are all, or mostly, in a direction that reflects a particular set of assumptions or a specific interest, and/or that encourages a particular sort of conclusion on the part of audiences. Furthermore, an underlying process – an individual or institutional orientation – must be shown to have been operating to produce those differences. Thus, explicit in Gillborn's (1998) critique of newspaper coverage of the Review, and in much research on the media's treatment of ethnic minorities, is the claim that there is *systematic* inaccuracy, and that this reflects the operation of an underlying social process, namely racism. Furthermore, this kind of bias in the media is viewed as reinforcing prejudice and discrimination within the wider society, so that what we have here is a functional process at the macro level, a process that feeds on itself.

There are severe limits to the evidence that my study can provide about this issue, given that I have no direct information about the production process or about audience reception of the media reports. Nevertheless, it is worth examining what it can offer, and above all what would be required in making judgements about this issue. In looking at coverage of the Review in the media for this purpose, we need to examine whether there are *patterns* of inaccuracy – across

---

12 The opposite of 'underachievement' is, of course, 'overachievement', and this term is also not used. But, in the context of the Review, 'achievement' also seems to be used as a contrast with 'underachievement'.

13 The absence of such specification may well have resulted from the substantial editing required by OFSTED in order to reduce the length of the initial draft of the Review.

the reports as a whole, or between different media, or within particular media. Is there a tendency for the media, or for parts of it, to distort the message of the Review in a specific direction, especially one that could imply or encourage discrimination against ethnic minorities? In trying to answer these questions, we will need to consider separately deviation from the two main interpretations of the message of the Review I outlined above.

Deviation from the first interpretation of the Review's message

As I indicated earlier, if we treat the Review as simply a list of findings, and treat accurate reporting as the reporting of any of the findings included in the Review and its summaries, then there is quite a high level of accuracy in most media reports. There is, of course, a strong tendency for them to foreground only a very small number of findings from the Review, and to leave quite a lot of findings unmentioned. Moreover, there is some inaccurate formulation, and there is also some false attribution of findings to the Review. Nevertheless, most of the inaccuracy, on this first interpretation of the Review's message, is not systematic in any obviously significant way.

Of course, we might still ask whether the selection and highlighting of particular findings reflected a discriminatory orientation or would encourage negative attitudes towards particular ethnic minorities on the part of audiences. For instance, does foregrounding the lower average level of educational achievement of some ethnic groups amount to, and/or generate, prejudice against those groups? Or does it indicate a concern with equity that is designed to lead, and perhaps *will* lead, to remedy? These are not questions that would be easy to answer.

One aspect of the issue, dealt with by much of the literature on media representation of ethnic minorities, is whether there is a tendency towards showing minorities in a bad light. We can link this to the question of whether media reports preserved the good news/bad news format characteristic of the short summaries, and the mixture of positive and negative findings to be found throughout the Review; or whether they deviated towards either emphasizing the positive or the negative. If we look across each of the media, we find rather different patterns.

In the case of radio, we are hampered by the fact that the data come from only one programme, and the news reports within it. Nevertheless, here, as we saw, headlines were generally formulated in terms of a contrast between the high achievements of some Asian groups and the lower average level of achievement of African Caribbean pupils. This could be interpreted as a balanced account that shows some ethnic minorities in a positive light and indicates that in the case of others there is a problem that needs to be tackled. This probably matches the intentions of the journalists concerned, and their expectations about how their audience would hear the reports. Yet these headlines and the reports following on from them *could* be read as suggesting that there is something defective about African Caribbean pupils, or their families and communities, given that they are unable to do as well as other ethnic minority groups.

In the case of television coverage, there are significant differences between the channels. The BBC bulletins begin with a good news/bad news formulation. And while the BBC education correspondent's subsequent reports tend to foreground the lower average level of achievement of African Caribbean pupils, a major part of these reports is concerned with how the situation can be improved. The ITN news report focused almost entirely on the lower average level of achievement of African Caribbean pupils, indicating that the educational performance of these pupils 'is getting worse'.[14] Channel 4 begins by reporting 'a growing gap in educational achievement among ethnic minority groups'. And the rest of the report makes clear that this is to be seen as a problem, so that the emphasis is on the fact that some ethnic minority groups are not doing as well as others. Indeed, it is possible that this opening headline would have been seen by many viewers as suggesting that there is an increasing gap between ethnic minority and majority pupils. Moreover, the Channel 4 report goes on to suggest, quoting comments from the Chief Inspector of Schools, that there is a limit to what schools can do in remedying this problem because it is generated by wider social factors. The emphasis in the television reports is mixed, then, but that of ITN and Channel 4 is very much on bad news.

In the case of newspapers, the good news/bad news format only occurred once in headlines: the *Asian Times* had one headline about the success of Indian pupils and another to the effect that 'Pakistani students face university places injustice'. Moreover, while both good and bad news findings were usually included within the body of newspaper reports, the predominant tendency in the national and local press was to emphasize the bad news. The main exceptions were among ethnic minority newspapers, where those serving Asian communities tended to stress the relative success of some pupils from those communities.[15]

It seems to me that the patterns identified here do not constitute strong evidence for the operation of a bias against ethnic minorities, or even against particular ethnic minorities, on the part of the media. While the effect, in many cases, is to highlight the lower average level of performance of African Caribbean pupils, it does not follow that the aim was to portray these pupils negatively, or that the journalists held a negative view of this ethnic group.[16] A more plausible explanation of this focus relates to the often-noted tendency of the media to concentrate on bad rather than good news. At the same time, it *is* likely that this aspect of the coverage would have encouraged stereotypes on the part of some

---

14 Furthermore, the qualifications that were present in the Review's summaries are stripped out.

15 One local newspaper, the *Wolverhampton Express and Star*, also led on the relative success of some Asian pupils.

16 An argument sometimes used in this context, as noted in the Introduction, is that racism has become more subtle, less overt. This may be so, but if this is the case we require more sophisticated methods to detect it; simply reading racist intent or function into the data is not sufficient.

audiences – though the effect will have varied considerably according to their prior dispositions.

Deviation from the second interpretation of the Review's message

We saw that, generally speaking, media reports did not focus on the recommendations of the Review, and hardly any foregrounded the idea that 'colour-blind' policies had failed, though this was sometimes mentioned. However, we cannot infer from this a tendency for journalists to assume that lower average levels of educational achievement on the part of some ethnic minorities under a 'colour-blind' policy simply reflects their lower capabilities (though some journalists may well have assumed this). There is a more obvious explanation for the fact that this finding does not get much attention. As I indicated earlier, this is that its meaning is not easy to understand, and would probably have been judged by journalists as unlikely to be immediately intelligible to many audiences. The complexity of the notion of 'colour-blind' policies probably discouraged the reporting of this finding. Given the emphasis journalists place on attracting and retaining the attention of audiences, it is likely to have been seen as a major drawback, which may well explain the low level of coverage of this finding. When asked why this had not been the top line of the story, one broadcast journalist involved in reporting the Review commented:

> I wouldn't have written the headline 'Colour-blind school policies do not help ethnic minority pupils, says OFSTED report' because it would have meant nothing to the bulk of our audience. It is a line written to be understood by other experts, e.g. academics and others 'in the know' e.g. some teachers.[17]

There was also relatively little prominence given to the finding that the performance of ethnic groups whose achievement levels are generally below average had been dramatically improved in some places by local policies. This was not emphasized in the BBC radio coverage, or on the ITN and Channel 4 news reports. It might be argued that BBC television reports did cover this, given their focus on two initiatives designed to improve the levels of educational achievement of particular groups. However, even here, it is uncertain whether the message that such initiatives can be successful – that change is possible – would have come across strongly to viewers. Also the fact that one of these initiatives was operating within the African Caribbean community could have been interpreted as implying that the problem belonged to that community, despite the alternative account offered by one of the workers involved in this initiative. In the case of newspapers, this message about the scope for improvement in the performance of 'underachieving' ethnic groups was sometimes mentioned,

17 Sue Littlemore, personal communication, August 1999.

but was only highlighted in a few cases, notably *The Guardian* and *Guardian Education*.

Another issue, as regards the second interpretation of the Review's message, concerns what I have called the explanatory implications of the language employed. We saw that the authors of the Review were themselves concerned about how use of the term 'underachievement' could encourage what they regarded as false conclusions on the part of readers. If we look at media reports in these terms, we do find a general trend: away from language reflecting the distribution metaphor, which was the predominant form within the Review, towards the competition model. It is not that the language of distribution is never used in media reports, but that, generally speaking, where it is used it is mixed in with (and often subordinated to) terms that imply competition; and where it is *not* used the competition metaphor usually predominates.

Once again, though, we cannot simply read off a bias against ethnic minorities. Here, too, the tendency towards the competition model may simply reflect an assumption on the part of journalists that the language of the distribution metaphor is less easily intelligible, and almost certainly not as familiar, to many audiences. Of course, what is intelligible to an audience, as well as journalists' judgements about this, depends on previous experience, which will have been shaped by the wider society and culture. Within the UK, and probably in many other societies too, the competition metaphor is a very common way of thinking about educational achievement. It is assumed that the education system approximates, or should approximate, to a meritocratic process in which pupils compete with one another, so that differences in achievement, for example as measured by qualifications, reflect their differential abilities and effort. By contrast, the language of the distribution metaphor is much rarer, though the rise of a discourse focused on the idea that education is 'delivered' by teachers and schools may open the way for it to become more widespread.

While there is a strong trend within the media reports towards the competition model, no explicit steer is usually given as to how the differences in performance are to be explained. As we have noted, the default explanation built into that model appeals to differences in ability, motivation, etc. between ethnic groups or in factors affecting these. For reasons already explained, on the evidence available, this assumption cannot reasonably be attributed to the journalists concerned, or even to the institutional processes in which they operate, though this may tell us how audiences will be likely to receive the message. Of course, in some of the reports, explanations *are* explicitly mentioned (for example in the two items on the *Today* programme, in the BBC television news, and in the Channel 4 news report, and, within newspapers, usually through the quoting of various commentators). There is a complex pattern here. Sometimes these were explanations in terms of particular characteristics of African Caribbean families and communities, thereby reinforcing the implicit message of the competition model. This was true of the *Today* programme, probably less so of BBC television coverage. There was no explanation offered in the ITN coverage. The Channel 4 report provided a rather ambiguous account: the term 'underclass' was attributed to the Review, but at the same time the danger of stereotyping was mentioned through the voice of a headteacher, and criticisms of the education system by black parents were reported.

In the case of the newspapers, there were significant differences both in terms of the explanatory implications that could be read as built into the reports and in terms of explicit explanations offered. As regards overall story line, the national Sunday and daily newspapers displayed a range of orientations, from those which adopted the competition model to those that focused on the government's response and/or on discrimination by teachers, as in the case of *The Independent*, the *Daily Telegraph*, and perhaps also the *Daily Mirror*. To some extent this matched the generally recognized political orientations of the newspapers, with those on the Right portraying ethnic groups as succeeding or failing in competition with one another, and those on the Left focusing on the role of teachers, schools or the government. The two specialist newspapers aimed at education professionals adopted almost entirely the latter emphasis. For the most part, local newspapers emphasized the competition model, though one or two focused on the role of government or teachers. The sharpest difference, however, was to be found among ethnic minority newspapers, with those serving Asian communities generally relying on the competition metaphor in highlighting the success of Indian pupils, while those serving the African Caribbean community tended to avoid the competition model in reporting the lower average level of achievement of pupils from that community.

There was also considerable diversity, not only across newspapers but also within particular reports, in the explanations presented, these usually appearing in reported comments from politicians, the Chief Inspector of Schools, representatives of various organizations with an interest in the topic, and so on. Some of these explanations contrasted with those presented in the Review, in that they appealed to, for example, the nature of African Caribbean families and youth culture. However, the fact that they were included as part of quotations from commentators means that they cannot in any straightforward sense be counted as indicating media inaccuracy, since it is not the Review's findings that are being reported here but reactions to them.[18] At the same time, these commentaries and the explanations they contain would probably have shaped the message received by readers.

My conclusion in relation to the second interpretation of the message of the Review is that some general tendencies can be identified. One is that there is a low emphasis given both to the findings that 'colour-blind' policies have failed and that in some localities the performance of lower-achieving groups of pupils from ethnic minorities has improved dramatically. Also, there is a strong trend towards presenting the ethnic inequalities reported by the Review in terms of the competition rather than the distribution metaphor. However, it seems likely that

18 There may, of course, have been some bias operating in the selection and reporting of what these other commentators said, but no evidence is available for making judgements about this.

many of these features reflect an often noted orientation on the part of journalists: a concern with ensuring that what they write is intelligible to their audiences. The linguistic formulations required by the distribution model are longer and probably less familiar to audiences than those of the competition model. And while reporting the findings in terms of the discrimination model *would* have been intelligible to audiences, the predominant use of the distribution metaphor in the Review, and especially in the summaries, probably discouraged this.[19]

Overall, then, my conclusion is that there is no clear evidence here for the claim that there was systematic bias against ethnic minorities, or against some ethnic minorities, in media reports of the Review. However, in order to come to any strong conclusion about this, more evidence would be required about the production processes that generated media reports. At the same time, it is clear that media accounts of the Review could have reinforced a bias against some ethnic minorities on the part of some audiences, depending upon their background attitudes; though it is also worth pointing out that even reports about the *success* of ethnic minority pupils might have done this too.

THEORIZING BIAS IN MEDIA REPRESENTATION OF SOCIAL RESEARCH

As I noted earlier, studies of media bias have often employed the traditional concept of ideology, or elements of it. Thus, news reports have often been presented as distorted representations of social reality that are generated by agents or forces within a society in such a way as to sustain the structures of that society, these structures usually being viewed by the analyst as inequitable, exploitative, and/or as embodying social class or 'racial' domination. This is true, most obviously, of the work of the Glasgow University Media Group and of that of the Centre for Contemporary Cultural Studies at the University of Birmingham in the 1970s and 1980s, and of much subsequent research influenced by it.[20]

As I noted in the Introduction, in more recent times, the element of this model referring to distortion of social reality has been played down or abandoned because of the influence of constructionism, and the epistemological scepticism associated with it. In my view this scepticism is misconceived: to say that the news reported by journalists is a product of their routine assumptions and practices, the institutional processes in which they operate, etc. does not imply that it has no referent – any more than pointing out that sociological findings are produced by sociological modes of production implies that sociologists create the

19 Here, there is a contrast with many of the studies that the Review covers, which do tend to employ the language of discrimination.
20 See Hall *et al.* 1978; Glasgow University Media Group 1976, 1980, 1982 and 1985. Many reviews of work in the field reflect this influence and rely on the ideology model, see, for example, Allan 1999.

phenomena they describe. Nevertheless, constructionism can lead to recognition of an important requirement for the social analysis of beliefs: in seeking to describe and explain them we should be indifferent to whether we judge them desirable or undesirable, or even true or false. To use a phrase that emerged within the sociology of scientific knowledge, we should adopt the principle of symmetry.[21] It is in the spirit of this principle that I have analysed both the Review and media reports in a manner that has (as far as possible) put on one side any evaluations I might be inclined to make about their quality, the validity of the knowledge claims they make, and so on. I have focused primarily on the relationship between the two of them, in terms of degree of correspondence between their messages.

So, while not accepting constructionist scepticism, I believe that the ideology model is defective in seeking to explain what are judged to be true and false, desirable and undesirable, beliefs differently, as if their desirability or truth were relevant to how they came to be produced or why they were accepted. However, there is another problem with the ideology model too. This is that it is used as an inference ticket for moving between (often speculative) identifications of motives for producing and accepting particular knowledge claims, interpretations about the accuracy of those claims, assessments of their political implications, and evaluations of the consequences of their being communicated to an audience.[22] Like many of the inference tickets we use routinely in everyday life, the concept of ideology is often employed by social scientists in a fashion that relies heavily on plausible interpretation, downplaying the need for evidence in support of all of its separate components. Thus, it frequently seems to be assumed that, given what are taken to be the political implications of some media report, perhaps supported by a belief that it involves misrepresentation, we can infer that an ideology is in operation, so long as some plausible link between motive and outcome can be supplied.[23] Furthermore, in identifying political implications, as with judging accuracy of representation, there is a tendency to assume that these can be read off in a relatively unproblematic fashion, neglecting the scope for alternative interpretations. Moreover, this has continued despite the emphasis by some constructionists on the extent to which the meaning of any text is constructed by audiences, and the ineradicable potential for multiple readings.

In the course of my research, I collected no direct data on the production of either the Review or of media reports, and only a relatively small amount of indirect data from interviews with the people involved in these production processes. On the basis of these data, and drawing on previous work on newspaper

21 See Barnes 1974 and Bloor 1976. For discussion of various interpretations of this principle, see Pickering 1992. A parallel concept in the sociology of deviance is 'appreciation'; see Matza 1969.

22 For an earlier critique of much media sociology along these lines, see Anderson and Sharrock 1979.

23 The inference ticket involved here is one that is also used in everyday life, memorably summed up by Mandy Rice Davies, in its conspiratorial form, as: 'they would say that, wouldn't they'.

and broadcast news, I have indicated some of the factors that probably affected the shape of media reports, notably time and space constraints and a journalistic concern with producing copy that will get through editorial gatekeepers as likely to be intelligible to, and to attract and keep the attention of, audiences. These factors are relatively uncontroversial, and many media analysts have noted them. It is also clear that the operation of these factors reflects, at least to some extent, the particular organizational arrangements within which media journalists operate. However, the ideology model requires that we move beyond these mundane factors to focus on what are seen as the effects on media production of larger social processes designed to reproduce the current structures of Western societies. In other words, it involves reliance upon a form of social reproduction theory that derives from Marxism or 'critical' research more generally. This analytic move seems to me to be, at best, premature. Not only does it involve very substantial demands for evidence, whose scale is usually underestimated, but it also requires some questionable theoretical assumptions.

As has often been pointed out, the social reproduction model parallels an earlier form of analysis in Western anthropology and sociology, in which particular processes and patterns within a society were treated as governed by functional relations through which the society sustained itself.[24] The most distinctive difference between these social reproduction and structural-functionalist analyses is that whereas the latter takes a neutral or positive attitude towards the reproduction of existing society, the former adopts a negative attitude towards this. Yet structural-functionalism was criticized on several other grounds besides its alleged conservative bias. Questions were raised about whether it made sense to see national societies as single, bounded systems, about the disadvantages of categorizing actions or institutional processes as either functional or dysfunctional (or, in the case of reproduction theory, as either serving dominant interests or resisting them), and about the cogency of explanations of human behaviour in terms of people following norms or serving objective interests (Demerath and Peterson 1967; Garfinkel 1967; Lemert 1967: ch. 1; Sharrock 1977; van Parijs 1981).

Taking proper account of these doubts about functional analysis, as they apply to reproduction theory, has important implications. It would require us to resist the temptation to assume that because we can interpret media reports as misrepresentations, and/or as carrying implications that support some aspect of the status quo or the interests of dominant groups, we can conclude that they actually function, and in some sense have been designed to function, so as to preserve existing social structures. Instead, we require more detailed investigation of the contexts in which, and processes by which, media reports are produced as well as of how media audiences 'consume' news reports and what role these play in

---

24 For the argument that Marxism, the model for social reproduction theory, is itself functionalist, see Cohen 1978. For two critiques of social reproduction theory, relating to the field of education but of more general application, see Hargreaves 1982 and Foster *et al.* 1996: 165–70 and 177.

their lives; and we need to do all this without jumping to conclusions about what *must* be going on in terms of social reproduction.

There will be, in all societies having mass media, attempts to shape media news reports in particular ways, for a variety of reasons, including their assumed political implications or consequences; and, in all those societies, any concern with attracting and retaining audiences is likely to lead to news reports using assumptions, metaphors and models that are already available to those audiences. Moreover, these background assumptions, metaphors and models will probably have developed because they serve important purposes for agents and institutions within those societies, including some that are below the level of general consciousness. At the same time, as more sophisticated versions of social reproduction theory recognize, there will be conflicts and contradictions among institutions and groups within any society, and these will shape both the production of media reports and their reception. And it is important to insist that this diversity and conflict may be an essential part of human social life, rather than assuming that it is a surface feature which obscures some single underlying process of systemic reproduction that is always operating 'in the last instance'.

In its reliance on social reproduction theory, much analysis of media news appeals to capitalism and/or to racism as the prime movers. Yet the term 'capital', or 'capitalism', is best viewed as an umbrella for various kinds of social formation involved in the production and distribution of goods and services, these taking different forms and having various relationships with one another.[25] That these types of social formation refer to structures with the capacity to generate and stimulate acceptance of various cultural and political forms is no doubt true, but how they do this in particular contexts will be a contingent matter that can produce diverse outcomes, including ones which may undermine particular capitalist relations. Moreover, these capitalistic institutional structures are not the only generative patterns operating even within contemporary Western societies.[26]

The term 'racism' is even more problematic as a causal factor. In its narrowest sense, as referring to differential attitudes towards people on the basis of 'racial' categories and differential treatment of those people in ways designed to favour or defend one's own 'racial' group, the term does pick out a relatively specific form

---

25 The different forms that capitalism can take has been widely recognized. For an analysis of its earlier forms see Pirenne 1914. Some of the more recent diversity is highlighted by discussions of the shift in power from owners to managers, and notions of 'state capitalism', the latter linking to the extent to which there is regulation of markets even in Western societies. There are differences in view about what are the essential features of capitalism, and even about whether the pursuit of profit is its driving force. Also relevant here are distinctions between different phases and forms of capitalism, for example commercial, industrial and finance capitalism (on the last of these, see Neal 1990). There are also phrases like 'monopoly capitalism' and 'welfare capitalism' that point to additional variations in institutional form. For a very useful brief discussion of the concept, see Cole 1964.

26 For a useful account of the criticisms and weaknesses, as well as the strengths, of Marxian analysis, see Giddens 1973.

of attitude and action. However, when the reference of the term is extended, as is usual today, to encompass any actions whose effects are judged by the social scientist to disadvantage 'racial' or ethnic minorities, this renders the concept unusable in analytic terms: it no longer offers any help in describing or explaining distinct types of social process, because it lumps together too much. While this extension in reference may be important for evaluative or political purposes, it undercuts its value in analytic terms.

In short, then, we need to avoid assuming that the phenomena being studied are primarily governed by some single functional process, what Hall (following Althusser) refers to as a 'structure in dominance' (Hall 1996: 11), in order to allow for the possibility that a variety of structured processes may be operating. Equally, these must be treated as contingent rather than fixed and teleological in character. Moreover, our accounts of these processes must be separated from any moral or humanistic meta-narrative or evaluation – of the kind derived from Marx, through Gramsci, by the radical tradition of media studies (Curran 1997).

Focusing more specifically on the media's reporting of social and educational research, there are important analytic advantages, I suggest, in beginning by seeking to understand any discrepancies between research reports and media accounts in terms of the different commitments and forms of social organization to be found within the two occupational communities involved. The media are not, and probably could never be, a transparent mechanism that simply transmits the findings of social research to its audiences. Rather, those findings, even when relatively simple and unambiguous, will be refracted through the distinctive social organization of the media, and this is likely to be the case whatever structures govern the wider society.

CONCLUSION

In this chapter, I have sought to draw together the evidence produced earlier in the book, exploring what is involved in coming to a judgement about whether the media were biased in their reporting of the Review, in particular by racism. I began by noting the various elements of the model of ideology on which claims about media bias frequently rely: that there are inaccuracies, that these are systematic in some relevant respect, and that there is an underlying mechanism which generated them. Furthermore, in the subsequent discussion I also took into account two other elements of that model, as typically applied to study of the news media: the idea that reports carry implications and have consequences that reproduce the socio-political status quo.

In the first part of the chapter, I summarized the main differences between the Review and media reports, in terms of the message presented, and I argued that any judgement about inaccuracy of media reporting of the Review is rendered complex by a number of factors. One is the very nature of communication, and in particular the fact that it must be recipient-designed: this means that in order to communicate a message to new audiences it will need to be reformulated in some ways.[27] A second factor is that reviews of research findings tend to have the character of lists, which places limits on the extent to which they can be organized effectively in terms of some single overall theme. Finally, I argued that the main message of the Review is ambiguous, and I examined media reports in terms of two very different interpretations of that message. Taking the Review as offering a range of specific findings, media reports showed considerable selectivity and quite a lot of reformulation but most of them involved what could probably be judged a low level of significant inaccuracy, although the good news/bad news format present in the short summaries was rarely retained. By contrast, taking a second interpretation of the Review's message, where the 'failure of "colour-blind" policies' is the main theme, the inaccuracy was much more substantial.

I went on to assess whether *systematic* patterns of inaccuracy could be identified, and whether it could be inferred that the media coverage would generate or reinforce a negative view of some ethnic minorities. I argued that there were some systematic differences between the message of the Review, on the second interpretation I had identified, and media reports. However, I concluded that this did not constitute strong evidence of racist bias, that it was more likely to be a product of more local features of the journalistic production of news, such as the greater weight given to bad news and the concern to ensure that messages are intelligible to audiences. At the same time, I argued that it was probably true that the reporting would reinforce the view, on the part of some audiences, that ethnic minorities achieving lower than average educational qualifications possessed lower levels of academic ability and/or motivation.

In the final section of the chapter, I identified some methodological and theoretical problems with the ideology model, and the associated concept of social reproduction that has informed much analysis of bias in media news. I suggested that it suffers from many of the well-known failings of functionalist analysis, and particularly that it tends to be applied in ways that amount to little more than plausible speculation. I noted how it assumed that different sorts of explanation are required depending upon the analyst's judgements of whether particular media accounts are true or false, good or bad; and I argued that this assumption is without justification. In addition, I pointed to questionable assumptions about the reproductive function of media accounts that are common in much of the literature, and the way in which these encourage the use of ideology as an inference ticket that circumvents the requirement that *all* its elements are grounded in evidence: that media accounts be shown to be systematically inaccurate, that underlying motives or processes be documented, and that purported implications and consequences are established. A better approach, it seems to me, is one that not only adopts the principle of symmetry, seeking to describe and explain media reports irrespective of whether they are judged by the analyst to be true or

---

27 Schegloff 1971 demonstrates this for one of the most mundane forms of communication: giving directions.

false, but also examines media reports, their production, and reception contexts, without *assuming* any functional links among these.

The sorts of grand conclusion to which social scientists studying the news media are often tempted, concerning the role of those agencies in social reproduction, can be no more than speculative given the present stage of development of sociological evidence and analysis. While theoretical ideas about ideology and social reproduction offer some potential insights, they can also very easily become a set of theoretical blinkers. Indeed, I suggest that, given these problems, any claim that the cognitive status of media sociologists' findings is greatly superior to that of journalists' own interpretations of the nature and function of their work is very questionable.[28] Moreover, where social scientists are studying media treatment of social research, there may be an even stronger inclination to move too rapidly to judgements about distortion, and to seek to explain what has happened in terms of the ideology model. In my view, this is a temptation that must be resisted if good quality social science is to be produced, despite the risk that such caution will lead to findings of low news value.

---

28 Both might be seen as reflecting occupational ideologies. Indeed, a reflexive sociology perhaps ought to examine the reproduction model as a form of 'occupational psychosis', a phrase invented by John Dewey, on which see Merton 1968: 251–2.

Epilogue: questions about the media, democracy and social science

In the Introduction to this book, I outlined what I called the 'democratic model' of the role of research in society and the key role this assigns to the mass media in communicating the results of social science so as to facilitate informed public discussion of policy issues. I suggested that this model lay behind many social scientists' views about the purpose of their work, and in part at least gave rise to their complaints about how it is treated by the media. In the body of this book I used this model as the framework for my analysis. So, in examining the case of *Recent Research on the Achievements of Ethnic Minority Pupils*, my concern was with the relationship between this review as source material and media reports about it. More specifically, the aim was to compare the two so as to identify what could count as inaccuracies, and what evidence there was of ideological bias, in reports of the Review's message.[1] At the same time, in the Conclusion I noted some serious difficulties involved in this task, a few relating to the character of the Review itself, others likely to apply more generally to any presentation of research findings to lay audiences, and some arising from the very nature of human communication.

It is important to reiterate that throughout the book my focus has been a factual one: I have not been *evaluating* – as good or bad, true or false – the work of journalists, or that of the social scientists who produced the Review, nor the role of OFSTED in sponsoring it. As I indicated in the Introduction, this limited focus reflects the adoption of a broadly Weberian conception of social inquiry, in terms of which its sole immediate goal should be the production of factual knowledge, albeit within a value-relevant framework. From this point of view, research should not claim to produce value judgements as conclusions.[2]

---

1 It is important to remember, of course, that what the media were reporting was not just the research findings offered by the Review but also the *event* of the Review's publication; indeed, it is events rather than issues that are the preoccupation of news media. From this point of view, the Review was a news object as much as a source.

2 This is, of course, at odds with the orientations of many social scientists, including those characteristic of 'critical' social science, of a 'public sociology' of some kinds (Agger 2000; Burawoy 2005), of 'interactive social science' (Caswill and Shove 2000), of 'mode 2 research' (Gibbons *et al.* 1994; Gibbons 2000) and of action research (see Hammersley 2004c). I have sought to justify my

So, throughout the book I have sought to avoid any implication that identifying factual inaccuracies automatically involves negative evaluation of them, or of those responsible for the accounts concerned. There has been no suggestion that media reports of the Review were of poor quality, nor have evaluative judgements been made of them on any other grounds. Indeed, my labelling of differences between the Review and media reports as 'inaccuracies' is no more than a conditional evaluation. In other words, it says that, if one were to adopt accuracy of reporting as the standard for evaluating media reports, then there are some differences between the Review and media reports that are likely to be judged inaccurate (though, as we saw, this depends a great deal upon which central message is attributed to the Review). I have simply used this value framework to pick out phenomena for study.[3]

While that was my orientation in previous chapters, in this epilogue I want to change tack, so as to explore the assumptions underlying the value relevance framework I employed. And this means stepping out of the restrictions just described, into the kind of normative orientation that is also essential in methodological reflection about how best to carry out research (Hammersley 2005d). Examining these assumptions is important for coming to any judgement about the proper relationship between social science and the media, and about their roles in the wider society. While these matters cannot be decided solely by means of research, or solely by researchers, they are important issues that researchers need to consider in pursuing their occupational task and thinking about their relationship to the mass media.

There are three topics I will focus on here: the nature of democracy and the role of social science in relation to it; how lay audiences, including journalists, ought to respond to the findings of social research; and, finally, limitations on the authority of social science within the public sphere.

DISCURSIVE DEMOCRACY AS REALITY AND IDEAL

Quite a lot of discussion about media reporting of social research has assumed that it contributes, or should contribute, to open public discussion of policy

orientation elsewhere: Hammersley 1995 and 2000. While I do not accept Weber's view that value commitments are ultimately irrational, I do believe that coming to reasonable conclusions about value issues cannot rely entirely on factual evidence but requires judgements in which competing value principles are weighed against one another in relation to the particularities of individual cases, and to some degree on the basis of the commitments of the person making the judgement. This means, in my view, that social scientists can have no distinctive authority in relation to value conclusions.

3 Here, I am contrasting conditional evaluations with actual, practically engaged evaluations. In the former, only the factual component of the evaluation is endorsed, whereas in the latter both factual and value elements are endorsed. Conditional evaluations are of the form: *if* we take this particular value framework, then this *would* (*or could*) be the evaluative conclusion reached. For further discussion of the notion of conditional evaluations, see Foster *et al.* 2000.

issues, this operating as a means of testing out the validity, desirability and viability of various policy options. One model for this sort of discursive democracy that is often appealed to is ancient Athens, in which all citizens, albeit by no means all inhabitants, of that city-state gathered together in order to discuss the problems facing it and how these should be addressed.[4] Another model, adopted by Habermas, is the 'bourgeois public sphere' of eighteenth-century Europe, this being treated as holding political authorities to account through public discussion (Habermas 1989), albeit again by no means involving the whole population.[5] However, while social scientists have often assumed some kind of discursive democracy as the backdrop to their work, in political science and elsewhere there has been considerable debate about both its viability and its desirability.

A useful starting point is to note that quite a lot of sociological research on the media denies the *current* existence of discursive democracy in Western societies, and perhaps also denies that this form of political organization is possible within present social structures: their capitalistic and/or neo-imperialistic nature is viewed as intrinsically anti-democratic in this sense.[6] Here, the media are portrayed not as feeding a process of open public deliberation but as tending 'faithfully and impartially, to reproduce symbolically the existing structure of power in society's institutional order' (Hall *et al.* 1978: 58). It is worth noting, though, that implicit in such analyses, very often, is the assumption that there is a form of society, achievable at least in principle, in which discursive democracy could operate or be approximated. Moreover, this capacity for discursive democracy is frequently treated as central to the desirability of that new society. In other words, these critics usually retain the *ideal* of discursive democracy even while denying its current *reality*.

By contrast, there are other commentators who dispute the general viability and/or the desirability of discursive democracy. Sometimes, in doing this they appeal to what are taken to be the realities of large, complex national or international states, arguing that in societies of this kind people cannot all be brought together, or otherwise enabled to participate, on an equal footing in the discussion of policy issues. Also influential are arguments against discursive democracy that cite human nature: it is suggested that the role of citizen assumed by this model is not one that most human beings could, or would want to, play. They do not have the necessary intelligence and knowledge; and/or they do not wish to be full-time citizens, or perhaps even part-time ones. It is argued that the model assumes cognitive and motivational capacities — and inclinations — that most people do not have, and are never likely to acquire. Moreover, sometimes this

---

4 On the background to Athenian democracy, see Davies 1978.
5 There is a considerable literature on Habermas's account of the public sphere. For a useful discussion of the historical accuracy of his account, see Raymond 1999. For discussion of the more sociological and philosophical aspects, see Calhoun 1992 and Crossley and Roberts 2004.
6 Indeed, Habermas himself argues that the bourgeois public sphere declined, being subjected to increasing commercial and/or state control.

argument takes an evaluative turn, to the effect that what is involved in the discursive democracy model is an attempt to legislate a particular mode of life, in which politics (and politics of a particular kind) is central, against other ways of living that have at least equal value, such as those focused on religious belief, the value of personal relationships, sport, literature, art, music and so on.[7]

In my view, these arguments against discursive democracy have considerable force. At the same time, their implications are often exaggerated. It is clear that the role the public plays in policymaking in Western societies today does not approximate closely to that implied in most conceptions of discursive democracy. However, there is a serious danger of overlooking the extent to which public discussion of policy issues and options *is* possible, *and actually takes place*, within present-day Western societies. A comparative perspective, and/or recognition of the full range of the scale implied by this ideal – from absence of discursive democracy to its complete achievement – ought to serve as a precaution against this tendency. What happens in these societies may not be as extensive, as open to the whole population and particular groups within it, or as effective in shaping state policies as we might wish, but it is greater in all these respects than in many other societies, past and present.

The argument that discursive democracy is either not viable in principle or is not desirable as an ideal also contains some truth. It does seem unwise to expect that participation in public policy discourse should be at the centre of everyone's life, since there are many other interests and ideals that people can have, and no one can be or do everything. Furthermore, we should not assume that the wider the participation the better will be the resulting policies. There is a fundamental problem here to do with the idea of discursive democracy, not just about assuming equality of cognitive and other capacities among the citizenry, but also with the assumption that such democracy involves a process that will lead to true conclusions. Habermas adopts this sort of model, with the idea that if we can approximate the ideal-speech situation in public deliberations this will maximize the chances of policy being based upon true, or at least consensual, value judgements.[8]

In relation to matters of fact, this seems to assume that public discussion of policy could operate on the same model that academic discussions are often supposed to follow, in which all participants are primarily seeking to discover the truth about some matter. Yet this is unlikely to be the case in public deliberations about policy, where various interests are operating even more strongly on

---

7 For useful discussions of many of these issues, in relation to the media, see Fiske 1989; Dahlgren and Sparks 1992; Curran 1997; and Corner and Pels 2003. Some of these points were raised long ago from a different angle and in a very different context by Graham Wallas and Walter Lippmann: see Wallas 1920 and Lippmann 1927. Part of Lippmann's argument was that government must be guided by committees of social science experts since public opinion could not be relied upon as a basis for wise policymaking.

8 For discussion of some of the complexities surrounding notions of 'the public', 'public opinion' and 'the public sphere', see Price 1992; Gitlin 1998; Calhoun 1992; and Crossley and Roberts 2004.

what people are motivated to argue and are willing to accept. Also, there is an assumption in academic discussions that all the relevant evidence can be made more or less explicit across personal differences in background experience and political or ethical commitment; whereas, for various reasons, this is not true of much of the relevant factual evidence in public discussions of policy. For example, some of it will depend upon distinctive forms of experience and/or on expert judgements that cannot be made completely accessible to those without that experience or expertise.

As regards value questions, there are good reasons to doubt whether, even in principle, there are single true answers to these, in the way that there are to factual questions, or whether a wide consensus can be reached about most of them. Instead, there will often be several more or less reasonable answers, because different frameworks of assumptions can be adopted. These differences in framework reflect both that there are conflicts even among the values that most people share, and that how people resolve these conflicts will often reflect their social roles and locations. Given this, there is no guarantee that public discussion of policies, which necessarily implicate values, will converge upon some true or agreed conclusion even in the long run, in the way that can reasonably be assumed, under certain conditions, in the case of factual matters. What is in the common interest is likely to be open to diverse reasonable interpretations.[9]

However, none of this undercuts the benefits to be gained from the public exposure of policy arguments to scrutiny and debate from a wide number of angles. Generally speaking, this seems likely to improve the quality of the decisions made. Moreover, social science can make an important contribution to such deliberations through opening up to question some of the factual assumptions on which participants rely, and by resolving disputes about factual matters where this is possible. From this point of view, accurate reporting of social science findings, along with provision of information about how they were produced, is an important responsibility of the media, though not the only one.

My conclusion, then, is that we need to be cautious in how far we push criticisms of discursive democracy and of the contribution that social science can make to it. It is not that there is no democratic deliberation about policy issues, but rather that in practice it falls short of what is often taken as the ideal. And this ideal should not be fully or exclusively endorsed. At the same time, public deliberation about policy issues is of value, and social science can help to correct factual errors in such discussions, some of which could be very consequential.

9 I have presented these arguments more fully elsewhere; see Hammersley 2005a.

HOW SHOULD LAY AUDIENCES RESPOND TO SOCIAL SCIENCE RESEARCH?

Built into the assumptions I used to frame the inquiry in this book is the idea that audiences – particularly journalists but by implication also their listeners, viewers, and readers – should accept at face value the validity of the research findings presented by the Review. In other words, a rather passive reception was assumed. The idea is that the media will 'receive' and 're-transmit' the messages coming from research, and that the public will accept those messages and incorporate them into their attitudes. This probably also underlies many complaints by social scientists about how the media treat their work. Thus, David Gillborn's (1998) criticism of newspaper coverage of the Review is, in large part, that journalists interpreted the Review's findings for themselves and re-presented these in terms that he judges to be racist.

There is a parallel here with the attitude that, until recently, governed research into the general public's understanding of natural science. In recurrent campaigns about this issue, for example by the Royal Society (1985), it was argued that advanced industrial societies need increased numbers of workers in science-based industries as well as a scientifically informed citizenry. And a considerable amount of research was done that documented the low level of scientific knowledge, or the false interpretations of natural phenomena, prevalent among the general public. However, more recently, this approach has come to be criticized for operating on a 'deficit' conception of lay knowledge, and for largely taking for granted scientists' own views about the nature of scientific inquiry, the knowledge it produces, and how this ought to shape policy and practice. In place of the previous contrast between scientists' knowledge, on the one hand – largely portrayed as universally valid and unsullied by social assumptions and interests – and public ignorance and prejudice, on the other, there has been an emphasis on the heterogeneous and socially constructed character of all knowledge, including that of scientists (see, for example, Irwin and Wynne 1996 and Irwin and Michael 2003). And this has led not only to recognition that lay audiences will always make sense of scientific knowledge for themselves, drawing on background knowledge and experience, but also to the implication that this is desirable.

This sort of critique could be applied at least as convincingly to ideas about the proper 'reception' of social science, and even more forcefully if we accept that the findings of social researchers are generally less well established than those of natural scientists. Certainly, we cannot ignore the fact that social scientific knowledge is fallible, and that there are other sources of valid factual information about the social world. Nor would most sociologists deny that they are part of the world they study, and therefore are themselves subject to the influence of a variety of preconceptions and interests. And this suggests that both journalists and their audiences may need to interrogate the results of social research, rather than simply accepting these on scientific authority. Moreover, this will require them to call on knowledge from other sources, including their own experience. So, we could reasonably see journalists as having a role in providing further resources for such interrogation on the part of audiences, and even in carrying out some of that interrogation themselves. And in doing this they would, necessarily, draw on lay understandings and sources of knowledge that social scientists may regard as defective.

An equally important point is that we must recognize that accuracy of reporting is not the only criterion by which journalists' reports are assessed within news organizations, and therefore not the only consideration that they must take into account in producing their reports. At least as important, as I have noted at many points in this study, is whether what they produce will attract and retain the attention and interest of audiences. Moreover, one way to do this is to be entertaining, and this may have significant implications for what is taken as the top line of a story and for how reports are written. With increased competitive pressure on news organizations over the past few decades, emphasis on this requirement has grown. And it is worth noting that it may also encourage journalists to offer what will appeal to their audience's prejudices, in that to some degree media organizations carve out market niches that represent particular politico-cultural orientations. It is in light of all this that many sociologists studying the media have come to question journalists' claims to objectivity, though equally influential here has been social constructionist scepticism about its very possibility.

While we may well deplore the results of these pressures within and on the media, and perhaps especially when we feel that our research has been misrepresented, it is important to recognize that journalists cannot ignore them. And if we take account of the arguments discussed earlier about the impoverished conception of human life that is built into the discursive democracy model – one that treats people as no more than narrowly rational political and economic actors, rather than as sensuous human beings who enjoy many modes of experiencing the world and of interacting with one another – we may have to treat these other journalistic criteria as something more than deviations from an ideal. Perhaps po-faced rejections of media reports as biased and/or sensationalist, like the dismissal of some newspapers as not 'serious', must simply be laughed away.[10]

Once again, there is some truth in these arguments. There is no reason to suppose that social scientists can guarantee the validity of their findings or that they have a monopoly on knowledge of the social world. It is also important not to treat journalism as if it had the same character as social research.[11] While the two activities have quite a lot in common, their purposes are significantly different, and they are carried out under quite discrepant social arrangements. At the same time, we must take care not to deny the findings of social research

10 Fiske 1992: 49 suggests that the dominant tone of much tabloid journalism is 'sceptical laughter'. Langer 1998 provides an analysis of entertainment-oriented news. See also Ang 1985; McGuigan 1992; Fairclough 1995.

11 For a critique of 'the journalistic field' which *does* seem to make this assumption see Bourdieu 1998.

all legitimate authority or to dismiss the *ideal* of objectivity as it applies both to journalism and social science.

While lay responses to social research must not be automatically dismissed because they do not match what is taken to be social scientific knowledge, it is important to remember that they may be based on false assumptions and/or on sham reasoning. And while it is true that science is also subject to the play of interests, misconceptions, foolishness, etc., it operates via institutional means that are specifically designed to reduce the chances of error from these sources. Generally speaking, there are no similar means in the case of lay knowledge.[12] It is not that lay people have no interest in what is true and false, it is that this is often subordinated to other concerns, and pursuit of the latter does not always facilitate gaining knowledge. There are losses as well as gains involved in specialized research, but it is important not to underplay the gains.

It is also worth saying that the shift to emphasizing entertainment within the media does not derive simply from celebration of other values than those built into the 'serious' worlds of politics and research. In our present society, it is fostered by powerful forces that can make a profit out of it, and for whom making a profit is a very serious business indeed, perhaps the only one that counts. And this points to the fact that the public sphere is as much a site for struggle among various interest groups, representing wider social forces, as it is a forum for rational public discussion or even a cultural playground. In some ways, the journalistic ideal of objectivity amounts to resistance against these trends. While it is no doubt true, as social scientists have pointed out, that this ideal is also used to protect the interests and status of journalists themselves, and is by no means always adhered to in practice, its value in this respect should not be denied.[13]

One conclusion that we ought to draw from all this, it seems to me, is that the media do have a responsibility to present the findings of social research as clearly and accurately as possible, and this requires those findings not to be obscured by journalists' own inferences and elaborations, or anyone else's. Here, in particular, the journalistic ideal of objectivity must be sustained. Media reports of the Review varied a good deal in how successful they were in this respect, in my judgement. Some of them provided relatively clear information about key findings from the Review, others filtered the information they provided

---

12 The most obvious exception to this is legal procedures.
13 Objectivity is not a simple concept. What I mean by the term here is a commitment to supply the relevant facts about whatever issue is being reported, and to take whatever precautions are feasible in avoiding error, whether the source of error comes from outside of or from within the news production process. It is worth noting that there is a conflict between social scientists' demands that the media report their findings accurately and the tendency of much recent work to question whether journalists can ever be 'objective', indeed to treat claims to objectivity as an occupational ideology (see, for example, Berkowitz 1997: xi–xii; Allan 1999). Also relevant here is the movement in the US towards so-called 'public journalism', which explicitly abandons notions of neutrality in favour of serving the public interest. On this, see Glasser and Craft 1998.

through headlines and leaders that misrepresented the main findings, while one or two gave little clear sense of those findings or a quite false indication of their character.

At the same time, we cannot reasonably expect social science research findings to be simply presented in their own terms by the media as absolutely authoritative. At the very least, it is the responsibility of journalists to locate these findings in the context of other sources of information and judgement about the same issue, and to present research findings in ways that are intelligible and of interest to their audiences. Moreover, if the media are to play the role ascribed to them in some versions of discursive democracy, for example that put forward by Dewey in which the task of journalism is to provide 'intelligence' to citizens, then they would need to interrogate the findings of social research *much more* searchingly, seeking to identify threats to validity and discount exaggerated claims (Dewey 1946; see Westbrook 1991: 54–5). None of the reports, not even the lengthy ones provided in the *Times Educational Supplement*, match this requirement. However, this may be to expect too much not just of journalists but also of citizens.

As all this makes clear, the question of how the media ought to deal with research evidence is caught up in more fundamental questions about what the function of newspapers, broadcast news and current affairs programmes can and should be; and beyond this about the nature of democracy, the role of the citizen and how sound policy decisions can best be made.

LIMITS TO THE AUTHORITY OF SOCIAL SCIENCE

In the previous two sections, I have suggested that, despite various qualifications, we should still see social science as capable of making a contribution to the public discussion of policies, that this is of value, and that it is the responsibility (albeit not the *only* responsibility) of the media to report its findings accurately. However, we must ask whether there are limits to the contribution of social research, in principle or in practice; and what the implications of these may be for how the media should report their findings. Furthermore, against this background, I will examine the Review's contribution to public knowledge.

Given my Weberian orientation, not surprisingly, I believe that we need to maintain the distinction between factual and value claims. In the case of the former, the limits to the contribution of social science were indicated in the previous section: probably even more than natural scientists, social researchers need to recognize that their conclusions are fallible, and that they do not have a monopoly on knowledge – that there are diverse available sources of experience and information about the social world. What follows from this, among other things, is that there must be clarity about how reliable (in the commonsense meaning of that term) particular knowledge claims produced by social scientists are, so that they can be properly assessed when they contradict information from other sources. At the same time, it is intrinsic to the nature of science, in my view, that social scientists ought to be able to argue that what is accepted as sound knowledge by the relevant research community is less likely to be false than knowledge claims coming from other sources. We should note, though, that some social science research communities do not currently operate in ways that closely approximate to what would be required to make this claim about reliability convincing.

As regards value conclusions, like Weber I do not believe that social scientists can reasonably claim any distinctive authority in relation to these.[14] It is true that researchers have access to a better command of much (though, as we have seen, not all) of the relevant factual material. It may also be true that doing research tends to inculcate some habits, for example careful argumentation, that may help in reaching sound value conclusions, enabling researchers to recognize hidden assumptions behind particular arguments that others tend to overlook. However, there is little involved in being a social scientist that, for instance, enables one to engage better than others in the careful weighing of different value concerns, both intrinsic and prudential, which is surely essential in coming to good policy decisions. Indeed, it could be argued that there are respects in which the work of social science makes its practitioners, like other intellectuals, rather ill suited to this kind of deliberation (see Hammersley 2005a) by comparison, for example, with those professions which, in dealing with clients, cannot but engage in this.

Nevertheless, social science findings are often phrased in ways that are either explicitly evaluative or are open to interpretation in this way (with authors doing little to discourage such interpretations). Some terms routinely used by social scientists are ambiguous in this respect, notable examples relevant to the area of research covered by the Review include 'inequality', 'discrimination' and 'racism'. These concepts are treated as if they were primarily descriptive in character, in the sense that explicit justification for evaluative implications is rarely presented, but in practice they are used only to identify what are taken by the analyst to be *illegitimate* differences and processes of differentiation. And there is often little clarity about the value assumptions involved. Moreover, it is not uncommon for explicit evaluations and recommendations to be derived by researchers from use of these terms, in the final sections or chapters of their work (see Foster *et al.* 1996 and 2000). Elsewhere, I have argued that it is an important requirement of a research community that it allows knowledge claims to be assessed exclusively for their validity, irrespective of whatever political, ethical or other implications might conceivably be derived from them on the basis of particular value assumptions (Hammersley 2005a). This is important in order to maximize the chances of reaching sound factual conclusions. Correspondingly, it seems to me that social scientists can make a significant public contribution, essential to discursive democracy, in reminding their audiences that value conclusions never follow automatically from factual premises, even those produced

14 For an account which captures the sophistication of Weber's position particularly well, see Bruun 1972.

by social science; and that, often, the value assumptions involved in routinized evaluations and prescriptions need to be made explicit and justified, since they are not a matter of general agreement.

If social scientists do not warn against drawing value conclusions immediately from research findings, and especially if they actually put forward such conclusions as research-based, then in my judgement this amounts to a form of scientism: in other words, excessive authority is being given to or claimed for research findings. Now, of course, it is far from being the case that social science is routinely attributed great authority by the media, by governments, or by the public at large. But this does not alter the fact that any demand on the part of social scientists that the media treat their findings as authoritative, when these amount to value conclusions, is illegitimate. This is true, not least, because it infringes the requirement of discursive democracy that participants do not make excessive claims for the authority of what they can contribute. If everyone were to do that, reaching decisions would become impossible via discursive means.

Of course, it may be argued that, even if this point is true in principle, given the imperfect state of discursive democracy in Western, and other, societies today, in practice there is some justification for social scientists to overstep their authority in this fashion. If the situation is closer to one where government and media, or the very mode of social organization of these societies, imposes a dominant ideology on the public, then surely any attempt on the part of social scientists to subvert this would be justifiable. There may be some force in this argument, though there are questions about the existence and role of any dominant ideology (see Abercrombie *et al.* 1980 and 1990). Furthermore, we should note its Machiavellian character: it proposes misuse of social science for what are deemed to be good purposes. In effect, the argument here, characteristic of some forms of critical social science, is that true democracy is not possible before fundamental structural change has taken place; and its corollary is that revolutionary activity must therefore be carried out by other means than democratic participation, including through 'ideological struggle'. But there is a serious question not just about the prospects of success but also about the scale of the damage likely to be done in this cause.

While I would not want to rule out Machiavellianism as always wrong, it is important to remember that because of its very character it makes much greater demands on us for justification than many other ethical stances. For one thing, it requires, in this case, very strong grounds for claiming that social scientists can know better than others what is in the common interest. And, for reasons already explained, I doubt such grounds are available. A second point is that it amounts to claiming that ends can justify means, allowing the use of methods that would normally be ruled out as unacceptable (Lukes 1985). While in this case the dangers and damage are not so obviously deplorable as in some others, notably that of terrorism, nevertheless anything that undermines trustworthy claims to knowledge is likely to render not just current society but any future society less capable of both social justice and prosperity. Of course, there may be those who deny this, who see the only proper function of social scientists today as to subvert all claims to knowledge, these being regarded as intrinsically hierarchical and oppressive, but in my view they are labouring under a deluded sense of the beneficial character of ignorance and illusion.

THE CASE OF THE REVIEW

Against the background of these limits on the contribution that social science can make to public discussion of policy, in the remainder of this section I want to look at the case of the Review, evaluating it as a source of authoritative social science knowledge. In many ways it is an illuminating example given that, even if not representative in all respects, it exemplifies the character of much recent social and educational research aimed at informing policymaking or practice.

We can start by noting that one of the Review's two possible main messages, identified in the previous chapter, is a practical evaluation: 'colour-blind' policies have failed. While this claim could be interpreted as a hypothetical or conditional evaluation, and therefore as basically factual in character, this is not how it is presented in the Review. The most we could say is that there is ambiguity about whether it is factual or evaluative; and, as I indicated, this sort of ambiguity is characteristic of many of the stated findings of social science research in this field and some others. Moreover, there are places in the Review where the authors put forward explicit practical evaluations. At one point they write: 'One of the clearest findings of this review is that if ethnic diversity is ignored, if differences in educational achievement and experience are not examined, then considerable injustices will be sanctioned and enormous potential wasted' (Gillborn and Gipps 1996: 7). And they also draw the conclusion from their review that the issue of ethnic inequalities in education should be moved back up the policy agenda. In the executive summary they state: 'During [the period since the Swann Report], issues of race and equal opportunity have tended to slip from policy agendas: this review demonstrates the need for this to change' (p. 1). This is clearly a prescriptive conclusion, in the sense of indicating what ought to be done. Moreover, it is claimed to follow directly from the research evidence that has been reviewed.[15] And, in this respect and others, the Review accurately reflects the character of most of the research in the field it covers. This research often presents practical evaluations of, and sometimes prescriptions for, the situations and processes it investigates, and does so as if they were factual matters (see Foster *et al.* 1996).

So, the conclusion that 'colour-blind' policies have failed – which, as we saw, was the message in terms of which claims about media bias in reporting the Review had most cogency – seems to be evaluative in character, and is therefore,

---

15 The lead author later reiterated these evaluations and prescriptions in the wake of the Macpherson Report on the police investigation of the murder of Stephen Lawrence; see Blair and Gillborn 1999 and Blair *et al.* 1999. See also Gillborn 2001.

in my view, itself illegitimate. Furthermore, the evaluative orientation of the Review extends beyond this conclusion. As I noted, the Review is structured by the belief that any lower level of average educational achievement on the part of ethnic minority groups is a product of some obstacle to their achievement within the education system. And we must ask about the status of this interpretive policy. Is it factual in character, and based on empirical evidence coming from research? Or does it rely upon value commitments about who is responsible for any ethnic inequalities in education?

This is a complicated question. In my view, explanations for any phenomenon necessarily depend upon using a value framework to determine what would and would not be relevant factors. We could never provide an explanation that included all of the factors that had a causal role in producing a phenomenon, since the number of these is always very large, if not infinite. After all, any particular cause we select will itself have been produced by other factors, and the latter were, in turn, themselves causal products, and so on. So, in developing an explanation we rely upon some framework of assumptions about what would be value-relevant explanatory factors. And this means, of course, that social scientists may put forward quite different explanations for the same phenomenon even when they agree more generally about what caused what – because they are operating on the basis of different relevancies.[16]

Given this, two requirements are placed upon social scientists putting forward explanations. First, they must make the relevancies by which they selected explanatory factors explicit. Second, they must not claim that the explanation they are presenting is the only true one: they must recognize that other true explanations are possible, based on different value relevancies, without implying that all candidate explanations are as valid as one another.

Now, the Review does not meet the first of these requirements entirely, and it certainly does not meet the second. Of course, it could be argued that this is acceptable because the assumptions which underlie the interpretative policy adopted by the Review's authors are in line with those of most researchers working in the field being reviewed, as well as with the stance of most anti-racists; and that they fit with a more general shift in attitude towards the operation of the public services across the political spectrum. The latter emphasizes the obligation of those services to 'deliver' what they claim to offer, to meet their targets, and so on.[17] Any failure on their part to do this is treated as culpable; thus, claims by practitioners that failure results from external constraints are liable to be dismissed as illegitimate excuses. This is the accountability ethos of the new public management. However, this value-relevance framework is clearly at odds with another still influential way of thinking, the competition model, according

---

16 It is important to remember the distinction between selecting what causal factors are value-relevant and selecting factors and treating them as causes solely on the basis of value relevance.

17 In a later book co-authored by David Gillborn a central concept is rationing, and this too seems to operate within the same discourse: Gillborn and Youdell 2000: 1–4.

to which the educational achievements of individuals reflect their own capacities and efforts, as shaped by their home and community backgrounds, an idea that informed much media reporting of the Review. There may be other perspectives as well, and social scientists cannot adjudicate among them. Yet the Review treats the distribution model as if it were the only legitimate one, and as if it had been validated by research.[18]

So, what I am arguing here is that the Review was not just evaluative in one of its conclusions – that 'colour-blind' policies have failed – but in a more thoroughgoing way. It was structured in terms of a particular conception of equality of opportunity, this being treated not just as one currently influential value-relevance framework but rather as the only appropriate one: the authors of the Review simply assume, presumably as a matter of political commitment, that if there are lower levels of average educational performance on the part of any ethnic minorities this is because resources have not been equally distributed and/or because there has been illegitimate discrimination against these groups.

In line with this orientation, as already noted, David Gillborn's criticism of newspaper coverage of the Review was not solely concerned with inaccuracy but also with what he takes to be the racism displayed in some reports.[19] And he uses the term 'racist' in a way that implies that its reference is determinate, rather than being relative to the value framework one adopts. As we saw in the Introduction, this is also true of much sociological research on the treatment of ethnic minorities in the media: the concern there was not just with bias away from the truth but also with bias in the sense of deviation from what the commentator

18 Both the distribution and competition models are metaphorical, and even the best metaphors only illuminate some aspects of a phenomenon, and potentially include irrelevant or misleading features. The competition model tells us something about the factors involved in differential educational achievement, concentrating on those to do with individual pupils and various factors which shape their intellectual and motivational capacities. Furthermore, in a credentialist society education can be turned into a race, with winners and losers. At the same time, this is not intrinsic to the nature of education, and particularly not at the aggregate level: ethnic groups do not compete as teams. The distribution model focuses on factors that the competition model neglects: it highlights the role of those working in the education system, and its policies and structures, both in determining what counts as education and educational success, and in allocating some of the resources that affect the chances of success. At the same time, it is misleading to think of education as something that can be distributed to people, or delivered. Nor are educational credentials distributed in any straightforward sense of that term (beyond the statistical, which is not part of the metaphor). Moreover, the distribution model neglects those factors shaping educational achievement that the competition model highlights. It probably does not make much sense to ask which of these metaphors is the correct one, they each illuminate different aspects of the same phenomenon, both of which will probably need to be taken into account for most purposes.

19 And this is very much in the tradition of research on media bias: for example the Glasgow University Media Group's landmark studies *Bad News* and *More Bad News* criticized coverage not just for inaccuracy but also for being 'skewed against the interest of the working class and organised labour' (Glasgow University Media Group 1980: 400), these two forms of bias being treated as correlated.

took to be justice. To repeat the point, this is to treat research as validating value conclusions, in this case about what should count as racism, when this is beyond its capacity and its authority.

So, in my view, this evaluative orientation on the part of the authors of the Review amounts to their stepping over the line between research and political activity, in effect using research to serve political purposes (see Hammersley 1995). This is illegitimate, first of all, because it gives the impression that research can in itself justify value conclusions, when it cannot do this (in the absence of some single, consensual or objective value framework). A second problem is that gearing research to political purposes in this way is likely to lead to factual error: it will encourage acceptance on inadequate evidence of factual conclusions that are desirable from the authors' political perspective; and/or it will discourage reaching conclusions that are judged to be politically undesirable even when the evidence for them is strong. This is not to say that error always results, simply that the chances of this are increased.[20]

In light of this, let me turn to an assessment of the factual component of the conclusions reached by the Review. Recent discussions about evidence-based policymaking and practice have presented the role of research as being to determine whether or not particular policies work, or which policy works best.[21] Clearly, the claim that 'colour-blind' policies have failed fits this model. So one way to begin is by comparing what advocates of the notion of evidence-based practice demand of research with what is offered in the Review.

Writings about evidence-based policymaking and practice portray it as based on research evidence that has been brought together in so-called 'systematic' reviews. What these require is an exhaustive search of the research literature, the use of explicit relevance and validity criteria to determine which studies should be included, and the employment of some systematic means of synthesizing findings from the studies. In these terms, the Review is not systematic: it does not report use of any procedure that would have more or less ensured exhaustive coverage, it is not very explicit about relevance and especially not about validity criteria, and what is provided is an *interpretation* of the findings rather than a formal synthesis.

Now, it should be said that there are good reasons to question the desirability of these requirements. They involve a questionable model of both research itself and of the task of reviewing, one that rests on the positivist assumption that it is possible and beneficial to reduce both these activities to the following of explicit procedures. They also ignore the trade-offs involved in carrying out a review, and the importance of careful interpretation of the findings of the studies being synthesized (Hammersley 2001 and 2005c). Nevertheless, these requirements do

---

20 For evidence of this across the whole field of research on educational inequalities, see Foster *et al.* 1996.

21 See Davies *et al.* 2000; Trinder with Reynolds 2000; Thomas and Pring 2004. Here, too, there is often ambiguity between conditional and practical evaluations: 'what works' tends to be treated as if it were solely a technical matter, rather than as also involving value assumptions about what counts as 'working' or 'failing'.

point to issues that need to be given attention by anyone reviewing a research field, and not all of them are addressed effectively by the authors of the Review. For example, in terms of relevance, as noted earlier, the authors adopt a definition of equity which they acknowledge is 'hotly contested' (Gillborn and Gipps 1996: 10) without examining what conclusions would follow if alternative senses of that term were employed. In effect, they assume that equality of average educational outcome between ethnic groups is the sole evaluative standard relevant to their inquiry and that it is a desirable one. Furthermore, the authors give the impression that the fact that, in recent years, research on the education of ethnic minority children has focused on factors internal to the education system reflects evidence that these factors are the most important ones, whereas it is clear that this shift was a product of change in the ideological climate, both within research communities and in the wider realm of public policy. Indeed, the motivation behind this focus is made clear by the authors of the Review in a later article, where they comment: 'We were also mindful of the fact that work on home and community influences in this field has historically been used to divert attention away from any shortcomings in the education system itself (Troyna, 1993)' (Gillborn and Gipps 1998: 632). This reveals that a concern with political impact shaped the very structure of the Review, and there is little doubt that it has also shaped much of the research in the field reviewed.[22]

As regards validity, some advocates of evidence-based policymaking and practice insist that wherever possible the studies included in a review should have involved the use of randomized controlled trials, this method being treated as the gold standard. A key exemplar is the kind of drug trial often used in medicine, where patients are randomly allocated to receive the drug being tested or a placebo, and the subsequent fortunes of treatment and control groups are compared in order to assess how effective the drug is, what its side effects are, and so on.[23] The rationale for emphasis on this research strategy is that random allocation of relatively large samples to treatment and control groups rules out confounding variables, putting us in a position to reach cogent conclusions about the effects of different treatments or policies. However, this is not an approach employed by any of the studies included in the Review.

Once again, there are good reasons for doubting the wisdom of this requirement. We can question whether randomized controlled trials are as powerful as some of their advocates claim, and we can challenge any suggestion that there is no other way in which we can identify the effects of policies convincingly (see Hammersley 2005b). At the same time, emphasis on the value of this method does point to an important problem that we all face in deciding whether a policy works or has failed in some specified respect. We need a way of distinguishing

22 For a more detailed discussion of these aspects of the Review, see Hammersley 2002: ch. 7.
23 Many trials examine several treatments, not just one. See Oakley's argument for the extension of this kind of research to fields of social and educational policy: Oakley 2000. See also Chalmers 2003.

the effects of the policy from those of other factors that are operating, perhaps in interaction with one another. Any study concerned with determining whether a policy 'works', or indeed with explaining something more generally, must have an effective way of dealing with this issue. Yet, to put it mildly, qualitative research, on which the authors of the Review place greatest emphasis, is not currently very strong in this department (see Gomm *et al*. 2000).

Looking specifically at the question of whether 'colour-blind' policies have failed, we would need, first of all, a reasonably clear definition of what form these policies take. No explicit definition of ' "colour-blind" policy' is provided in the Review, but what seems to be intended is an approach in which teachers and other school personnel do not vary their treatment of pupils according to the latter's ethnicity. Two obvious alternative policies would be where teachers treat members of some ethnic group in a way that is intended to disadvantage or to favour them. The first is typically labelled 'discrimination', though it might be better to call it 'negative discrimination'; and the second policy is one possible interpretation of the term 'positive discrimination'. However, neither of these is, I am sure, what the authors of the Review are recommending as an alternative to 'colour-blind' policy.

The problem here is that, as indicated earlier, the term 'discrimination' has both descriptive and evaluative senses. In descriptive terms, it refers simply to acting on the basis of some consideration that differentiates people. On this definition, we discriminate not only if we treat people so as to disadvantage or favour some among them, but also if we award prizes to winners in races on the basis of their performance, treat people at the front of queues first on the grounds of fairness, and so on. By contrast, as already indicated, the evaluative sense of 'discrimination' is now almost always negative: what it refers to is differential treatment on the basis of some consideration that is deemed by the commentator to be unjustifiable. And, again, the phrase 'positive discrimination' is often interpreted by its critics as the mirror image of this: as the favouring of some category of person on illegitimate grounds. Clearly, the crucial issue here is what are and are not appropriate grounds for differential treatment of people in the context of the activity concerned.

What the authors of the Review are arguing for, presumably, is treatment of pupils by the education system in such a way as to take account of factors that *illegitimately* disadvantage members of ethnic minority groups. These could include the need to acquire facility in a second language, and also the effects of racism and of wider social inequalities on the differential capacities of children from various ethnic groups to succeed within the education system. Thus the Review's criticism of 'colour-blind' policies is that the education system does not take account of all the factors that depress the performance of pupils from particular ethnic minorities that *ought* to be taken into account if treatment is to be equitable.

It is worth noting that there are two rather different ways in which disadvantaging factors could be tackled. The compensatory strategy provides extra resources so as to enable groups that are 'under-performing' to improve their level of achievement. By contrast, what we might call the restructuring strategy modifies existing features of the education system – in other words, it requires changing some of the rules of the game, for example curricular and/or assessment practices – so as to remove any feature that illegitimately represents a higher barrier for members of particular ethnic groups.

However, it is important to recognize that what is and is not a relevant consideration that ought to be taken into account in judgements about equity is a complicated and contentious matter, and is often open to reasonable disagreement (see Williams 1962 and Mackinnon 1986). As a result, both of the strategies outlined above, and perhaps especially that concerned with restructuring the system, are almost always open to reasonable challenge. Moreover, the grounds for challenge concern not simply whether one group is being wrongly advantaged at the expense of others, but also considerations beyond those of equity: about what should be taught and how it should be assessed in particular sectors of the education system, about how effective in terms of facilitating learning of particular kinds various organizational practices are, such as banding and setting, and so on.

These questions about what are and are not relevant considerations in dealing with ethnic minority pupils, and why, are not addressed by the authors of the Review, nor by most of the studies they cover. This makes it very difficult to be sure what would count as illegitimate 'colour-blind' treatment, and what in specific terms the authors of the Review are recommending as a more appropriate strategy.[24] Yet we need to be clear about both if we are to be able to come to any reasonable conclusion about the success or failure of 'colour-blind' policies.

Putting this on one side, the next requirement in evaluating such policies would be to identify cases where they and contrasting policies are in operation, and to compare the levels of achievement of relevant ethnic groups under these different conditions. However, as far as I can tell, there is no study among those covered by the Review that carries out any comparison of this kind, nor do the authors claim that this has been done. Instead, almost all of the research reviewed is concerned with charting the performance, or comparing the treatment, of pupils from different ethnic groups within parts of the education system, on the basis of which claims are made about the effects of differential treatment on aggregate educational outcomes.[25] Moreover, many of the qualitative studies discussed argue that there is unconscious or inadvertent discrimination on the part of teachers against some ethnic minority groups. For example, the authors of the Review point to studies which have suggested that teachers operate on the basis of stereotypes of Asian and African Caribbean pupils which lead to differential treatment and differential outcomes (Gillborn and Gipps 1996: 54–5). This raises the question of whether colour-blind policies are actually currently in operation within the British education system, or at least about whether they are

---

24 David Gillborn has addressed the latter issue elsewhere, though without providing the sort of clarification of value assumptions that I am suggesting is required: Gillborn 1995.
25 For discussion of some of the problems with such inferences, see Foster *et al.* 1996.

being applied consistently. And if they are *not*, then we cannot reasonably draw conclusions about whether or not they work on the basis of aggregate evidence about performance within that system.[26]

Of course, it would be possible to examine those situations where these policies *have* been properly applied, but as already indicated none of the studies discussed seems to meet this requirement.[27] Furthermore, many of those studies have been subjected to criticism for lacking adequate descriptions of the cases investigated, for over-generalizing, and for failing to address the issue of competing explanations effectively (Foster 1990b, 1991, 1993a–c). These criticisms are given no weight in the Review. Instead, they are dismissed as resulting from reliance on an unattainable requirement of 'absolute proof', and an implied bias arising from a concern with defending teachers – though neither of these charges is substantiated (Gillborn and Gipps 1996: 56).[28] Not just in terms of the exhaustiveness requirement of systematic reviews, but also according to the canons of traditional reviewing, this amounts to neglect of relevant literature.

In the Review there is some evidence reported of more positive discrimination, presumably of a compensatory kind. For example, the authors write that:

> The London Borough of Tower Hamlets houses almost a quarter of all Bangladeshi children aged 5–15 in England. The borough has made a priority of identifying and targeting the needs of Bangladeshi pupils, especially through the use of Section 11 funds. Recent years have seen improvements in the average exam scores of pupils in each of the borough's ethnic groups, but the achievements of Bangladeshi pupils are especially dramatic ...; as a group, Bangladeshi pupils now achieve higher average exam scores than both white and 'Caribbean' pupils in the borough. This is despite experiencing greater levels of economic disadvantage. It would appear, therefore, that Bangladeshi pupils in Tower Hamlets are able to transcend social class relatively more than their white and Caribbean peers; nevertheless, social

26 This goes back to the problem of what is meant by '"colour-blind" policies'. It could refer to a situation where teachers declare their commitment to treating pupils the same irrespective of 'race'/ethnicity, allowing the possibility that in practice they do deal with them differently on these grounds. This would be the situation where teachers operate on the basis of largely unconscious stereotypes. Alternatively, it could refer to the situation where teachers do indeed treat pupils the same irrespective of 'race'/ethnicity but where there is a systematic relationship between this variable and some other one that is relevant to educational performance, with the result that some ethnic groups have a lower level of academic achievement than others.

27 The only recent study I am aware of which does report teachers operating in a 'colour-blind' way is largely dismissed by the authors of the Review (Foster 1990a). Like some other commentators, they imply that Foster simply overlooked discrimination against particular ethnic minorities by setting too high an evidential standard (Gillborn and Gipps 1996: 55). So, in their view, presumably, even in the school that he studied a 'colour-blind' policy was not being effectively applied.

28 For attempts to understand the dispute over Foster's work, see Hammersley 1995: ch. 4 and 2000: ch. 5.

class continues to be strongly associated with achievement in as much as each group attains below the national average. (Gillborn and Gipps 1996: 26)

There are, however, questions about this as evidence for the success of non-'colour-blind' policies. We are told nothing about what 'targeting the needs of Bangladeshi pupils' amounted to here: we have none of the qualitative data about processes that the authors emphasize the value of elsewhere in the Review. Furthermore, we do not know whether it was this policy, rather than some other factor, that was responsible for improvement in the educational achievements of these Bangladeshi children. Despite the claims about 'transcending' social class, no data are presented about the social class profiles of the different ethnic groups in Tower Hamlets. As the authors go on to note, a key factor affecting the performance of these children seems likely to be growing competence in the English language, and to some degree this would probably have occurred without any intervention within the education system. Moreover, while assistance with the learning of English seems likely to increase achievement levels, such assistance was by no means restricted to Tower Hamlets. Finally, even if this form of intervention is generally successful, it does not mean that other kinds of non-'colour-blind' intervention, whether compensatory or restructuring, would be; nor can we assume that because this one is fair and legitimate all others would be. There are, then, very serious weaknesses in the evidence that the authors of the Review rely on in evaluating 'colour-blind' policies.

To a large extent, in attempting to show that there is negative discrimination in the system, or that 'colour-blind' policies are not working, the authors of the Review rely on statistics about differential levels of average achievement among ethnic groups. As noted earlier, their assumption is that if an ethnic minority group is performing at a lower level on average than other ethnic groups, this is *prima facie* evidence of culpable failure on the part of the education system, or at least of the need for action to remedy the situation. This is not a strong argument, however. While such differences should certainly stimulate investigation, they do not provide sufficient grounds for inferring direct or indirect discrimination, or policy failure.

There are several reasons for this, over and above those already mentioned. One is that the samples of pupils from various ethnic groups present in particular areas and schools, and even within the UK as a whole, are not necessarily representative of the ethnic groups concerned. These samples may well have different profiles from one another on other relevant variables, including social class.[29] This is acknowledged in the Review, and emphasized by David Gillborn in the interview

29 There is a more fundamental issue than representativeness here, to do with the very identification of particular ethnic groups. Aside from the problem of how ethnic labels are used across contexts (Sharrock 1974), there is also the question of what should be counted as essential to an ethnic identity. After all, even across the world and over time there may be some stable differences among ethnic groups in social class profiles, assuming that we can give some reasonably stable meaning to 'social class' across this range of application.

reported on BBC television news. However, this factor is taken account of only selectively. We must recognize that not only may the higher social class profile of Indian pupils explain their relative success in particular areas, but also that it is likely that those ethnic groups who have a lower average level of achievement than the white majority do so because they too have a different social class profile. In other words, if one were to allow for social class, one might find that inequalities among ethnic groups would be substantially reduced. At the very least, the effects of this and other relevant variables need to be assessed before research-based conclusions can be reached about discrimination on ethnic grounds. Yet, sound national evidence is not currently available to allow this.

Of course, even if it were true that what appeared to be ethnic inequalities actually arose from social class divisions, it could be argued that this simply indicates that the education system discriminates against working-class children generally. However, this raises a difficult issue that was mentioned earlier: we need to be clear about what are and are not legitimate considerations in treating pupils differently. The fact that some category of pupil achieves at a lower average level than another is not in itself a sign of unacceptable discrimination, either by commission or omission. For example, it may be that if we allowed for differences in academic ability there would be little difference in performance between working class and middle class children, or that the differences would be significantly reduced. The problem is that we are a long way from being able to come to any conclusion about this. One reason is that 'ability' can be defined and measured in different ways, producing different results.[30] It is not just that many intelligence tests can be criticized for favouring middle class children, they can also be criticized for not taking into account all that is involved in academic ability. A second point is that ability is not, and arguably should not be, the only determinant of educational success: motivation and effort are usually included in the meritocratic formula. And these factors are even more difficult to measure than ability. Finally, it is important to recognize that at present we have little reliable national data about the performance of ethnic groups and social classes that takes account even of ability.[31]

Given all this, in my view the only reasonable conclusion to be reached is that we cannot know *on the basis of research evidence* whether or not variations in the average level of performance of ethnic groups is inequitable, or what policies 'work' and should be adopted to deal with the problem. Moreover, even the factual components of these questions, which research *can* address, are a great deal more difficult to tackle than is implied in the Review. Rather than making

---

30 Much the same is true of social class.

31 The problems, and the scope for variation in interpretation, are illustrated in the recent debate about how far meritocracy is operating in Britain, see Saunders 1995, 1996, 1997 and 2002; Marshall and Swift 1993 and 1996; Lampard 1996, Savage and Egerton 1997; Breen and Goldthorpe 1999, 2002, and 2002; and Cooper 2005.

the problems explicit and warning readers that they have serious implications for the reliability of any conclusions reached, the authors of the Review put forward strong evaluative and prescriptive, as well as factual, claims as if these had been validated by research.

In this section, I have suggested that social science may not always operate in a fashion that justifies its contributions to public policy discussions being accorded the authority that it could, in principle, claim. And I argued that the Review does not meet the requirements here, and that its authors should have been a great deal more cautious in the conclusions they drew on the basis of the research reviewed.

CONCLUSION

In this epilogue I have moved outside the sphere of empirical inquiry in order to engage in a broader, normative discussion about the role of research and of the media in the public sphere. I have examined three areas of doubt about the arguments underpinning the democratic model that I used as a framework for the research reported in this book, and which is widely adopted by social scientists. I noted the various criticisms that have been directed against the notion of discursive democracy, both in terms of whether it is currently realized in Western societies and also of whether it is a viable and desirable ideal. I recognized that the importance of public policymaking, of discursive democracy, and of the role of social research in relation to these can easily be overplayed. At the same time, I argued that the criticisms by no means entirely undermine the value of the model, and that one important justification for social research, and especially for its state funding, is its capacity to serve public deliberation about policies.

Second, I examined the assumption, built into this democratic model, that journalists, and perhaps even their audiences, should accept the authority of social science findings at face value. I argued that there were various reasons why this ought not to be the case, not least the availability of alternative sources of information about the social world with which research knowledge must be combined. At the same time, I suggested that, in principle, social science findings warranted being given some distinctive authority, on the grounds that the institutional framework within which they are produced, if operating properly, minimizes (though cannot eliminate) the danger of error.

In the final section I explored the limits to that authority. First of all, I argued that it does not extend to value conclusions, only to factual ones. Second, I suggested that, even in relation to the latter, it depends upon social researchers operating in a way that minimizes the chances of their producing false conclusions. And, examining the Review that has been the focus of this book, I argued that it fails on both counts: it makes or implies value conclusions, and it ignores serious threats to the reliability of its findings. On this basis, one might even conclude that it was given more respect by most of the media than it deserved.

However, any such judgement relies on assumptions about what social research can and should supply, about what the proper functions of the media are, and about how public decisionmaking can best be pursued. As my discussion will have made clear, if it was not obvious already, these are matters on which there is currently considerable room for reasonable disagreement, yet they are ones which require serious attention by social scientists.

Appendix 1   Newspaper headlines

National sunday newspapers

Newspaper	Main headline	Secondary headline	Editorial
Independent on Sunday	Black pupils falling behind at school in 'cycle of failure'		
The Sunday Times	Indian pupils outclass all other groups		

National daily newspapers

Newspaper	Main headline	Secondary headline	Editorial
Daily Express	Race checks to help our black pupils work better		
Daily Mail	The ethnic underclass	Black pupils 'falling behind' whites and Asians in school performance	
The Daily Mirror	Probe on expelled blacks		
Daily Star	Black to the drawing board	Kids turning to crime because they hate Sir	
The Daily Telegraph	West Indians 'fail because teachers expect them to'		
The Guardian	Ministers in school anti-racist drive	'Do well' imperatives boost Asian children Where ethnic mix proves no barrier to success	

(Continued)

National daily newspapers (cont'd)

Newspaper	Main headline	Secondary headline	Editorial
The Independent 06.09.96	Teachers to be monitored for racial harassment		Moore column: The post-racist bubble bursts: we knew it all along.
10.09.96	Pupils can expect to do better and better in exams, unless they are black. Why?		Now even Ofsted admits the link between race and educational achievement Letter: Schools cannot right race legacy
The Sun	Asian pupils top whites in classroom		
The Times	Ministers act to help failing black pupils		

Education supplements

Newspaper	Main headline	Secondary headline	Editorial
Guardian Education	About face on race	Alarming evidence of under-achievement among some ethnic minorities is shaking up thinking in Whitehall and town halls Tower Hamlets Leicester	
The Times Educational Supplement 06.09.96	Ethnic gap growing in many areas	Frances Rafferty on the major report that finds white teachers creating conflict with their African-Caribbean pupils	Editorial: Still far to go
13.09.96	Race inequality 'as bad as ever'	Reva Klein looks at the background to a new report that shows black children still get a raw deal from the education system	Letter: Long overdue
20.09.96	Black sociologist attacks race 'doom and gloom'		

Ethnic minority newspapers

Newspaper	Main headline	Secondary headline	Editorial and comment
Asian Times	Indians ahead as academic race gap widens	Pakistani students face University places prejudice	
Asia Weekly	Indian students excel in Britain		
Caribbean Times	Are black boys really the problem?		
The Journal	Making progress Change the school menu		
Eastern Eye	Top of the class	New education report puts Asian students ahead again	Editorial: Making the grade Letter: Simply the best
Muslim Times	Ethnicity matters		
The Voice			
10.09.96	Our kids are still missing out	Report highlights lack of progress in tackling Afro-Caribbean performance in schools	Editorial: Standing up for our children's schooling
17.09.96			Observer column: Schooled in doing badly Sewell column: Everyone's losing the skin game in school
24.09.96	Exam figures that miss the mark	Official statistics say that Black pupils fail at school. But is that a true picture? This is the success story that government figures don't show	
The Weekly Gleaner	Underachievement of black boys		

Local press

Newspaper	Main headline	Secondary headline	Editorial
Birmingham Evening Mail	Cash plea for ethnic pupils		
The Birmingham Post	Report highlights ethnic under-class in schools		
Bradford Telegraph & Argus	Pupils Progress Mixed reports for ethnic pupils		
Derby Evening Telegraph	Help plan for ethnic schoolkids		
The Leicester Mercury	School pupils: 'Don't fall into stereotyping trap'		
London Evening Standard	Colour-blind policies 'are failing pupils from ethnic minorities'		
Manchester Evening News	Afro-Caribbeans do worse at school		
Oldham Evening Chronicle	Afro-Caribbean 'underclass' in education		
South London Press	Black kids suffer	Gap widening between Afro-Caribbean children and other ethnic pupils	
The Western Mail	African Caribbean youths trail badly		
Wolverhampton Express and Star	Asian pupils top the exam tables		
Yorkshire Evening Post	'Underclass' in the classroom		
Yorkshire Post	Schools plan set out in black and white	Scheme to target ethnic-minority pupils attacked	Bottom of the underclass

Appendix 2   Incidence of findings in the national newspapers

Findings	Frequency
1) Lower than average performance of African Caribbean pupils	
Express × 2^a, *Times* [combines this and next], *Mail* [combines this and next] × 4, *Guardian, Telegraph* × 2, *Sun, Star, Sunday Times, Independent on Sunday*	9
2) African Caribbean boys more likely to be excluded than others	
Express, Times, Mail, Guardian, Telegraph, Independent × 2, *Mirror, Sunday Times* × 2, *Independent on Sunday*	9
3) Growing gap in performance between pupils from different ethnic groups	
Sun: 'But blacks – particularly Afro-Caribbean boys – are falling further behind'	
Express, Times, Mail × 3, *Guardian, Telegraph* × 2, *Independent* × 2, *Sun, Sunday Times* × 2, *Independent on Sunday* × 2	9
4) Asian/Indian pupils achieving at higher levels, on average, than other groups	
Star: Top of the form were Indian students	
Express, Times, Telegraph × 2, *Sun* × 2, *Star, Sunday Times, Independent on Sunday*	7
5) Conflict between white teachers and African Caribbean pupils	
Times, Mail, Guardian, Telegraph, Independent, Sunday Times	6
6) Teachers' actions could create and amplify/were creating and amplifying conflict	
Mail, Telegraph, Independent, Mirror, Independent on Sunday	5

[a] ×2 indicates that this finding is mentioned twice in the Daily Express's report. Other multiple mentionings are indicated similarly.

(Continued)

Findings	*Frequency*
7) Some Asian groups have dramatically increased their performance level	
Times, Mail, Guardian, Independent, Independent on Sunday	5
8) Teachers had low expectations of African Caribbean pupils	
Telegraph × 2, *Independent, Mirror, Independent on Sunday*	4
9) For all ethnic groups achievement depended on social class/economic background	
Mail, Telegraph, Independent	3
10) 'Colour-blind' policies have not succeeded	
Times, Guardian, Telegraph	3
11) Girls/white girls tend to do better than boys at 16+	
Mail, Telegraph	2
12) Dramatic improvements in the performance of Bangladeshi pupils in Tower Hamlets	
Telegraph, Independent	2
13) In Birmingham, more than 40% of Indians got five or more top GCSEs last year, next to 35% of whites and 22% of blacks. [This is slightly inaccurate, the reported figures are 39.4% for Indians, 35.7% for whites and 17.6% for African Caribbeans (Gillborn and Gipps 1996: Note 43, p33).]	
Sunday Times, Sun	2
14) In Brent in northwest London the average GCSE points score for Asian teenagers rose from 30 to 38 between 1991 and 1993. By contrast, white pupils increased their performance from 26.9 to 25.6/32.3 in the same period (*Telegraph* adds: West Indians from 19.1 to 25.6). [These figures are slightly inaccurate. Reading off the graph in the Review, the score for Asians goes from 30.5% to 42%, for whites from 28% to 34%, and for African Caribbeans from 13% to 20%. Here it seems that the *Telegraph* did not simply copy the information from the *Sunday Times*. The correct figures are that Asian pupils moved from 31.0% to 43.3%, white pupils moved from 28.4% to 34.8%, and African Caribbean pupils moved from 13.0% to 19.8%.]	
Sunday Times, Telegraph	2

(Continued)

Findings	Frequency
15) Gender also plays a part in differences between ethnic minority groups' performance	
Telegraph, Independent	2
16) Schools should carry out more detailed monitoring	
Sunday Times	1
17) In some areas performance of African-Caribbean pupils has worsened	
Mail	1
18) There were, however, some exceptions, where young black pupils were ahead of their white classmates – outperforming them in tests in the ages of five and six in some city areas	
Sunday Times	1
19) Asian pupils more likely to be bullied	
Guardian	1
20) Overall increases in examination performance across ethnic groups	
Telegraph	1
21) Gulf between experience of many black pupils and equal opportunities	
Telegraph	1
22) Teachers view Asian pupils as better behaved and more able [*Telegraph*]/quiet and compliant	
Telegraph	1
23) Black pupils' experience of school less positive than other groups	
Telegraph	1
24) Teachers had negative stereotypes of Asian pupils [*Independent*]	
Independent × 2	1
25) Teenagers from all ethnic minority groups stayed in education for longer than white students	
Independent	1
26) Ethnic minority students less likely to apply to a traditional university and more likely to go to a former polytechnic	
Independent	1

(Continued)

Findings	*Frequency*
27) One in two Asian and white girls achieved five or more GCSE passes at grade C or better, compared with less than one in four West Indian girls. For boys, the figures were one in three Asian and one in four whites compared with one in six West Indians. But almost one in ten white boys left without any GCSE passes, compared with one in 25 West Indians and one in 200 Asians [Figures relate to Brent]	
Telegraph	1
28) In Bradford, Pakistani pupils achieved a better average examination score than Bangladeshi pupils but below Indians, whites and blacks, in that order	
Telegraph	1
29) Bangladeshis [are] often less fluent in English than other ethnic minorities. In the London borough of Camden they were below blacks and well below whites but in the London borough of Tower Hamlets, which has almost a quarter of all Bangladeshi children aged 5–15 in England, Bangladeshis have higher average examination scores than both white and Caribbean pupils.	
Telegraph	1
30) Pupils of black African background often achieve relatively higher results than those of black Caribbean background	
Telegraph	1
31) On average, Caribbean young men achieve significantly below their potential.	
Telegraph	1
32) The pattern of girls outperforming boys was true only for white pupils [This is presumably derived from Table 2.1 in the Review, though it should be noted that African Caribbean female pupils from manual backgrounds outperformed boys from the same background]	
Telegraph	1
33) In Birmingham, 1 in 12 African Caribbean boys gained A–C grades in maths compared to 1 in 3 whites	
Independent on Sunday	1
34) Chinese pupils are least likely to be disciplined [What is meant by 'disciplined' here is 'excluded']	
Sunday Times	1
35) The total number of exclusions has risen from 2,900 in 1990 to 10,000 last year [This information comes from an endnote in the Review]	
Independent on Sunday	1

Appendix 3   Incidence of findings in the ethnic minority newspapers

Findings	Frequency
1a) Asian/Indian pupils achieving at higher levels, on average, than other groups.	
Eastern Eye × 6, *Asian Times* × 2, *Asia Weekly* × 2, *Muslim News*	4
1b) African-Caribbean boys more likely to be excluded than others	
Weekly Gleaner, Caribbean Times × 2, *Voice* × 2, *Eastern Eye*	4
3a) Lower than average performance of African-Caribbean pupils	
Weekly Gleaner × 2, *Caribbean Times, Voice*	3
3b) Growing gap in performance between pupils from different ethnic groups	
Weekly Gleaner × 2, *Caribbean Times, Voice*	3
3c) General rates of educational achievement have improved over the past 10 years [For Asian Times the reference is to South Asian groups]	
Weekly Gleaner, Asian Times, Weekly Journal	3
3d) Conflict between white teachers and African-Caribbean pupils	
Weekly Gleaner, Caribbean Times, Voice	3
7a) Bangladeshi pupils suffer the greatest level of poverty and are the least fluent in English	
Asian Times, Muslim News	2
7b) Indians are more likely to stay on at school after the age of 16	
Eastern Eye, Asia Weekly	2
7c) Colour-blind policy has failed	
Voice, Muslim News	2

Muslim News: 'To end with a positive note, one of the clearest findings of this review is that if ethnic diversity is ignored, if differences in educational achievement and experience are not examined, then considerable injustices will be sanctioned and enormous potential wasted.

(Continued)

Findings	Frequency
10a) Teachers have behavioural stereotypes of African Caribbean pupils	
Caribbean Times	1
10b) Teachers' have low expectations of African Caribbeans' academic performance	
Caribbean Times	1
10c) Teachers' actions could create and amplify/were creating and amplifying conflict. Star: racist attitude of teachers	
*Weekly Gleane*r	1
10d) For Asian pupils in Brent average GCSE marks rose from 30–38% 1991–3, this is in contrast to white pupils 26.9–32.3	
Eastern Eye	1
10e) More than 40% of Indian GCSE entrants achieved 5 or more A–C grades last year, compared with about 35% of whites and 22 per cent of Afro-Caribbeans	
Eastern Eye	1
10f) Asians continue to perform well once they go on to further education – especially at degree level	
Eastern Eye	1
10g) Pakistani and Bangladeshi schoolchildren struggle at school	
Asian Times	1
10h) Pakistani and Bangladeshi schoolchildren face discrimination in access to university places	
Asian Times × 2	1
10i) No single pattern of achievement amongst Pakistani pupils but they are said to be performing less well than any other group in certain urban areas [No single pattern reported, and achieving at lower levels than some other groups in some areas, but no evidence that they are achieving 'less well than any other group in certain urban areas'. The reference in the executive summary is to their doing less well than whites in many areas]	
Asian Times	1
10j) Black Caribbean pupils continued to be significantly less likely to be admitted to university	
Voice	1
10k) Although black children are widely perceived as underachievers, when they enter the school system at age 5 they actually out-perform their white peers [This relates to data from Birmingham]	
Weekly Journal	1
10l) 5 year old black children in Birmingham perform at the levels expected of 6 or 7 year olds.	
Weekly Journal	1

(Continued)

Findings	Frequency
10m) Achievement depends on economic background/social class	
Muslim News × 2	1
10n) Asian pupils more likely to be victimised by peers	
Muslim News × 2	1
10o) Outside London white pupils leave with highest average achievements [This finding is presumably based on the data from Birmingham, which has the largest population of South Asians, where the average GCSE performance of whites marginally exceeded that of Asians as a whole, though not of Indian pupils]	
Muslim News	1
10p) Complicated interplay of sociological factors helping to grind down and demotivate ethnic minority pupils	
Muslim News	1
10q) Racial harassment not always recognised by teachers	
Muslim News	1
10r) Negative and patronising stereotypes towards Asian pupils	
Muslim News × 3	1
10s) Gender a contributory factor towards success	
Muslim News	1
10t) Even when previous achievements taken into account, people do not share an equal chance of admission into Higher Education	
Muslim News	1

Findings not in the review included in ethnic minority newspapers

Indians are better behaved in the classroom	*Eastern Eye, Asia Weekly*
There are growing variations in standards of behaviour between ethnic groups	*Eastern Eye*
The research does not entirely blame black pupils for their low success rate	*Weekly Gleaner*
Many Muslim parents do not appreciate significance of National Curriculum stages 1 and 2	*Muslim News*
Interviews by the researchers with 55 young Muslim women, predominantly of Pakistani background, indicated that around a third of their parents were unequivocally opposed to their daughters pursuing higher education. It seems that enlightened Islamic principles are ignorantly cast aside or misunderstood [This seems to be a reference to another piece of research, not the Review]	*Muslim News*
Biology [...] is still a contributory factor towards success	*Muslim News*

Appendix 4   Incidence of findings in the local newspapers

Findings	Frequency
1 African-Caribbean boys more likely to be excluded than others	
Birmingham Evening Mail, Birmingham Post, Bradford Telegraph and Argus, London Evening Standard, Leicester Mercury, Manchester Evening News, South London Press, Western Mail, Wolverhampton Express and Star, Yorkshire Post × 2	10
Sometimes reported as higher than average level of exclusions among African Caribbean pupils, not just boys	
2 Lower than average performance of African Caribbean pupils	
Birmingham Evening Mail, London Evening Standard, Leicester Mercury, Manchester Evening News, Oldham Evening Chronicle × 2, South London Press, Western Mail × 2, Yorkshire Post × 2	8
3a Achievement at 16 depends on economic background across all groups	
Birmingham Post, Bradford Telegraph and Argus, Manchester Evening News, Oldham Evening Chronicle, Western Mail, Wolverhampton Express and Star, Yorkshire Evening Post	7
3b Girls tend to do better than boys	
Birmingham Post, Bradford Telegraph and Argus, Manchester Evening News, Oldham Evening Chronicle, Western Mail, Wolverhampton Express and Star, Yorkshire Evening Post	7
3c Asian/Indian pupils appear consistently to achieve more highly than others from South Asian backgrounds	
Birmingham Post, Bradford Telegraph and Argus, Manchester Evening News, Oldham Evening Chronicle, Western Mail, Wolverhampton Express and Star, Yorkshire Evening Post, Wolverhampton Express and Star	7
6 Pakistani pupils achieve less well than whites in many areas, although there is no single pattern of achievement	
Bradford Telegraph and Argus, Manchester Evening News, Oldham Evening Chronicle, Western Mail, Wolverhampton Express and Star, Yorkshire Evening Post	6

Findings	Frequency
7a Ethnic minorities have not shared in generally improving rates of achievement, and in some areas their performance has worsened	
Birmingham Post, Manchester Evening News, South London Press, Western Mail, Yorkshire Evening Post	5
7b GCSE performance has improved across the board, but not all groups have shared in the trend	
Birmingham Post, Oldham Evening Chronicle, Western Mail, Wolverhampton Express and Star, Yorkshire Evening Post	5
7c Bangladeshi pupils, with less fluency in English and greater levels of poverty on average, generally do less well than other groups	
Oldham Evening Chronicle, Manchester Evening News, Western Mail, Yorkshire Evening Post, Bradford Telegraph and Argus	5
7d Unusually high degree of conflict of African Caribbean pupils with white teachers	
Manchester Evening News, Western Mail, Wolverhampton Express and Star, Yorkshire Post, Yorkshire Post editorial	5
11a Colour-blind policies failing ethnic minority pupils	
London Evening Standard × 2, *Yorkshire Post*	2
11b Asian secondary school pupils making better progress than their white counterparts	
Bradford Telegraph and Argus × 3, *Yorkshire Post*	2
11c Participation in post-16 education is higher for young people from all ethnic minority groups than for whites	
Yorkshire Evening Post, Birmingham Evening Mail	2
14a Ethnic origin is important in determining a pupil's progress from infant school through to university	
Bradford Telegraph and Argus	1
14b Pakistani and Bangladeshi students consistently underperform at primary school	
Bradford Telegraph and Argus	1
14c Widespread incidence of harassment against some pupils, not always recognized by teachers	
Wolverhampton Express and Star	1
14d Educational performance of all ethnic groups had improved	
Yorkshire Post	1

(Continued)

Findings	*Frequency*
14e Review warns that 'failure to take into account social differences between pupils will lead to a further decline in the performance of many'	
London Evening Standard	1

'Findings' reported that are not in the Review

Findings	*Frequency*
1) Ethnic underclass in schools	
Birmingham Post, Manchester Evening News, Oldham Evening Chronicle [headline and first line], *Western Mail, Wolverhampton Express and Star, Yorkshire Evening Post* [headline and first line], *Yorkshire Post* editorial	7
2) Thousands of children are being left on the educational scrap-heap because politically correct schools are failing to tackle the problems faced by children from ethnic minorities	
London Evening Standard	1
3) Experts have accused teachers of ignoring differences in racial lifestyles and of holding the misguided view that pupils should not be singled out for special treatment	
London Evening Standard [This is false if the experts referred to are the authors of the Review]	1

Appendix 5   Sequencing of findings in national newspapers

The Sunday Times: **Indian pupils outclass all other groups**   Indians most highly qualified, and better behaved, than blacks, particularly Afro-Caribbean boys; latter are falling further behind; more likely to be expelled; widening gap; more detailed monitoring recommended; danger of black underclass; Indians consistently achieving in excess; educationists believe that among Asians cultural commitment to education and family support helps them to shine; variations in standards of behaviour; unusually high degree of conflict between white teachers and Afro-Caribbeans; but are exceptions where black pupils head of their classmates; situation too varied to speak of underachievement.

Independent on Sunday: **Black pupils falling behind at school in 'cycle of failure'**   These pupils falling further behind; locked into a cycle of failure; Indians and Pakistanis doing better than ever; those at the bottom likely to become disaffected; more likely to be excluded; teachers often underestimate them and find them more intimidating and give less encouragement; while all groups improved GCSE scores, Afro-Caribbean pupils improved far less than some other groups.

Daily Express: **Race checks to help our black pupils work better**   Watchdog highlighted poor performance of Afro-Caribbean youngsters; spotlighting the growing gap in performance between pupils from different ethnic backgrounds; Indian pupils consistently doing better; but experts alarmed at poor performance of Afro-Caribbean boys; and that they are six times more likely to be kicked out of school than other pupils.

Daily Mail: **The ethnic underclass, Black pupils 'falling behind whites and Asians in school performances**   An educational underclass revealed containing increasing numbers of African Caribbean youngsters; they are falling drastically behind in both examinations and school attendance; black youngsters had not shared in the generally improving rates of achievement; in some areas their performance had worsened; paradoxically the report records dramatic increases in the examination performance of some ethnic minorities, especially Indians, even in poor areas; but in many authorities, the achievements of African Caribbean youngsters, particularly boys, were 'significantly lower than other groups'; they were between three and six times more likely to be excluded from school than whites; report blames teachers for some of the problems and highlights the 'unusually high degree of conflict between white teachers and African-Caribbean pupils'; despite their best intentions, there was evidence that teachers' actions could create and amplify conflict.

Daily Mirror: **Probe on expelled blacks** Probe into why Afro-Caribbean pupils six times more likely to be expelled than whites; report said that teachers might jump the gun; have low expectations and think these pupils will cause trouble; Indian youngsters perform better in GCSEs than whites or blacks; doubling of Bangladeshi pass rates helped by extra teaching support; yet funding cuts.

Daily Star: **Black to the drawing board: Kids turning to crime because they hate Sir** Thousands of black youngsters face future of drug taking and street crime because of their hatred of teachers, claimed yesterday; new report revealed Afro-Caribbean kids were starting to form a menacing new underclass in the educational system; race watchdogs blamed racist attitude of some teachers for the poor performance of black youths; Chris Myant of CRE says that mutual distrust has developed between black boys and their teachers, many teachers have low expectations of young black males that become self-fulfilling; government inspectors found that while black girls gave no major cause for concern, black youths had hopelessly missed out on generally improving rates of achievement; top of the form were Indian students; they were among the most diligent, disciplined and hard-working and proportionately achieved the best exam passes; experts say this is because they respect both their teachers and parents; and know good exam results will make or break their future lives; Mr Myant said many black youths from poor homes had no role models because fathers and bothers unemployed; this created a high degree of apathy, resentment and trouble; last year Scotland Yard boss said that 80 per cent of muggings in inner London were committed by young black males.

The Daily Telegraph: **West Indians 'fail because teachers expect them to'** Children from a West Indian background are doing less well than other ethnic groups partly because teachers expect them to; report shows that Indian students achieve better examination results than any other group, while black fall further behind; Ofsted warns that disproportionately high number of black children have been expelled; and colour-blind policies are allowing inequality of opportunity to persist; report warns of 'considerable gulf between daily reality experienced by many black pupils and the stated goal of equal opportunities for all'; authors say teachers often view Asian pupils as better behaved, more highly motivated and more able than black children; by contrast, black pupils' experience of school is less positive than other groups 'regardless of ability and gender'; there was often conflict between black pupils and white teachers; teachers may play 'an active (though unintended) part' in creating conflict with West Indian pupils 'thereby reducing black young people's opportunity to achieve'; social class remains more important than ethnic background in determining achievement; and gender is also important; West Indian children, of both sexes, 'achieved below the level attained by the other groups; Asian pupils did as well or better than whites of the same class and gender; the pattern of girls outperforming boys was true only for white pupils.

The Guardian: **Ministers in school anti-racist drive**   Government has reversed its attitude instructing schools to adopt anti-racist and multi-cultural programmes; colour-blind policies in schools had failed; the performance of African and Caribbean pupils – six times more likely to be expelled – was of particular concern said Ofsted; in the past 10 years had been dramatic improvement in exam results among some minority groups, such as Bangladeshis in inner London; but the gap between highest and lowest achieving groups was growing; Asian pupils most likely to be bulled; there was 'an unusually high degree of conflict between white teachers and African-Caribbean pupils'; government proposed schemes to tackle racial stereotyping.

The Independent: **Teachers to be monitored for racial harassment**   Schools to face ethnic monitoring programme to eliminate racial harassment and stereotyping by teachers; report revealed 'unusually high' degree of conflict between white teachers and black pupils; African-Caribbean pupils were up to six times more likely to be excluded from school; Asian pupils were subjected to 'negative and patronising' stereotypes, with staff often assuming their English was poor and that girls would be expected to marry early and stay at home; report showed that while some ethnic minority groups, particularly Indians were doing better than ever, others were improving only very slowly; it added that initiatives in some local authorities had made a huge difference, e.g. Tower Hamlets; teenagers from all ethnic minority groups stayed in education for longer than white students; however less likely to apply to a traditional university and more likely to go to a former polytechnic.

The Independent: **Pupils can expect to do better and better in exams, unless they are black: Why?**   Black boys, according to some race relations experts, are often more lively, more boisterous, more chatty than their classmates. Could this be the reason why they are six times more likely to be excluded?; while most ethnic groups are doing better than before, African Caribbean boys are slipping further behind; Ofsted report said that teachers were creating and amplifying conflicts with black pupils; far from seeing them as energetic and enthusiastic, they interpreted their behaviour as threatening and aggressive; they expected them to achieve little at school; Asian pupils, meanwhile, were seen as quiet and compliant; not surprisingly both groups tended to live up to their stereotypes; the researchers did add that social class and gender both played an important part in the failure of those young people but in seeking both causes and solutions they turned to the school system.

Bernie Grant: the schools are failing them, talk back more because of feeling they are being discriminated against, *Carlton Duncan*: absence of strong supportive family.

Box listing 'the theories'. And then photos and brief biographies of three pupils representing Asian, white and African Caribbean pupils.

Unusually high degree of conflict, exclusion, Asian pupils subjected to stereotypes, initiatives in some areas made huge difference, more likely to be excluded, 'slipping further behind, teachers creating and exemplifying conflicts, stereo-types, researchers did add that social class and gender are also important factors.

The Sun: **Asian pupils top whites in classroom**   Asian pupils are outclassing their white schoolmates in exam results, the reason is greater discipline at home, says the Institute of Education, but blacks – particularly Afro-Caribbean boys, are falling further behind, in Birmingham more than 40 per cent of Indians got five or more top GCSEs last year, next to 35 per cent of whites and 22 per cent of blacks.

The Times: **Ministers act to help failing black pupils**   Focus on A/C pupils: 'falling behind', but then 'schools not doing enough, Indian pupils performing much better, conflict, expulsions.

References

Abercrombie, N., Hill, S. and Turner, B. S. (1980) *The Dominant Ideology Thesis*, London: Allen and Unwin.

Abercrombie, N., Hill, S. and Turner, B. S. (eds) (1990) *Dominant Ideologies*, London: Unwin Hyman.

Abercrombie, N. and Longhurst, B. (1998) *Audiences: a sociological theory of performance* and *imagination*, London: Sage.

Agger, B. (2000) *Public Sociology: from social facts to literary acts*, Lanham, MD: Rowman and Littlefield.

Alexander, R. (1997). *Policy and Practice in Primary Education: Local initiative, national agenda*, London: Routledge (second edition).

Allan, S. (1999) *News Culture*, Buckingham: Open University Press.

Altheide, D. L. (1974). *Creating Reality: How TV Distorts News Events*, Beverly Hills: Sage.

Anderson, D. C. and Sharrock, W. W. (1979). 'Biasing the news: Technical issues in "Media Studies", *Sociology* 13, 3: 368–85.

Ang, I. (1985) *Watching Dallas: Soap opera and the melodramatic imagination*, London: Methuen.

Baker, M. (1994) 'Media coverage of education', *British Journal of Educational Studies*, 42, 3: 286–97.

Ball, S. J. and Gewirtz, S. (1997) 'Is research possible? A rejoinder to Tooley's "On school choice and social class"', *British Journal of Sociology of Education*, 18, 4: 575–86.

Barnes, B. (1974) *Scientific Knowledge and Sociological Theory*, London: Routledge and Kegan Paul.

Barth, H. (1976) *Truth and Ideology*, Berkeley: University of California Press.

Bassey, M. (2000) 'Reviews of educational research', *Research Intelligence*, 71: 22–9.

Bell, A. (1991). *The Language of News Media*, Oxford: Blackwell.

Benjamin, I. (1995) *The Black Press in Britain*, Stoke on Trent: Trentham Books.

Bennett, A. (ed.) (1995) *Readers and Reading*, London: Longman.

Bennett, T. (1982) 'Theories of the media, theories of society', in M. Gurevitch, T. Bennett, J. Curran and J. Woollacott (eds) *Culture, Society and the Media*, London: Methuen.

Berkowitz, D. (1997). 'Overview' in Berkowitz, D. (ed.) *Social Meanings of News*, Thousand Oaks, CA: Sage.

Blackburn, S. and Simmons, K. (eds) (1999) *Truth*, Oxford: Oxford University Press.

Blair, M. and Gillborn, D. (1999) 'Face up to racism', *Times Educational Supplement*, 5 March.

Blair, M., Gillborn, D., Kemp, S. and MacDonald, J. (1999) 'Institutional racism, education and the Stephen Lawrence Inquiry', *Education and Social Justice*, 1, 3: 6–15.

Bloor, D. (1976) *Knowledge and Social Imagery*, London: Routledge and Kegan Paul.

Blunkett, D. (2000). 'Influence or irrelevance: can social science improve government?', *Research Intelligence*, 71: 12–21.

Bohman, J. (1996) *Public Deliberation*, Cambridge, MA: MIT Press.

Bourdieu, P. (1998) *On Television and Journalism*, London: Pluto.

Braham, P. (1982) 'How the media report race', in M. Gurevitch, T. Bennett, J. Curran and J. Woollacott (eds) *Culture, Society and the Media*, London: Methuen.

Breen, R. and Goldthorpe, J. H. (1999) 'Class inequality and meritocracy: a critique of Saunders and an alternative analysis', *British Journal of Sociology*, 50, 1: 1–27.

Breen, R. and Goldthorpe, J. H. (2001) 'Class, mobility and merit: the experience of two British birth cohorts', *European Sociological Review*, 17, 2: 81–101.

Breen, R. and Goldthorpe, J. H. (2002) 'Merit, mobility and method: another reply to Saunders', *British Journal of Sociology*, 53, 4: 575–82.

Brooker, W. and Jermyn, D. (eds) (2003) *The Audience Studies Reader*, London: Routledge.

Bruun, H. H. (1972) *Science, Values and Politics in Max Weber's Methodology*, Copenhagen: Munksgaard.

Burawoy, M. (2005) 'For public sociology', *American Sociological Review*, 70: 4–28.

Calhoun, C. (1992) *Habermas and the Public Sphere*, Cambridge MA: MIT Press.

Campbell, C. P. (1995) *Race, Myth and the News*, Thousand Oaks, CA: Sage.

Carey, J. W. (1989) *Communication as Culture: Essays on media and society*, Boston: Unwin Hyman.

Caswill, C. and Shove, E. (2000) 'Introducing interactive social science', *Science and Public Policy*, 27, 3: 154–8.

Centre for Contemporary Cultural Studies (1977) *On Ideology*, Birmingham: Centre for Contemporary Cultural Studies, University of Birmingham.

Chalmers, I. (2003) 'Trying to do more good than harm in policy and practice: the role of rigorous, transparent, up-to-date evaluations', *Annals of the American Academy of Political and Social Science*, 589; 22–40, September.

Clayman, S. (1988) 'Displaying neutrality in television interviews', *Social Problems*, 35: 474–92.

Clayman, S. (1992) 'Footing in the achievement of neutrality: the case of news-interview discourse', in P. Drew and H. Heritage (eds) *Talk at Work: interaction in institutional settings*, Cambridge: Cambridge University Press.

Clayman, S. and Heritage, J. (2002) *The News Interview: journalists and public figures on the air*, Cambridge: Cambridge University Press.

Cohen, G. A. (1978) *Karl Marx's Theory of History*, Oxford: Clarendon Press.

Cohen, S. and Young, J. (eds) (1973) *The Manufacture of News: Social problems, deviance and the mass media*. London: Constable.

Cole, G. D. H. (1964) 'Capitalism', in J. Gould and W. L. Kolb (eds) *A Dictionary of the Social Sciences*, London: Tavistock.

Cooper, B. (2005) 'Applying Ragin's crisp and fuzzy set QCA to large datasets: social class and educational achievement in the National Child Development Study', *Sociological Research Online*, 10, 2. <http://www.socresonline.org.uk/10/2/cooper.html>

Corner, J. and Pels, D. (eds) (2003) *Media and the Restyling of Politics*, London: Sage.

Cottle, S. (1993) *TV News, Urban Conflict and the Inner City*, Leicester: Leicester University Press.

Cottle, S. (ed.) (2000) *Ethnic Minorities and the Media: changing cultural boundaries*, Buckingham: Open University Press.

Crisell, A. (1994) *Understanding Radio*, Second edition, London: Routledge.

Crossley, N. and Roberts, J. M. (eds) (2004) *After Habermas: new perspectives on the public sphere*, Oxford: Blackwell.

Curran, J. (1991) in P. Dahlgren, and R. Sparks (eds) *Communication and Citizenship: journalism and the public sphere in the new media age*, London: Sage.

Curran, J. (1997) 'The new revisionism in mass communication research: a reappraisal', in Curran *et al.* (eds).

Curran, J. and Seaton, J. (1991) *Power without Responsibility: the press and broadcasting in Britain*, Fourth edition, London: Routledge.

Curran, J. and Seaton, J. (2003) *Power without Responsibility: the press and broadcasting in Britain*, Fifth edition, London: Routledge.

Curran, J., Morley, M. and Walkerdine, V. (eds) (1997) *Cultural Studies and Communications*, London: Arnold.

Dahlgren, P. and Sparks, C. (1992) *Journalism and Popular Culture*, London: Sage.

Davies, H. T. O., Nutley, S. M. and Smith, P. C. (eds) (2000) *What Works? Evidence-based policy and practice in the public services*, Bristol: Policy Press.

Davies, J. K. (1978) *Democracy and Classical Greece*, London: Fontana.

Davis, H. and Walton, P. (eds) (1983) *Language, Image, Media*, Oxford: Blackwell.

Demerath III, N. J. and Peterson, R. A. (eds) (1967) *System, Change and Conflict*, New York: Free Press.

Dewey, J. (1946) *The Public and its Problems*, second edition, Chicago, NL: Gateway Books.

Dickinson, R., Harindranath, R. and Linne, O. (eds) (1998) *Approaches to Audiences*, London: Arnold.

Drew, D. and Gray, J. (1990) 'The fifth year examination achievements of Black young people in England and Wales', *Educational Research*, 32, 3: 107–17.

Dryzek, J. S. (1990) *Discursive Democracy: politics, policy, and political science*, Cambridge: Cambridge University Press.

Dunning, E. (1994) 'The sociologist as media football: reminiscences and preliminary reflections' in C. Haslam and A. Bryman, (eds) *Social Scientists Meet the Media*. London: Routledge.

Eagleton, T. (1991) *Ideology: an introduction*, London: Verso.

Eason, D. (1988) 'On journalistic authority: the Janet Cook scandal', in J. W. Carey (ed.) *Media, Myths, and Narratives: Television and the Press*, Newbury Park, CA: Sage.

Elster, J. (ed.) (1998) *Deliberative Democracy*, Cambridge: Cambridge University Press.

Epstein, E. J. (1973) *News from Nowhere: Television and the News*, New York: Random House.

Ettema, J. S. and Whitney, D. C. (eds) (1994) *Audiencemaking: how the media create the audience*, Thousand Oaks, CA: Sage.

Evans, W. (1995) 'The mundane and the arcane: prestige media coverage of social and natural science', *Journalism and Mass Communication Quarterly*, 72: 168–77.

Evans, W. A., Krippendorf, M., Yoon, J, H., Poluszny, P. and Thomas, S. (1990) 'Science in the prestige and national tabloid presses', *Social Science Quarterly*, 71, 1: 105–17.

Eysenck, H. J. (1994) 'Media vs. reality?', in C. Haslam and A. Bryman (eds) *Social Scientists Meet the Media*. London: Routledge.

Fairclough, N. (1995) *Media Discourse*, London: Edward Arnold.

Fenton, N., Bryman, A., Deacon, D., with Birmingham, P. (1998) *Mediating Social Science*, London: Sage.

Finlayson, J. G. (2005) *Habermas: a very short introduction*, Oxford: Oxford University Press.

Fishman, M. (1980) *Manufacturing the News*. Austin, TX: University of Texas Press.

Fiske, J. (1989) *Understanding Popular Culture*, Boston, MA: Unwin Hyman.

Fiske, J. (1992) 'Popularity and the politics of information', in P. Dahlgren and C. Sparks (eds) *Journalism and Popular Culture*, London: Sage.

Foster, P. (1990a) *Policy and Practice in Multicultural and Anti-racist Education*, London: Routledge.

Foster, P. (1990b) 'Cases not proven: an evaluation of two studies of teacher racism', *British Educational Research Journal*, 16, 4: 335–48.

Foster, P. (1991) 'Cases still not proven: a reply to Cecile Wright', *British Educational Research Journal*, 17, 2: 165–70.

Foster, P. (1992) 'What are Connolly's rules? A reply to Paul Connolly', *British Educational Research Journal*, 18, 2: 149–54.

Foster, P. (1993a) 'Teacher attitudes and Afro-Caribbean achievement', *Oxford Review of Education*, 18, 3: 269–82.

Foster, P. (1993b) 'Some problems in identifying racial/ethnic equality or inequality in schools', *British Journal of Sociology*, 44, 3: 519–35.

Foster, P. (1993c) 'Equal treatment and cultural difference in multi-ethnic schools: a critique of teacher ethnocentrism theory', *International Studies in the Sociology of Education*, 2, 1: 89–103.

Foster, P., Gomm, R. and Hammersley, M. (1996) *Constructing Educational Inequality*, London: Falmer.

Foster, P. and Hammersley, M. (1998) 'A review of reviews: structure and function in reviews of educational research', *British Educational Research Journal*, 24, 5: 609–28.

Foster, P., Gomm, R. and Hammersley, M. (2000) 'Case studies as spurious evaluations: the example of research on educational inequalities', *British Journal of Educational Studies*, 48, 3: 215–30.

Franklin, B. and Murphy, D. (eds) (1998) *Local Journalism in Context*, London: Routledge.

Freeden, M. (2003) *Ideology: a very short introduction*, Oxford: Oxford University Press.

Fuller, M. (1980) 'Black girls in a London comprehensive school', in R. Deem, (ed.) *Schooling for Women's Work*, London: Routledge.

Fuller, M. (1982) 'Young, female and black', in E. Cashmore and B. Troyna, (eds) *Black Youth in Crisis*, London: Allen and Unwin.

Fuller, M. (1983) 'Qualified criticism, critical qualifications', in L. Barton and S. Walker (eds) *Race, Class and Education*, London: Croom Helm.

Galtung, J. and Ruge, M. H. (1965) 'The structure of foreign news', *Journal of Peace Research*, 2, 1: 64–91.

Gans, H. J. (1979) *Deciding What's News*, New York: Pantheon.

Garfinkel, H. (1967) *Studies in Ethnomethodology*, Englewood Cliffs NJ: Prentice Hall.

Genette, G. (1997) *Paratexts: thresholds of interpretation*, Cambridge: Cambridge University Press. (Translation of *Seuils*, Paris, Editions du Seuil, 1987.)

Gibbons, M. (2000) 'Mode 2 society and the emergence of context-sensitive science', *Science and Public Policy*, 26, 5: 159–63.

Gibbons, M., Limoges, C., Nowotny, H., Schwartzman, S., Scott, P. and Trow, M. (1994) *The New Production of Knowledge: the dynamics of science and research in contemporary societies*, London: Sage.

Giddens, A. (1973) *The Class Structure of the Advanced Societies*, London: Hutchinson.

Gillborn, D. (1995) *Racism and Antiracism in Real Schools: theory, policy and practice*, Buckingham: Open University Press.

Gillborn, D. (1998) 'Policy and research in "race" and education in the UK: symbiosis or mutual abuse?', paper given at 14th World Congress of Sociology, Montreal, July.

Gillborn, D. (2001) '"Raising standards" or rationing education? Racism and social justice in policy and practice', *Support for Learning*, 16, 3: 105–11.

Gillborn, D. and Gipps, C. (1996). *Recent Research on the Achievements of Ethnic Minority Pupils*, London: Office for Standards in Education/Her Majesty's Stationery Office.

Gillborn, D. and Gipps, C. (1998) 'Watching the watchers: research, methods, politics and equity', *British Educational Research Journal*, 24, 5: 629–33.

Gillborn, D. and Mirza, H. S. (2000) *Educational Inequality: mapping race, class and gender – a synthesis of research evidence*, London: OFSTED. (Available at www.ofsted.gov.uk)

Gillborn, D. and Youdell, D. (2000) *Rationing Education: policy, practice, reform and equity*, Buckingham: Open University Press.

Gitlin, T. (1998) 'Public sphere or public sphericules', in T. Liebes and J. Curran (eds) *Media, Ritual and Identity*, London: Routledge.

Glasgow University Media Group (1976) *Bad News*, London: Routledge and Kegan Paul.

Glasgow University Media Group (1980) *More Bad News*, London: Routledge and Kegan Paul.

Glasgow University Media Group (1982) *Really Bad News*, London: Writers and Readers Cooperative.

Glasgow University Media Group (1985) *War and Peace News*, Milton Keynes: Open University Press.

Glasser, T. L. and Craft, S. (1998) 'Public journalism and the search for democratic ideals', in T. Liebes and J. Curran (eds) *Media, Ritual and Identity*, London: Routledge.

Goffman, E. (1972) *Interaction Ritual*, Harmondsworth: Penguin.

Goffman, E. (1981) *Forms of Talk*, Oxford: Blackwell.

Golding, P. and Elliott, P. (1979) *Making the News*, London: Longman.

Gomm, R. (2001) 'Unblaming victims and creating heroes: reputational management in sociological writing', *Discourse: studies in the cultural politics of education*, 22, 2: 227–47.

Gomm, R., Hammersley, M. and P. Foster (eds) (2000) *Case Study Method: key texts, key issues*, London: Sage.

Greatbatch, D. (1992) 'On the management of disagreement between news interviewees', in P. Drew and H. Heritage (eds) *Talk at Work: interaction in institutional settings*, Cambridge: Cambridge University Press.

Grice, P. (1978) 'Further notes on logic and conversation', in P. Cole (ed.) *Syntax and Semantics: Pragmatics*, Vol. 9, New York: Academic Press.

Gutmann, A. and Thompson, D. (1996) *Democracy and Disagreement*, Cambridge, MA: Harvard University Press.

Habermas, J. (1989) *The Structural Transformation of the Public Sphere*, Cambridge, MA: MIT Press. (First published in German in 1962.)

References

Habermas, J. (1992) 'Further reflections on the public sphere', in C. Calhoun (ed.) *Habermas and the Public Sphere*, Cambridge, MA: MIT Press.

Hall, S. (1990) 'The whites of their eyes: racist ideologies and the media', in M. Alvarado and J. O. Thompson (eds) *The Media Reader*, London: British Film Institute.

Hall, S., Critcher, C., Jefferson, T., Clarke, J. and Roberts, B. (1978) *Policing the Crisis: Mugging, the state, and law and order*, London: Macmillan.

Hall, S. 'Signification, Representation, Ideology: Althusser and the post-structuralist Debates', in Curran, J., Morley, D., and Walkerdine, V. (eds) *Cultural Studies and Communications*, London, Edward Arnold 1996.

Hammersley, M. (1981) 'Ideology in the Staffroom: a critique of false consciousness', in L. Barton and S. Walker (eds) *Schools, Teachers and Teaching*, Brighton: Falmer Press.

Hammersley, M. (1992) *What's Wrong with Ethnography?* London: Routledge.

Hammersley, M. (1995) *The Politics of Social Research*, London: Sage.

Hammersley, M. (2000) *Taking Sides in Social Research: Essays on partisanship and bias*, London: Routledge.

Hammersley, M. (2001) 'On "Systematic" reviews of research literatures: a "narrative" reply to Evans and Benefield', *British Educational Research Journal*, 27, 5: 543–54.

Hammersley, M. (2002) 'Research as emancipatory: the case of Bhaskar's realism', *Journal of Critical Realism*, 1, 1: 33–48.

Hammersley, M. (2003a) *Discourse Analysis: bibliographical guide*, available at http://www.cf.ac.uk/socsi/capacity/Activities/Themes/In-depth/guide.pdf

Hammersley, M. (2003b) 'Conversation analysis and discourse analysis: methods or paradigms?', *Discourse and Society*, 14, 6: 751–81.

Hammersley, M. (2004a) 'Literature review', in M. Lewis-Beck, A. Bryman and R. F. Liao (eds) *The Sage Encyclopedia of Social Science Research Methods*, Thousand Oaks, CA: Sage.

Hammersley, M. (2004b) 'Get real! A defence of realism', in H. Piper and I. Stronach (eds) *Educational Research: Difference and Diversity*, Aldershot: Ashgate.

Hammersley, M. (2004c) 'Action research: a contradiction in terms?', *Oxford Review of Education*, 30, 2: 165–81.

Hammersley, M. (2005a) 'Should social science be critical?', *Philosophy of the Social Sciences*, 35, 2: 175–95.

Hammersley, M. (2005b) 'Is the evidence-based practice movement doing more good than harm? Reflections on Iain Chalmers' case for research-based policymaking and practice', *Evidence and Policy*, 1, 1: 1–16.

Hammersley, M. (2005c) 'Systematic or unsystematic, is that the question? Reflections on the science, art, and politics of reviewing research evidence', in A. Killoran *et al.* *The Evidence-Based Approach to Public Health*, Oxford: Oxford University Press.

Hammersley, M. (2005d) 'Methodology, who needs it?', unpublished paper.

Hannay, A. (2004) *On The Public*, London: Routledge.

Hargreaves, A. (1982) 'Resistance and relative autonomy theories: problems of distortion and incoherence in recent Marxist theories of education', *British Journal of the Sociology of Education*, 3, 2: 107–26.

Harrison, M. (1985). *TV News: Whose bias?* Reading: Policy Journals.

Hartley, J. (1982) *Understanding News*, London: Routledge.

Haslam, C. and Bryman, A. (1994a) 'The research dissemination minefield', in Haslam and Bryman (eds). *Social Scientists Meet the Media*, London: Routledge.

Heritage, J. (1985) 'Analysing news interviews: aspects of the production of talk for an "overhearing" audience', in T. van Dijk (ed.) *Handbook of Discourse Analysis, vol. III: Discourse and Dialogue*, London: Academic Press.

Heritage, J. and Greatbatch, D. (1991) 'On the institutional character of institutional talk: the case of news interviews', in D. Boden and D. H. Zimmerman (eds) *Talk and Social Structure: Studies in ethnomethodology and conversation analysis*, Cambridge: Polity Press.

Hirsch, E. D. (1967) *Validity in Interpretation*, New Haven, CT: Yale University Press.

Holub, R. C. (1984). *Reception Theory: A critical introduction*, London: Methuen.

Hutton, Lord (2003) *Report of the Inquiry into the Circumstances Surrounding the Death of Dr David Kelly C.M.G.* (The Hutton Inquiry), available at http://www.the-hutton-inquiry.org.uk/content/report (accessed on 26.08.05).

Irwin, A. and Wynne, B. (1996) *Misunderstanding Science? The public reconstruction of science and technology*, Cambridge: Cambridge University Press.

Irwin, A. and Michael, M. (2003) *Science, Social Theory and Public Knowledge*, Maidenhead: Open University Press.

Keane, J. (1991) *The Media and Democracy*, Cambridge: Polity Press.

Kress, G. and van Leeuwen, T. (1998) 'Front pages: (the critical) analysis of newspaper layout', in A. Bell and P. Garrett (eds) *Approaches to Media Discourse*, Oxford: Blackwell.

Lacey, C. and Longman, D. (1997) *The Press as Public Educator: cultures of understanding, cultures of ignorance*, Luton: University of Luton Press.

Lampard, R. (1996) 'Might Britain be a meritocracy? A comment on Saunders', *Sociology*, 30, 2: 387–93.

Langer, J. (1998) *Tabloid Television: popular journalism and the 'other news'*, London: Routledge.

Larrain, J. (1979) *The Concept of Ideology*, London: Hutchinson.

Leach, E. (1976) *Culture and Communication: the logic by which symbols are connected*, Cambridge: Cambridge University Press.

Lemert, E. M. (1967) *Human Deviance, Social Problems and Social Control*, Englewood Cliffs, NJ: Prentice-Hall.

Levinson, S. (1988) 'Putting linguistics on a proper footing: explorations in Goffman's concepts of participation', in P. Drew and A. Wootton (eds) *Erving Goffman: Exploring the interaction order*, Cambridge, Polity, Press.

Lichtheim, G. (1967) *The Concept of Ideology and Other Essays*, New York: Vintage.

Lippmann, W. (1927) *The Phantom Public*, New York, Macmillan. (Re-published, New Brunswick, NJ: Transaction Books, 1993.)

Lister, R. (1996) *Charles Murray and the Underclass: The developing debate*, London: Institute of Economic Affairs, Health and Welfare Unit.

Lukes, S. (1985) *Marxism and Morality*, Oxford: Oxford University Press.

McGuigan, J. (1992) *Cultural Populism*, London: Routledge.

McIntyre, D. (1997) 'The profession of educational research', *British Educational Research Journal*, 23, 2: 127–40.

Mackinnon, D. (1986) 'Equality of opportunity as fair and open competition', *Journal of Philosophy of Education*, 20, 1: 69–71.

Macksey, R. (1997) Foreword, in Genette (1997).

Macpherson, W. (1999) *The Stephen Lawrence Inquiry*, CM 4262-1, London: HMSO (The Macpherson Inquiry).

Manning, P. (2001) *News and News Sources: A Critical Introduction*, London: Sage.

Marshall, G. and Swift, A. (1993) 'Social class and social justice', *British Journal of Sociology*, 44, 2: 187–211.

Marshall, G. and Swift, A. (1996) 'Merit and mobility: a reply to Peter Saunders', *Sociology*, 30, 2: 375–86.

Matza, D. (1969) *Becoming Deviant*, Englewood Cliffs, NJ: Prentice-Hall.

Merton, R. K. (1968) *Social Theory and Social Structure*, second edition, New York: Free Press.

Mirza, H. S. (1998) 'Race, gender and IQ: the social consequence of a pseudo-scientific discourse', *Race, Ethnicity and Education*, 1, 1: 109–26.

Moore, C. (1996) 'Media Guardian: a military operation', *The Guardian*, 13 May.

Moores, S. (1993) *Interpreting Audiences: the ethnography of media consumption*, London: Sage.

Morley, D. (1986) *Family Television: cultural power and domestic leisure*, London: Comedia.

Morley, D. (1992) *Television, Audiences and Cultural Studies*, London: Routledge.

Myers, G. (2004) *Matters of Opinion: Talking about public issues*, Cambridge: Cambridge University Press.

Neal, L. (1990) *The Rise of Financial Capitalism: international capital markets in the age of reason*, Cambridge: Cambridge University Press.

Nino, C. (1996) *The Constitution of Deliberative Democracy*, New Haven, CT: Yale University Press.

Oakley, A. (2000) *Experiments in Knowing: gender and method in the social sciences*, Cambridge, Polity Press.

Philo, G. (1987) 'Whose news?', *Media, Culture and Society*, 9, 4: 397–406.

Pickering, A. (ed.) (1992) *Science as Practice and Culture*, Chicago, IL: University of Chicago Press.

Pirenne, H. (1914) 'The stages in the social history of capitalism', *American Historical Review*, 19, 3, 494–515. Reprinted in R. Bendix, and S. M. Lipset (eds) *Class, Status, and Power: social stratification in comparative perspective*, second edition, New York: Free Press, 1966.

Pomerantz, A. (1984) 'Agreeing and disagreeing with assessments: some features of preferred/dispreferred turn-shapes', in J. M. Atkinson and J. Heritage (eds) *Structures of Social Action: Studies in conversation analysis*, Cambridge, Cambridge University Press.

Price, V. (1992) *Public Opinion*, Newbury Park, CA: Sage.

Raymond, J. (1999) 'The newspaper, public opinion, and the public sphere in the seventeenth century', in J. Raymond (ed.) *News, Newspapers, and Society in Early Modern Britain*, London: Frank Cass.

The Royal Society (1985) *The Public Understanding of Science*, London: The Royal Society.

Rubin, Z. (1980) 'My love–hate relationship with the media', *Psychology Today* 13: 7–13.

Ryan, A. (1995) *John Dewey and the High Tide of American Liberalism*, New York: W. W. Norton.

Saunders, P. (1985) 'Might Britain be a meritocracy?', *Sociology*, 29, 1: 23–41.

Saunders, P. (1996) *Unequal but Fair? A study of class barriers in Britain*, London: Institute of Economic Affairs.

Saunders, P. (1997) 'Social mobility in Britain: an empirical evaluation of two competing explanations', *Sociology*, 31, 2: 261–88.

Saunders, P. (2002) 'Reflections on the meritocracy debate in Britain: a response to Richard Breen and John Goldthorpe', *British Journal of Sociology*, 53, 4: 559–74.

Savage, M. and Egerton, M. (1997) 'Social mobility, individual ability and the inheritance of class inequality', *Sociology*, 31, 4: 645–72.

Schegloff, E. A. (1971) 'Note on a conversational practice: formulating place', in D. Sudnow (ed.) *Studies in Social Interaction*, New York: Free Press.

Schlesinger, P. 1987. *Putting 'Reality' Together: BBC News*, second edition, London: Methuen.

Schumpeter, J. (1952) *Capitalism, Socialism, and Democracy*, fifth edition, London: Allen and Unwin.

Shannon, C. E. and Weaver, W. (1949) *The Mathematical Theory of Communication*, Urbana, IL: University of Illinois Press.

Sharrock, W. W. (1974) 'On owning knowledge', in R. Turner (ed.) *Ethnomethodology*, Harmondsworth, Penguin.

Sharrock, W. W. (1977) 'The problem of order', in Worsley (ed.).

Sigal, L. V. (1986) 'Sources make the news', in R. K. Manoff and M. Schudson (eds) *Reading the News: a Pantheon guide to popular culture*, New York: Pantheon Books.

Smith, E. (2003) 'Failing boys and moral panics: perspectives on the underachievement debate', *British Journal of Educational Studies*, 51, 3: 282–95.

Smith, G. (2000) 'Research and inspection: HMI and OFSTED 1981–1996 – a commentary', *Oxford Review of Education*, 26, 3–4: 333–52.

Sperber, D. and Wilson, D. (1986) *Relevance: communication and cognition*, Oxford: Blackwell.

Swann, Lord (1985) *Education for All: Final Report of the Committee of Inquiry into the Education of Children from Ethnic Minority Groups*. Cmnd 9453. London: HMSO.

Taylor, M. J. (1981) *Caught Between: a review of research into the education of pupils of West Indian origin*, Windsor: National Foundation for Educational Research–Nelson.

Taylor, M. J. (1986) *Chinese Pupils in Britain: a review of research into the education of pupils of Chinese origin*, Windsor: National Foundation for Educational Research–Nelson.

Taylor, M. J. (1988) *Worlds Apart? A review of research into the education of pupils of Cypriot, Italian, Ukrainian, and Vietnamese origin, Liverpool Blacks, and Gypsies*, Windsor: National Foundation for Educational Research–Nelson.

Taylor, M. J. with Hegarty, S. (1985) *The Best of Both Worlds? A review of research into the education of pupils of South Asian origin*, Windsor: National Foundation for Educational Research–Nelson.

Thomas, G. and Pring, R. (eds) (2004) *Evidence-based Practice in Education*, Maidenhead, Open University Press.

Thompson, J. B. (1984) *Studies in the Theory of Ideology*, Berkeley, CA: University of California Press.

Thompson, J. B. (1995) *The Media and Modernity: a social theory of the media*, Cambridge: Polity Press.

Todorov, T. (1984) *Mikhail Bakhtin: the dialogical principle*, Manchester: Manchester University Press.

Tompkins, J. P. (ed.) (1980) *Reader–Response Criticism: from formalism to post-structuralism*, Baltimore, MD: Johns Hopkins University Press.

Toynbee, P. (1999). 'Interview (with Liam Murphy)', *Network, Newsletter of the British Sociological Association*. 72: 20–23.

Trinder, L., with Reynolds, S. (eds) (2000) *Evidence-based Practice: a critical appraisal*, Oxford: Blackwell Science.

Troyna, B. (1993) *Racism and Education: research perspectives*, Buckingham: Open University Press.

Tuchman, G. (1978) *Making News: A Study in the Construction of Reality*, New York: Free Press.

Ussher, J. (1994) 'Media representations of psychology: denigration and popularization, or worthy dissemination of knowledge', in C. Haslam and A. Bryman (eds) *Social Scientists Meet the Media*. London: Routledge.

van Dijk, T. A. (1991) *Racism and the Press*, London: Routledge.

van Dijk, T. (2000) 'New(s) racism: a discourse analytical approach', in Cottle (ed.).

van Parijs, P. (1981) *Evolutionary Explanation in the Social Sciences*, London: Tavistock.

Walum, L. R. (1975) 'Sociology and the mass media', *American Sociologist*, 10, 1: 28–32.

Wallas, G. (1920) *Human Nature in Politics*, third edition, London: Constable.

Weigel, R. and Pappas, J. (1981) 'Social Science and the press: a case study and its implications', *American Psychologist*, 36, 5: 480–84.

Weiss, C. and Singer, E. (1988) *Reporting Social Science in the National Media*, New York: Russell Sage Foundation.

Westbrook, R. (1991) *John Dewey and American Democracy*, Ithaca, NY: Cornell University Press.

Williams, B. (1962) 'The idea of equality', in P. Laslett and W. G. Runciman (eds) *Philosophy, Politics and Society, 2nd Series*, Oxford: Blackwell.

Williams, B. (2002) *Truth and Truthfulness*, Princeton, NJ: Princeton University Press.

Worsley, P. (ed.) (1977) *Introducing Sociology*, second edition, Harmondsworth: Penguin.

Index

Page numbers for tables have suffix t, those for notes have suffix n.

KWESI mentoring project in Birmingham
73, 74, 77, 79, 80

Labour Party 77
Lacey, C. 2, 43, 89, 89n, 125, 126
Lambeth (London Borough) 29
Lampard, R. 176n
Langer, J. 162n
Larrain, J. 136n
Lawrence, Stephen 135
Leach, E. 138n
Leicester 113
Leicester University 131
The Leicester Mercury 89, 96;
    discriminatory model for headlines 104;
    headlines on reaction 91; local teachers
    views 117–18; main headline on
    stereotyping 95, 103; refers to Review
    as a survey 107
Lemert, E.M. 151
Levinson, S. 110n
Lewis Lynch High School, Barbados 116
Lichtheim, G. 136
Lippman, Walter 2n, 159n
Littlemore, Sue 52, 54, 55, 56, 58, 67, 69,
    73, 146, 146n
London Boroughs: Brent 39, 48, 50, 68,
    69, 184, 188; Lambeth 29; Tower
    Hamlets 27, 28, 29, 39, 58, 70, 86, 114,
    119, 130, 131, 174, 175, 184, 186, 195
London Evening Standard 89, 98;
    distribution model for headlines 104;
    headlines on the Review 91; main
    headline failure of colour-blind
    policies 95
London Institute of Education *see* Institute
    of Education, University of London
Longhurst, B. 9n
Longman, D. 2, 43, 89n, 125, 126
Lukes, S. 166

MacKinnon, D. 28n, 173
Macksey, R. 17n
McGuigan, J. 162n
McIntyre, D. 11
Macpherson, W. 46, 135
Macpherson Report 167n
Manchester Evening News 89; competition
    model for headlines 104; headlines on
    the Review 91; main headline on
    African Caribbean pupils 95, 99
Manning, P. 15n
Marshall, G. 176n
Marx, Karl 153

Matza, D. 150n
Merton, R.K. 155n
Michael, M. 161
Mirza, Heidi 27n, 108n, 118n, 130
Moat Community College, Leicester 118
monitoring achievements and needs 36
Moore, C. 126
Moores, S. 9n
More Bad News (Glasgow University
    Media Group) 169n
Morgan, Steven 115
MORI (Market and Opinion Research
    International) 89n, 125, 126
Morley, D. 9n
Murphy, D. 89n
The Muslim News 91, 96
Myant, Chris 113, 194
Myers, G. 59n

narratives, causal 121–34; competition
    model *(The Sunday Times)* 123; in the
    education supplements 129–32; ethnic
    differences caused by teaching *(Daily
    Mirror)* 123; ethnic differences partly
    caused by teachers *(Daily Telegraph,
    Daily Mail)* 125–9; in ethnic minority
    newspapers 131, 132t; in local Press
    132–4; in national newspapers 122t;
    need for action by teachers *(Guardian)*
    124; two main causal narratives,
    competition model or distribution
    model 122
Naughtie, James 56, 60, 61, 63, 64
Neal, L. 152
news in the media: problems of objectivity
    9; reception by audiences 9–10;
    sociological research on bias 8
newspaper coverage of the Review
    85–134; balance of focus in newspaper
    reports 105, 106t; competition model
    98–101; coverage in national daily
    newspapers 87t; direct discriminatory
    action 101; discrimination model
    101–4; distribution model 97–8; ethnic
    minority newspapers headlines 94t;
    ethnic minority press coverage 88t;
    findings in the headlines of national
    newspapers 93t; findings in the reports
    of newspapers 118–21; focus on the
    Review or on reactions to it 91t;
    headlines 90–7; local newspapers
    findings 95t; location and extent of
    coverage 85–90; the Review as